Growing Up On the Mississippi

Growing Up On the Mississippi:

The 1950s in Winona, Minnesota

A joyous autobiography containing stories, local histories and snippets of life found in the river town of my youth.

Kent Otto Stever

NORTH STAR PRESS OF ST. CLOUD, INC.

St. Cloud, Minnesota

Printed in the United States of America

Published by
North Star Press of St. Cloud, Inc.
P.O. Box 451
St. Cloud, MN 56302

www.northstarpress.com

Facebook - North Star Press

Twitter - North Star Press

Table of Contents

Chapter Seven

Chapter Eight

Chapter Nine

Chapter Ten

Chapter Eleven

Preface

I have had a lifetime love affair with the life and times and places of my youth.

Being raised in the bluffs, hills and valleys of the Mississippi River in southeastern Minnesota, I lived and grew amidst the most beautiful of God's creations. Somehow He allowed that glaciers wouldn't flatten the earth around Winona. He held up his hand and said, "Stop! I want this valley preserved."

He allowed the rivers and streams to course through limestone hills, planted the hardwood forests and created a natural richness of valley farmland. Farmers learned a few lessons about planting and erosion control and eventually preserved the land. Along the river, my small city became a place of industry, recreation and reflection. It truly became "God's Country." And I was at the center of it all.

In the pages following, I have brought together stories, histories and snippets of life as a youth in the late 1940's and early '50's in the Winona area. It is a New Departure in theme—a term taken from the single-wheeled coaster brake on the back wheel of my constantly reassembled bike. My life depended upon that brake (and my mechanical expertise) as I roared down steep country roads. So, too, my life has depended upon lessons learned from family, neighbors, teachers and friends.

My children encourage me to write some of my thoughts of the town, of independence, responsibility and freedom. They can't believe the freedom of youth—or the expectations or responsibilities taken on by the very young— of which the stories resonate. Kids I have served as principal, teacher and guide over many years in the schools have also offered support.

As I meted out discipline, they listened to my stories and my themes of expectations—and even sometimes applauded the fact that I would stand up and tell them (in spite of a bad behavior) that they were good. They simply needed to be responsible. Upon leaving with their punishment, they often said, "Thank you."

Adults of all ages have encouraged me to share my stories. They "feel as if they are there" as I describe a scene, or they "wish that they had had these expectations placed upon me as a young person." They believe that my stories are "Moments to Remember," one of the named stories.

I dedicate these remembrances to a special family of the 1950s, to extended family members of the Winona neighborhood evident in stories, and to my wonderful family of today.

Introduction

Enclosed are stories of the heart—stories of life and struggle and joy and outcomes. They are stories of wonderment, stories of real life. My kids love to hear them. In bits and snatches, these stories (and others) emerged with a pattern of thought that they suggested I share with others.

They read my stories and they wonder. Why is the way their children are developing so very different from the ways of their grandfather? How did he have such freedom to come and go and do as a child, and simultaneously become so responsible? Who told him what to do? How did he possibly get to the places he did without having someone tell him and guide and nurture him?

How could he not be sad and alone and unsure? Was there a force that led him that he didn't see? How could he independently find small jobs in the neighborhood, gather rags and metal for resale and build forts in the woods without someone's permission and direction?

My eclectic short stories are interspersed in the following pages between brief histories of topics I selected and researched. Hopefully, these histories support the stories and the stories support the history. The "whole is greater than the sum of its parts."

Back then, Boy Scouts happened because one independently joined up and took campouts in the woods. With a can of beans, a big brother's knapsack and a change of underwear, I was ready for outdoor adventure. A "Mulligan Stew" or "Arms of Steel" or "Hold the Torch High" story followed.

I played basketball in the city league on Saturday mornings of winter, and baseball in the days of summer, all without direction and "carpooling." We simply jumped on our bikes or trudged through the snow. There were no cell phones on which to call and report whether one made it or not.

"Checking in" wasn't necessary, since we were doing what we said we would be doing. There were no coaches, no parents involved—actually no interference in our growth. We just went and did and became—and returned for supper.

These stories may in part be about the sense I have that something is afoul in our lives today. Parents seem to have taken their own learned moments of childhood and set them aside. They don't seem to remember the treasures from whence they came. Many seem to get engaged in only the here and now. They are so focused on "talk therapy," the self and the need to feel good that they have lost sight of who and what they really are.

We are simple people who are to take the wonderful experiences that made us, absorb those experiences and pass them on. Today it's as if the natural decision-making within each of us has been set aside in order to focus on someone else's interpretations. What happened? When and why did we give up our rights and our truths? How can we not remember what we know to be good and true? Why do we not proceed with the strength that we know we have?

These may be stories that won't appear on the afternoon television shows, won't make it into *Parents Magazine*. Some may seem more fitting for the world of nostalgia. But, like the temporary cure for a toothache that I offered just moments ago to an ailing laborer—a clove held between the teeth—each has a place—for remembrance, wonder and application to the growth of children and families.

Enjoy the ride on the New Departure.

Chapter One

Arms of Steel

Fifty members strong, Troop 5 of Madison School assembled in the heart of downtown in front of the Woolworth Store on Third Street—as directed by the scoutmaster at our Monday night meeting. We had half-stepped and hustled in the early morning haze and humidity past the well-known landmarks of our steamy river valley town to get there well in advance, following the motto of Boy Scouts to "Be Prepared."

Ours was the largest of the troops—and we were the newest members. I was there to march as a full-fledged Boy Scout for the first time. The sensational Fourth of July parade down Main Street was a high point of our summer. Lining up in the fashion of World War II veterans, we each took our place in ranks assigned by the scoutmaster.

I was so proud of my new Boy Scout shirt, the yellow, official BSA kerchief and its knotted neckerchief slide holder to keep the kerchief in place. With "BSA" emblazoned over my right front pocket, I was truly in the form of the Boy Scouts I saw pictured in *Boys' Life* magazine.

Since age eight or so, I had been a member of the Boy Scouts. With the blue Cub shirt, I attended den meetings in the school neighborhood—learning my way through Fox and Wolf books, which covered everything from astronomy to knot-tying. We had den meetings in the warm environment of Rich Johnson's house.

In the oversized kitchen of his parents' old Victorian house on the finest street of Winona, we were led through the techniques of scouting by Rich's mom. She was a wonderful teacher who guided us through baking, woodcarving and the study of the stars. Completing the steps to Webelos was our crowning achievement—the completion of pre-scouting rigors that allowed us into the full Boy Scout experience.

Today was our first "official" appearance. Waiting in our semi-straight lines, we readied for final assembly, inspection and inspiration. The scoutmaster announced that he was looking to the ranks of the "tenderfoots" for a trio of volunteers to carry the flags at the front of the troop. One was to carry the U.S. flag, another the Minnesota flag, and the third the Boy Scout troop flag.

I was thrilled to be chosen and outfitted with the leather strap and holder to become the carrier of the troop flag. Imagine being at the head of the troop to march with the bands, floats, dignitaries and other scouts down Main Street, to arrive at the band shell at Lake Winona for the program to honor our veterans and the birth of our country. To be in full uniform at the head of the pack was the greatest honor to which I had ever been selected.

I had put on my school patrol belt for several years in elementary school and held that flag daily, had been a strong Cub Scout member who earned the necessary "notches" of the scouting program—but had never imagined that those experiences would allow me to lead and carry a flag of honor for the most distinguished troop in town on such a momentous day.

The scoutmaster reviewed for us the proper procedure of flag carrying—to show the highest respect for the American flag. It would lead the troop. The state and troop flags would be two steps behind. All flags were to be carried "aloft and free"—never flat or horizontal. With instructions clearly in mind, the troop was called to attention. A salute to the flag was given and all recited the Pledge of Allegiance.

Rich was at the lead with the U.S. flag. Davey held the state flag as my partner in the second row. With the Harley-Davidson three-wheeled police motorcycle escort at the head of the parade, followed by the VFW Honor Guard and the high school band, the parade was in motion.

We headed down Third, took a sharp left onto Main and set off through the throng of parade viewers lining the route for the next mile. In the blocks ahead I spotted neighbors, school friends and several of my teachers as I proudly held the flag at what I thought was the correct angle. They shouted greeting and encouragement—knowing that this was a special honor for me.

Having passed by the teachers college at the midway point of our parade, we were well on our way to successful completion, with the lake park area only blocks ahead. We were holding our positions and marching in time with the band when we suddenly saw Rich, the U.S. flag carrier, veer off to the left of center.

We knew that as a lefty, he had a tendency to favor everything to the left side. He seemed to always have a bit of a tilt to the left in his walk and posture—as if a heavy weight were in his left hand and he couldn't get upright. But we had never seen him take such a pronounced departure from normal. He was headed for the crowd at curbside! The flag was in the proper position, but his direction was askew.

The next thing I knew, Rich was directly in front of me, having made up the several yards between us, and was now on a collision course. I was concerned for his safety, but also concerned for the flag and our duty to hold the colors aloft. He was upright—but somehow drifting in his own world—right in front of me.

Using quick Boy Scout action, I stepped beside Rich, grabbed his left arm with my right and attempted to aim him toward the lake. By now the scoutmaster, who had been marching to the left side of the troop, moved up quickly to resolve the situation.

Putting his arm around Rich, he rescued the flag and handed it to me—with quick instructions to keep the American flag to the right of the troop flag. I knew that I was now in the lead—with the dual responsibility of troop and country. With hardly a beat missed, we had completed the unanticipated maneuver, now to the applause of the watching crowd.

Rich was whisked to curbside and safety where the scoutmaster and observers came to his aid. As I marched forward—certain of my task and uncertain of my abilities, I felt a strong hand on my right shoulder. Marching next to me was my oldest brother Frank, a senior member of the troop and a Life Scout, a ranking second only to the ultimate Eagle Scout. He quietly directed me to remove the troop flag from its holder, hand it to him and replace it with the U.S. flag. Once accomplished, I was to take over front and center with the "Stars and Stripes."

He fell in to my former spot at left of center—a few paces behind me. I was now leading the total troop—and my big brother.

I must have shown arms of steel in that position of honor—for my flag never wavered, save for the slight breeze created by the brisk march in the morning sunshine. We completed the journey to the lake park, placed our flags in the fixed holders of the band shell and enjoyed the festivities of the day. Rich was found to be okay, with a bit of heat stroke—coupled with the excitement of the assignment.

We had marched. We had brought honor to our troop and country. We were thrilled beyond belief. Oh, what a glorious day to actually see the Scout slogan of "Do A Good Turn Daily" come into play.

Lucky, the Wonder Dog

One day Davey showed me how smart his dog Lucky was. She was a rag-tailed mutt with legs too long for her body, a friendly disposition, a white spot on her chest and what seemed to be an ever-present smile. Davey wanted me to see how much he had taught her.

Lucky was a wonderful dog—most often tied up in the small front yard kitty-corner from Deilke's grocery. Her job in life seemed to be to lie in the front yard all year long and monitor the movements of kids to school and into the school playlot across the street. She also kept a watchful eye on the delivery truck drivers and customers who frequented Old Man Deilke's grocery.

She was kind, attentive, friendly and alert. Being smart, however, was not one of the traits that she showed best. It could be that she had not been trained in the tricks of the dog world. But more likely, she hadn't been born with exceptional good sense.

It might explain why she was always tied in the front yard. Nevertheless, Davey was out to show Lady Lucky's new trick to me. It wasn't to be just a ball toss and return or a "roll over." Of course not! Davey had to impress me with the biggest trick he could manage.

He maintained that Lucky could cross the street to the grocery store, open the screen door by herself and bring home a bone from Old Man Deilke's meat market counter in the back of the store. He had practiced the trick with Lucky and the cooperative J.L.F. Deilke many times. The stage was set.

It was a quiet moment after school. Before we moved on to tricks, we needed to settle down with a cup of hot cocoa and tell Davey's Ma of the day's event.

We had just come to Davey's house from Miss O'Meara's classroom—our fifth grade teacher. Miss O'Meara was not one of the picture book teachers whom we had seen depicted in the Dick and Jane books that we read in earlier grades.

Those teachers (always female) were beautiful, fit and dressed in simple, well-fitting dresses. They were a cross between the most beautiful moms we had seen and the models we occasionally glanced at on the calendar in my older brother's room. Miss O'Meara was none of these.

She epitomized the ugly duckling grown up—and fitted with half-glasses. There was nothing attractive about our teacher's clothes. Her dresses were in the range of the gingham dresses and house robes Davey's Ma wore around the house.

Miss O'Meara may have had a total absence of style but she had a good heart. She tried hard to keep us engaged. With the distraction of evolving female frames in our class and thoughts of outdoor adventure, her words seemed to fall on deaf ears. Somehow, she just couldn't grab our attention.

Bruce, a classmate in Miss O'Meara's room, was sort of a non-entity whose main feature was his ability to raise the biggest farts in the room. Even though he was bigger than us, he was harmless, quiet and soft flab. We had been with Bruce over a few years and had accepted him for his docile nature. He had never acted up or been a challenge on the playground—for we could all run circles around him. Today had been different.

Bruce lost it!

In the quiet of Miss O'Meara's class, something that she said to him set him off. He stomped and puffed and ballooned red in the face. His ranting continued to escalate. And then he attacked. He swung his open palm and slapped Miss O'Meara square across the face.

She was about the same size as Bruce and had never been seen as a physical person. But with a twist of her body and a whap from her ever-present hardwood yardstick, she whomped him into submission. The principal soon arrived to escort Bruce away in a principal's favorite hold for errant youth—a firm hold by strong ex-Marine fingers on Bruce's left ear.

Davey's Ma was shocked, but she had heard worse. Over the many years we had been together at the kitchen table, she always listened raptly to our stories and offered her bit of advice. She was our daily confessor and friend.

With our nerves settled by hot cocoa, we moved out to see the wonder dog, Lucky. All the kids had made their way home from school, the delivery men had finished the day's deliveries to the store and life was generally settled as fathers began to make their way home from their labor. She jumped and frolicked when released from the clothesline rope tether. Maybe she knew that she was about to take center stage.

Davey had two simple commands for Lucky—"Bone" and "Go." With a swing of his hand in the direction of the small store, Lucky took off. She bounced quickly across the street and headed for the old wood-framed screen door that served as the entry to the old store with its polished plank flooring.

We hustled off after her. Arriving at the store, she took a seat on the limestone step in front of the door with the weathered metal "Little Miss Sunbeam" sign. Hanging down from the weathered brass door pull was a small piece of rope with a knot in the end. Over the years, Mr. Deilke had found that the handle was just a bit high for the little ones to enter his store on errands for Mom, so he installed the small piece to assist with door opening.

Davey again said "Bone" and "Go" and Lucky grabbed the knot and gave a pull. Once she had opened the door a few inches, she stuck her nose in the opening and wedged herself into the store interior. In a flash, she headed past the glass cases of candy, the water-cooled Coke dispenser and the wooden chairs toward the back of the store.

Mr. Deilke, the white-haired, burly German storekeeper in a white shirt, green apron and shaded hat, saw Lucky pass by. He rose from his small desk at the side of the store to head toward the meat cooler in the back.

We always wondered why he wore the half-hat, half-accountant's shade on his head. But with his apron, shirt and tie, a pencil behind his ear and the shade, he had the appearance and pleasant demeanor of a focused shopkeeper. He was always there to greet us like an old friend when we arrived for a loaf of bread or a two-pound roll of butter, on a mission from home.

He was also very cooperative and friendly when we were there to hang out on his front stoop. We could get a cold bottle of pop from the cooler and a couple of jawbreakers from the candy counter and sit on the limestone slabs outside the store, facing toward the school playground and Davey's house.

The bottle of pop (Pepsi for me) was eight cents, the jawbreakers two for a penny. Deposit on the bottle was two cents. Mr. Deilke didn't charge us the extra two cents for the deposit, since he knew us to be good customers who would return our bottles to the wood case at the side of the cooler.

Lucky waited patiently at the side of the meat case as Mr. Deilke opened the sliding door on the back. Finding just the right size bone for Lucky's small mouth, he passed it to her with a pat on the head. With a thank you to Mr. Deilke and a "Home" to Lucky, we followed Lucky out the door and back to her favorite spot in the front yard.

Davey was thrilled. I was amazed. The wonder dog had done her trick. I had seen the Krause brothers, owners of the local Vets Cab Company, work with their black lab in their yard. Their dog would retrieve the large canvas-padded dummy when they tossed it every which way. They kept the dog in shape for field trials, contests and duck hunting in the back sloughs of the Mississippi River. But I had never seen a dog pull off a "trick" or retrieve such as Lucky's. Unbelievable!

Before adjourning for the day and heading home for my own chores, I suggested that we give some thought to showing off Lucky's trick to other classmates. Maybe Davey could bring Lucky to school and get our teacher and the class onto the playground to observe. They wouldn't believe it!

Looking through my papers from school at home, I set out my homework and the papers returned by Miss O'Meara. It was always my routine to get out school papers and set them on the kitchen table so Pa could do his review of my progress. I was happy to have a starred paper or two to share with Pa today.

It was a good day when you got a shiny, colored star on your paper. In the midst of my papers and notes passed across the classroom (not to be shared with Pa), I found a small colored paper that I had been handed by Terry as I left class for the day. Terry was in the next grade. He lived in a big house less than a block from school. The paper announced that Terry was having his "carnival" this Saturday.

Several times each year, especially in the summer when the play-ground was full of kids, Terry set up a number of games in the big garage be-hind the house and invited willing participants to risk their nickels and pennies.

We enjoyed games of chance at the carnival when it came to town in the summer for Steamboat Days. With ring tosses around pop bottles, pennies rolled across the numbered squares, and the "Digger" in the glass cases filled with corn and prizes, we all attempted to be a winner.

We might win a cap gun or a silver dollar in the Digger, a shiny metal horse or stuffed animal in the ring toss or a plate or cup in the nickel toss—if the nickel landed in one or the other. Terry's setup mimicked the carnival booths on the levee downtown, but in a smaller way.

One of our favorites that we knew that Terry would have was the coin roll. Setting our coin upright in a slot on the side of a square table, we rolled the coin out on the table. Terry would announce with each roll, "you takes your chances."

With squares just larger than coins, each was marked off with numbers and dividing lines. We rolled for 1x, 2x, 3x, 5x and the ultimate, 10x. Terry would pay off the number listed times the coin you had used. If you landed on the line—no pay. If you landed perfectly in the square, he reached into his carpenter's apron and paid off the appropriate number of coins.

All of the games were fun and Terry provided a special carnival for the kids of the neighborhood. He had games of chance for the bigger kids and the floating rubber duckies and balloons for the little ones. He was quite the entrepreneur. We never thought much about the potential profit that Terry realized. We only knew that we were having fun.

Since it was only Tuesday, Davey and I could set up and capitalize on Terry's audience in the neighborhood to show off Lucky. I called Davey to let him know of my idea and asked him to come over after supper. We would meet in the shed behind the house (our fort and workshop) and work out the details.

With paper and carpenter's pencil, we laid out the plan. We would offer shows on the hour at 12:00, 1:00, 2:00 and 3:00. By charging observers a dime for the experience of seeing Lucky the Wonder Dog, we had the possibility of making a few dollars.

We would need to pay a few nickels to Mr. Deilke for the bones and figured we could exchange notices with Terry so that our customers went his way and vice versa. By setting up a couple of boards across cement blocks, we could have seating for ten at each performance on the school side of the street, with a full view of Davey's house and Deilke's Grocery.

Our first task was to make up our notices to hand out in class the next day. Using a couple of pieces of carbon paper borrowed from Miss Kissling, our neighboring teacher, we were soon able to scratch out multiple copies for distribution.

By the end of our meeting we had all the notices printed and cut, plans laid out and responsibilities defined. I would be the ticket seller and crowd organizer, while Davey would take responsibility for handling Lucky. It was agreed that for authenticity Davey would remain in his front yard, to further amaze the crowd.

The week went by quickly as we advertised the happening and organized our materials. On Saturday, we were up early and raring to go. We constructed our seating, put up a few signs at the store (with Mr. Deilke's permission) and stopped by Terry's to see that all was in place.

Since he wanted our nickels and pennies, we assured him that we would come by between shows to play his games of chance. He reciprocated by stating that he would do everything in his power to send us more paying customers.

The first show began at high noon with an audience of seven. We were a bit disappointed with the sparse turnout, but Lucky performed admirably and we had seventy cents in the can. The second show brought us more than our ten seats could hold. We even had two adult paying customers who had stopped by the store and saw our notice.

Our third show was a smash. We sold twenty-seven tickets! The carnival at Terry's was in progress, the neighboring adults decided to come out and the sun was shining. Lucky faltered just a bit on her way across the street in the midst of the third show. One of the kids had her cat with her and Lucky decided to chase it across the playground. Once settled, she went about her performance with stunning precision. Our final show was equally successful. Lucky earned a standing round of applause when she came out the door with her fourth bone of the day.

We thanked our audience, put away our benches, paid Mr. Deilke for the bones and petted Lucky incessantly for her performance. In addition to our gratitude, she resided comfortably on the front yard with four well-earned bones.

We headed to the cellar, counted our net profits and gave ourselves thirty cents each from the can for the carnival. With change in our pockets and six dollars safely secured in the can in our secret hiding place in the cellar, we headed off to Terry's house.

It was our Lucky day!

A Walk Down Memory Lane:
Madison School Revisited

One perfect summer evening while visiting in-laws, I decided it was time for a walk.

Starting in the blocks of Goodview on the outskirts of Winona, I soon found my way down Fifth Street—passing Cheer's Barber Shop and the liquor store. Angling around the parked trucks of Kujak Trucking Company on the corner, I stopped at the in-town Dairy Queen on the west end of Broadway—home of the trademark "Curl on Top." The DQ has been operating in the same small space since long before the Blizzard was born.

Heading nowhere in particular, I soon found myself licking a twist cone on the streets of my old Sunday paper route. As a boy, I had delivered a route for the St. Paul *Pioneer Press* that seemed to be centered at the West End Theatre on Ewing and West Fifth streets—where tickets for a Saturday or Sunday matinee "show" were twelve cents. With an additional nickel tacked on by Pa for good behavior, I got a Holloway Sucker to last through half of the Geronimo or Gene Autry show.

Tires on the bricks of West Fifth caused a rubbery rumble in the hot night as cars passed me outside EB's Tavern. Those bricks had been in place since the late 1800s—about the time horse-drawn streetcars were extended out that way. The West End Hotel, Libera's Grocery and EB's Tavern were all there then. A couple of blocks over on Wabasha Street were the sites of the Winona General Hospital, the Lutheran church of my Christmas and Easter youth and the school of my history and dreams—Madison.

On this summer night as I walked down Wabasha, I was back there as a boy—playing baseball, finding my way in early for school patrol, swinging on the bars in the back lot, or handing out prizes at the "Fish Bowl" of the evening school carnival.

With my wandering, I was centered in the middle of my old school/home neighborhood. For seven years in the late 1940s and early 1950s, Madison was my life, my everything. From Dick and Jane readers of grade one to basic algebra of grade six, I was immersed. Along with others in my family (three of four kids in the family in the same school at the same time), we set a record at Madison for *all* having perfect attendance and no tardies in the same year. We must have loved the environment.

This school of my youth had been laid out about the time of the street bricks on Fifth. In 1874, bids were let. With add-ons for third-floor finishing, trees, ground improvements and classroom seating all accomplished by the end of 1875, the "Jewel of the West" stood facing Winona's finest street for the grand sum of $24,845.00.

In 1882, a riverboat captain, William Woodin, building a cabin only two blocks from Madison, commented, "Steam boaters all like Winona." A near neighbor to him and to Madison had a family afflicted with dysentery in 1883, causing the death of two of the children. Physicians blamed it on "poor water and the too-free use of new potatoes."

Around the same time period, the newspaper reported that there were some "Bad Boys" in the Madison area. A group of twelve- or thirteen-year-olds decided to build a shanty as a "club" that overlooked the sawmill (probably near the steam boater!). They were often truant to outfit their shanty with pictures and stolen furniture. They probably used the money (three to four dollars) stolen from Miss Tawney's room at Madison, in 1886, to buy supplies for "the boys'" hostel. Some sixty-plus years later, a couple of Madison boys (in my class) burned down one of the boathouses along the river from which they had been stealing. They may have been descendants of the early "bad boys."

It was getting to be a bit late as I slowly crossed the playground behind the building. It was where I shot hoops, played tetherball, swung high and skated after school. I practically lived all summer at the playground, and occasionally had eight cents for a bottle of Pepsi at Deilke's Grocery at the corner of the playground. I passed the store hundreds of times as I went to school and back, twice per day for seven years.

On the Wabasha Street corner, the Madison Meat Market flourished with Mr. Bergemann in 1900. Next to the Kindt Grocery, Mr. Schumacher (a favorite of ours) succeeded Bergemann and smoked his sausages in a small, tall, wood building behind the shop. Delicious smells drifted across the street to the playground to give olfactory pleasure to pupils at recess time.

As I stood at Deilke's corner, I looked across the street to discover that Mrs. Pahnke was out in the warm night with her small dog. I crossed the street and approached gently, since it was a dark night and it had been more than twenty-five years since she had last seen me.

I called her name and identified myself and was soon in conversation. In a fashion of the many after-school visits to her home, to David's room, and to our "fort" in the cellar, she accepted me with ease. It was a glorious reminiscence in the soft light of the street lamp.

In 1886, there was concern over the use of a basement room at Madison for class use. The objecting director to that use (Stewart) also declared at the school board meeting that Algebra at the high school was "a superfluous study" and should be eliminated. In spite of "superfluous" thoughts, the 1890s became boom years for Madison.

There wasn't sufficient room in the school for large gatherings of school entertainment, so programs were held at the West End Hall, located on the second floor of Libera's General Store at Fifth Street and Ewing.

By 1915, the PTA was active, encouraging "all women to bring their sewing" to the 3:45 p.m. social/meeting on November 8. That same year the playground apparatus of teeters, swings and slide we so enjoyed was installed. In 1919, Madison parents were astir, perceiving a crisis in the education profession with quality teachers leaving due to low salaries.

From school, I wandered homeward—a couple of blocks from the back door of Madison to my home of fifty years ago on Grand Street. As I wandered, I could name every neighbor and isolate every apple and pear tree in backyards from which we stole in the middle of the night. I took a moment to stand under one of the four known catalpa trees in a three-block radius that provided beautiful flowers in springtime and twelve-inch "whips" for us to carry in summer.

The Madison neighborhood was my paper route, my playground for years. Day and night, I slammed the screen door on the back porch of home and headed out across Madison-area blocks to ever more adventure. Every step across imprinted sidewalks of cement artisans of the 1900s was a step toward excitement with school pals at the playground or to new learning.

Madison was in my bones.

In 1897, Miss Jessie Brammer became the new principal for the kindergarten through eighth grade school. She continued on for many years— a possible run of nearly forty years. Jessie was the founder of the Madison

PTA. She was also instrumental in bringing in some of our favorite teachers, who themselves had long runs at Madison—including Fern Kinzie at the kindergarten level, Mildred Kjome at first grade, Ruth Kottschade at second grade, Grace McLeod (1926) at third grade, Genevieve Carroll (1936) at fourth grade, Neva King at fifth grade (1944), and Orloue Nordby at sixth grade.

Miss Grace Kissling, the music teacher and my next-door neighbor, appeared throughout the years at Madison, as early as 1919. She taught us how to make "bean-hole" beans in our backyard. I have a very nice picture of many of our favored teachers from September 15, 1953, including the single male teacher, Ev Mueller. Ev taught me the jump shot in the school gym—and later became Assistant Superintendent of Winona Schools.

Jessie was dedicated to children making a difference in the world. Her efforts were shown through Thrift Stamp sales efforts that helped the WWI effort. She organized a letter- and packet-writing action that went to "Our Soldier Boy" (one of many) somewhere in France—to often receive a return letter of thanks and gracious appreciation.

Miss Brammer led 400 children at Madison to become members of the Junior Red Cross in 1918. It was a "patriotic group" to "aid in the read-justment and alleviation of poverty after the war." Her efforts continued over more than twenty-five years. One of her projects was sending Christmas pack-ets to English children during World War II. We received letters of thanks back in 1945. This writer participated with classmates in the late 1940s to cre-ate and send CARE packages overseas to war survivors in Europe.

Miss Brammer also shepherded the changeover from an eight-grade school to a six-grade school, with graduation of sixth graders first shown in 1935. This probably coincided with the opening of the new Madison School in 1933. Plans and referendum were considered for the building in November, 1931, with furniture bought in 1933—along with dirt, grading and tilling of grounds.

The story about building the new school describes it as "acclaimed as one of the best in the northwest" when it opened eighteen rooms, for a total cost of $176,000.00. Although purchases included teacher desks, kinder-garten furniture and seating for the 500-seat gymnasium/auditorium (with opera seats), there was not sufficient money to keep everything flowing in the heart of the Depression. The district had to cut the salaries of all janitors by ten percent.

The teachers, principals and janitor (Bill Groves) of Madison made daily impact on our lives. They reinforced the expectations of parents and went beyond to create a more global perspective in each of us, through Boy Scouts, School Patrol, academics, behavior, and the Junior American Red Cross.

They followed the tenets laid out in the Madison, Wisconsin conference in 1884, which suggested: "This course should be so planned that at whatever stage the pupil leaves it he will have received the best preparation for life possible in the time at school. The wants of the child's nature must also be considered broadly in planning the course."

We were not only considered, we were included in building the structure of the school and of our future lives. To a person, we "graduates" of Madison, from our ninety-three-year-old great-grandmother, to this wizened grandfather, to a twelve-year old great-grandson of today, the spirit of Madison has spoken to everyone. We were fortunate to be a part of the building processes of school and life.

Miss Mary McIver carried on as principal (1941–49) during my time there, following the dedicated Miss Brammer. The Cub Pack of Boy Scouts was formed at Madison in 1944, organized by the school and led by elected officers. I was soon a member. James Kroner led the very active Boy Scouts in 1950.

With an enrollment of 315 students in 1945, Miss MacIver coordinated the Cub Scout Supper in 1947, the evening X-rays in 1948, the Summer Roundup in 1949, and all the aspects of curriculum and guidance throughout each and every day. Verdi Ellies was named principal in the early 1950s, continuing the tradition of excellence.

At the Annual Madison Fun Frolic in 1952 (admission was forty cents, with 1,000 in attendance), the Cub Scouts had the Fish Pond and the Boy Scouts the pop stand. The principal coordinated the very popular "Cake Walk." Verdi is shown as Cake Walk Lead, being assisted by long-term school secretary Marilyn Neitzke. She knew those of us well who occupied the long hard bench outside the principal's office, waiting our turn. Mr. Ellies was a gracious and caring leader, the first male to serve as principal of Madison.

In my case, esteemed teachers and principals have been easily named and remembered. When a kindergarten classmate and I were recently asked (at the funeral of a ninety-three-year-old Madison graduate) by a young adult how we could remember teachers' names from so long ago, we quickly and mutually responded that they were a part of our lives. They stepped out and made a difference—and "looked out for the wants of the child's nature."

Walking west, I followed the familiar bus route of Howard Street ("Lake Line") past Thorn's Grocery at Dakota Street, until I ran out of Madison territory. My walk took the better part of a late, quiet and beautiful evening. I had suggested to my wife that I was going for a walk. She didn't know that it would be a marathon. I never did run out of memories and sensate pleasures. Ah—the mood, the remembrances, the smells, the quiet night sounds and the goodness of life in West Winona!

After several hours—and only moments before my wife was to send the Goodview constable out looking for me—I appeared on the western fringe of Winona. As with this essay, I had simply taken a walk down memory lane, having not a care in the world.

The complete story was originally created for the Winona Education Sesquicentennial, with a posting of the story to the school district's website. A copy was sent to the Madison School principal and staff.

Girls:
When They Finally Existed

We never meant for girls to enter our lives.

Ever since kindergarten, we knew that they were there. They were the ones who cried a lot when they skinned their knees on the gym floor or fell off the slide. They were known—but only just there—as we moved from grade to grade and age to age. They didn't cause any particular harm. For the most part they stayed out of the way.

They weren't a part of our playground softball games or after-school walks to the surplus store. But they were ever-present. They gave us nice valentines and candy and even invited us into their kitchens now and then to sample chocolate chip cookies baked by their mothers. They knew how to treat us right. Their cards were nice, but you didn't dare admit it.

"Naw," and "I don't care" were the most likely responses heard when the valentines or notes from them came our way. Then they started that "I like you" sign system that did nothing more than embarrass the receiver. But somehow, secretly, it felt good.

We saw them daily in our classes and bumped into them at the pencil sharpener and on the way into the coat closet. Except for the occasional warm, sweet smell that they seemed to generate when we entered the landing at the same time or when we had to work with one or more of them on small group projects in school, they seemed not to be in our thought process.

They just weren't a part of our awareness. They didn't have comic books. Or if they did, they were probably *Archie and Veronica* or some similarly sappy stuff. But in any case, they weren't part of the comic book trading action that occurred after school in small rooms at our homes. Only now and then did they appear where we were.

They didn't seem to like to fish, so they weren't at the lake. They didn't camp out or play baseball or basketball or serve with us on our military maneuvers. Where were they? We really didn't think of them.

Only now and then did you catch a glimpse of one or another. That was usually downtown on Saturday or at Christmas shopping time with their mothers. They could occasionally be seen in the summer riding bikes in doubles or triples. They were never to be seen alone.

Davey and I discussed the possibilities one late summer morning as we rested on the top of a hill after our hike.

"Are the girls at the bathing beach?" Davey wondered.

"I don't remember seeing them. We'll have to look around. There are always a lot of kids there. Some of them must be girls."

"Do girls swim?" he asked.

"They must. Esther Williams swims like a dolphin." She was s gorgeous movie star for whom all the boys showed up for Saturday afternoon movies at the State Theatre, and one of our favorites.

"Today when we hit the beach, we'll have to check it out."

The city beach was located on the river across from the town levee. It was the spot where we spent our summer days. We each grabbed a towel from home, jumped on our fenderless bikes and headed off across the bridge. With a nickel, we rented a small locker in the bathhouse to contain our clothes and valuables as we swam. For our nickel, we could also enjoy a shower of river water in the bathhouse to rinse off the sand.

Coming off the wood steps that led down from the bathhouse to the sand beach, we almost stepped on a blanket containing four girls. They were lounging around with sun lotion, potato chips and Kool-Aid. I was struck immediately with the bright colors of their swimsuits and the smell of coconut oil. It all seemed so delicious.

I gave a kick and spread some sand across the blanket and hustled off to do a running belly flop into the water. Davey followed—after knocking over their thermos of Kool-Aid. We knew they were there. They were out in the real world. We thought that they were always at home—snapping the ends off string beans from their mothers' gardens or playing with dolls.

We aimed for the diving platform beyond the bounds of the wooden dock walkway that kept non-swimmers contained by lifeguards. Girls didn't go there. If they did, they certainly weren't into our high-risk ventures on the wood diving platform with crash dives from the high board leaving us red from one end to the other. Maybe that's why we were so adventurous. No one was there to make us feel embarrassed or stupid if we belly-flopped. We really didn't give it a second thought as we headed into action.

After a few crash dives, we lounged on the platform and looked in to shore where the girls had been sitting. They were tossing around a beach ball on the sand. Davey suggested that maybe we should swim in and bomb them with mud balls from the murky bottom. We didn't.

Somewhere it happened. An accumulation of soft smells, the "I like yous" signaled across the classroom and the domestic, sensitive nature they presented all called to the "man of the wild" within us. There was something about their pretty dresses in church and the way they rode their bikes that caused us to stop our planning for the next field trip and recognize that something had changed.

There was no turning back. Once they started to be recognized it was as if they were everywhere. You went to the store for a loaf of bread and Boom!—There they were. Individually, in small groups or in the midst of many, they started to show up. It was a new sensation to hear the soft-stated "Hi" at the candy counter from one of them or to find that your bike was suddenly diverted two or more blocks out of the way just to ride by a girl's house.

It wasn't intended. Pretty soon it was a joint phenomenon that struck several of us at once. Our bike trips grew more frequent and wider-ranging, until we were covering virtually the whole town.

We don't know what caused it to happen. Whatever the reason, it seemed to hit all of the young ruffians at the same time. We just weren't in control. Like magnetic attraction of the needle of a compass to north, we were drawn to a new quarry. Our lives had changed forever.

Connie was a special friend. Her father was in the military. One day while we were at her house for an after-school visit, her father called from Hawaii. We couldn't get over it. Somehow, my bike kept wandering toward her house.

One day Davey and I were headed across the playground on our way to somewhere important when Diana and her friend Sharon met us. They were sitting on the snow bank on the side of the city-plowed ice rink just about to take off their new white skates. It must have been sixth grade or so, since we were still at the neighborhood school.

"Where are you guys going?" Diana asked.

"Off to Deilke's store to get a Pepsi," I responded.

"My dad's out of town and my Mom has gone to work until midnight. Do you want to come over to the house?" Diana's charming smile offered.

It was the first time that we had been invited to go to a girl's house without parents being present. How to respond? It was a new situation in life. Our regularity of supper at six at our houses had precedence over anything else. If you didn't get there you didn't eat—and you had to explain your whereabouts. Deciding in a flash is a strong male strength, especially when risk and adventure present themselves. Forgoing the Pepsi, we accepted the invitation and headed off to a new experience.

It was only a couple of blocks to Diana's. Walking together with the girls carrying their own skates, we saw several of our classmates headed in the same direction. Apparently Diana had invited more than a few—girls and boys alike. She opened the door to the assemblage and we all found our way to the refrigerator for a bottle of Coca-Cola. Diana assured us that there were hundreds of bottles of pop in the house, since her dad ran a downtown bar and had lots of stock on hand at home—a few wouldn't be missed.

We gathered in a circle on the floor in the large living room and Diana explained the rules of the house: we were free to visit the rooms, but everything should remain untouched; we needed to pick up after ourselves—and that the game was about to begin.

She had learned from her older sister or brother a game called "Spin the Bottle." She said we could all play it together. Using one of the empty Coke bottles in the center of the circle, a player would spin the bottle and watch it turn until it stopped. If it stopped facing one of the game players of the same sex as the spinner, then one would simply pass the bottle on to the next person. If, however, it landed with the top of the bottle facing another of the opposite sex, then the spinner was required to give that person a kiss on the lips.

For all—with the possible exception of Diana, who always seemed a bit more advanced than the rest of us—this was a new game and a new process of discovery. The game went on for an hour or so. After initial fumbles and inept moves across the circle that were met with hoots and whoops of the other players, we got into the rhythm of the game.

Most certainly it was a game of chance with a big or little reward, depending upon the final stop of the bottle and the accumulated fervor we held toward certain of the players. It soon became evident that the boys were anticipating their chances of the bottle coming to rest at Diana's place. She seemed to have a real verve for the game—and we were getting to understand the payoff.

The game went well that day. We spun the bottle and left the house with heads similarly spinning. There were many more days and nights at Diana's house over the years ahead that led us into the ranks of puberty.

We appreciated her training and were saddened when she moved away with her family, as we were about to enter high school. By then, we had become somewhat accomplished in our approach to girls—and absolutely aware that the soft sensate pleasures of girls were etched into our male psyche for all the years to come.

Chapter Two

The Pride of Work

I had a contract at age eight.

Every time it snowed, I was responsible to clean the walk at the Brunberg's house across the street. Before school, I grabbed the metal shovel off the front porch and quickly cut a path through the light snow from our porch to the sidewalk, then cut across the street.

Get there early. Get the job done.

Upon completion, Mrs. Brunberg opened the door and my adrenaline pumped. She was always gracious, always reasonable. Payment in full! A big half-dollar coin filled my small hand; even more on days when the snow was deep. It was a steady source of income (if it snowed)—like a government job.

After completing my contracted job, I moved around the neighborhood to additional opportunities. Finding two or three inches of snow before school was a special treat. Anticipation was that the work would be quick and the potential income great. Fifty cents here and seventy-five cents there added up to a pretty good wage before the day had even begun.

I did have to factor in the lady on the corner with an impaired daughter who needed my assistance—with no pay expected. It was a suggestion from Pa that we do this favor whenever it snowed.

Around the corner I would finish out the Hicks walkway and side drive so they could get their 1932 Plymouth coupe out of the garage. I soon warmed in the still, early and cold morning. Fully warmed, I finished without any more noise than the scrape of my single shovel.

The Hicks were pleasant old folks who sometimes did it themselves. Other times they were happy to pay. I just needed to check. The key to paying jobs was to beat the residents and any other young shovelers to the snow.

If you waited until after school, you were too late—someone else would get there or the homeowners did it themselves. If you were there by 6:30 a.m., then you most likely would have the job. There was no guarantee of pay.

Sometimes I finessed my way around the Hicks's home after school and was rewarded financially. If paid, then great. If not, then no big deal. There was reason for their inability to pay and that was understood without statement. Next time, maybe. They were friends, after all. I especially enjoyed the moments with Mr. Hicks in his little workshop in their warm, small basement with a furnace.

The only income or "allowance" that there was for me as a young boy was that which could be earned through the sweat of one's own brow or the ingenuity of one's own mind. These were creative moments of salesmanship, of creating one's own opportunities through a self-assured approach to a neighbor lady by offering to complete a chore or shovel the fresh snow.

I recall vividly what seemed to be one of my first "real income" jobs at about the same time. A nearly exact pair of single, elderly sisters lived around the corner and down the block. One was a nurse (retired) and the other a teacher (soon to retire). The two "Miss Carrolls" had me raking leaves and carrying things up and down the stairs.

I worked hard for them, earned my pay, knew it and felt good about the process from start to finish. My visit to their home got the job done and culminated in a fresh-baked item and cold drink in their immaculate small kitchen.

In the summer, I sold subscriptions for prize rewards (not real money) for the Minneapolis *Tribune*. I also collected rags and newspapers and metals for recycling.

By rapping on neighbors' doors I would provide a free serviceby hauling away some of their junk—and earn income along the way. A wagonload (the height of a stack allowed in and around my old Radio Flyer wagon) was taken to the Weisman's metal-paper-rag salvage yard at the end of our street.

It might bring fity-one cents or eighty-seven cents or a dollar and twelve cents, all dependent upon the content and quantity of collected goods. After weighing all of the goods separately on his Fairbanks-Morse scale with the sliding brass weights, Mr. Weisman reached inside his bib overalls to extract a large leather coin purse to pay the exact amount. It was "fair pay for fair trade"—with a businessman who treated an eight-year-old like a partner.

To earn income in this way was as much a matter of pride and achievement as it was of receiving the actual cash income. I learned from years of unpaid challenge at home and in helping neighbors that work had its own rewards. Pay received was just frosting on the cake.

Every winter, my brothers and I dutifully sawed six-foot side sections of sawmill cuts. Stored on the dirt floor of the old "Barn" in our backyard, we cut the sections into pieces for woodstoves of the kitchen and middle room heating our small house. With a buck saw and slabs on a wooden stand, we sliced the lengths, split the pieces with an axe, and stacked resulting chunks on our sled for careful movement to the porch.

There were moments of pay and there were moments of gift, and there were moments that fell in the middle. Working for Grandma or the elderly neighbor or the person who asked a favor didn't warrant pay. There were times when you just did it.

I would regularly hustle off to Grandma's at the end of the school day and take out the "clinkers" from her coal-burning furnace, carefully cut the new asparagus in her garden or run an errand to the store. It was my pleasure to serve. The occasional cash reward was a nickel or so that she carefully extracted from her worn, long leather coin purse with the metal clasp— as I was sent across the alley to the store for an item or two.

I earned a penny a minute from Mrs. Curtis in her garden which allowed me to occasionally hang out at Deilke's Grocery Store on summer days, which in turn caused me to spend eight cents for a cold twelve-ounce bottle of Pepsi. In the process, I got to know the comings and goings of the Sunbeam Bread deliveryman, Walt Woegen. Observing his full arms every time he entered the store, I sometimes assisted him with the large packs of donuts and bread and "coneys," all with the Little Miss Sunbeam logo.

I soon became Walt's assistant on the truck and stayed with him through the summer to handle the slides of bread (ten loaves in a re-foldable carton) and the deliciously scented baked goods from the Federal Bakery. We began our day at 4:00 a.m. Walt cruised by my home from his home down the street to pick me up at curbside.

At the darkened bakery in early morn, we entered the fully loaded truck and headed off to small town grocery stores across the Mississippi River where we unlocked doors and stocked shelves with soft, fresh bakery goods. By 7:00 a.m., we were back in town for a stop at Nick's Diner on Highway 61, where Walt introduced me to his favorite breakfast of eggs sunny-side up.

From there, we continued around the west end of town and visited virtually every small grocery store to greet owners and provide fresh-baked goods of the day. Our circuit finished at the SkyVu Drive-In Theatre near the airport, where we provided hundreds of coney buns for hot dogs served to a full house of theatre patrons each night.

Our day ended around 1:30 p.m., when Walt did his accounting with the office manager and I ventured around the bakery to get to know the bakers and the excellent products they were creating. For each day of work, I received two dollars in cash from Walt when he dropped me back at home. It was a job made in heaven—as Little Miss Sunbeam truly shined on me.

My days on the milk truck route began at age eleven or so, taking me throughout the county—first as assistant on a huge milk truck, then as novice driver at age thirteen of a huge, double-shifted Dodge "Job-Rated" truck, finally to gain a personal truck and route of my own by age fifteen.

With my driver's license at age fifteen, I continued on with jobs of car washer and floor sweeper at the Owl Motor Company. By age sixteen, I progressed to trusted driver of all the new models of Fords and Edsels arriving at this most successful dealership. I drove the shop pickup everywhere, delivered massive Gateway Motor Company delivery trucks back to their terminal after service and was encouraged by the manager to stay on at the dealership to become Assistant Service Manager after high school and Ford Company training.

My jobs continued over all the years of high school, college and marriage. To survive, I always seemed to be working at least two jobs. Truck driver and cab driver, clothing salesman and cab driver, beginning teacher and Dayton's suit salesman, the jobs never stopped. Through the extra hours and earnings I was able to take care of current needs and to save a bit for all the rainy days.

I am so thankful for the trust and expectation of the many whom I served over the years. They took a risk with me by giving me a job—and I learned to perform.

Work has been a blessing for me since that first shoveling contract—and first wagonloads heading down Grand Street. The reward is in the doing.

Mulligan Stew:
Meatballs and Meaning

*F*ive *or six hobos join in this. Only a pot and a fire are required.*

One builds a fire and rustles a pot. Another has to procure meat; another potatoes; one fellow pledges himself to obtain bread, and still another has to furnish onions, salt and pepper. If a chicken can be garnered, so much the better. The hobo who puts it together is known as the "mulligan mixer."

The whole outfit is placed in the pot and boiled until it is done. If one of the men is successful in procuring "Java," an oyster can is then used for a coffee tank—also put on the fire to boil.

—A 1900 version of Mulligan stew.

Hobos rode the rails into the heart of our small city along the Mississippi River—and into my heart.

Daily arrival of freight trains in the 1940s and 1950s brought us these open-air riders. Often seen standing in the open doors of the multitude of freight train cars passing through town, they sometimes chose to stop. Approaching a small home or two of the neighborhood after World War II, they entered or knocked on the screen door of the back porch, asking for a gift of a tomato from the garden, an apple from the tree or a sandwich to spare—and quietly inquired if there was any work they could do in exchange.

"Mulligan" was a stand-in for any Irishman. Mulligan stew is simply an Irish stew that includes meat, potatoes, vegetables and whatever else can be begged, scavenged, found or (occasionally) stolen. In their camps, American hobos created their own recipes.

It is reported that California hobos always put a "snipe" in their coffee, to give it that delicate amber color and to add to the aroma. "Snipe" is hobo slang for the butt end of a cigar that smokers throw down in the streets. All hobos had large quantities of snipes in their pockets, for both chewing and smoking purposes.

The Mulligan stew I ate as a young boy came in a tin bowl with a spoon and a tin cup of Kool-Aid or "nectar." Prepared and served by volunteers associated with the playgrounds and recreation department of my hometown, the donated thirty-gallon potful (from the Hot Fish Shop) was an elixir of the gods on a warm summer afternoon. It was a plate of sustenance to an ever-growing pre-teen body, a treasure from heaven, a gift of goodness, a celebration of life. The cups and dishes may have been a part of the city's inventory remaining after serving the World War II German POW camp outside our town.

On the designated summer Hobo and Gypsy Day, kids from all the playgrounds of the city gathered at the bandshell of Lake Park for an afternoon of games and Mulligan stew. With 300 kids present and king and queen candidates chosen from each playground, an overall King and Queen of the day was then chosen. It is interesting to note that the King of Hobo Day of 1948 was future Winona priest and Monsignor Thomas Hargesheimer.

Winona had a history of Mulligan stew, having been served at the Red Men's Club and Eagles Club in the 1950s, and in the local jail in 1935, to "thirty-day residents who demanded more than the daily nickel sandwiches served by the jailers." The Boy Scouts served it at their Armory scouting demonstration of 1929.

Priced at two cans for twenty-nine cents, it was available at Consumers Food Market in 1934. In 1917, Company Cook Gus Koschel of the Machine Gun Company of the Second Minnesota was "ranked by company members with some of the famous cooks of the U.S.,"having served the likes of sauerkraut, wieners, hot bologna and Mulligan stew.

In our house, with no convenience foods in the icebox, meals were homemade. At home, some of us were of a generation of hobos and cobblers of meals. Tomatoes of the summer garden were a special afternoon treat, a fresh-baked loaf of bread from Grandma a delicacy.

When Pa was working, Turner's ring-bologna or liver sausage sandwiches were fried for lunch. That special Saturday lunch he, the butcher, and the bakers of Mahlke's (who wrapped their white bread in white, imprinted wax paper) prepared a delicacy.

On lean winter days, goose-grease was spread and salted on a piece of Mahlke's Bread to suffice as breakfast. Goulash or buckwheat pancakes for six kids and Pa was typical "supper at six." With plenty of glass-bottled Winona Milk, it sustained us.

In winter, the hobos must have stayed in warmer climes, and good they did. Food of cold days and through Pa's unemployment limited our assortment to buckwheat pancakes, coon and beans, boiled potatoes with Pa's gravy over an occasional pork chop, a goose or a slab of venison provided by a hunting uncle or other home-created soups or stews from the bushel baskets and burlap bags of vegetables stored in the cellar under the kitchen floor. Goulash was a specialty of the house—not unlike the hobo stew of summer.

A stew is a combination of solid food ingredients that have been cooked in liquid and served in the resultant gravy. Ingredients in a stew can include any combination of vegetables (such as carrots, potatoes, beans, peppers and tomatoes) and meat—especially tougher meats suitable for slow cooking, such as beef. Poultry, sausages and seafood are also utilized when available.

While water can be used as the stew-cooking liquid, wine, stock and beer are also common. Seasoning and flavorings may also be added. Stews are typically cooked at a relatively low temperature (simmered, not boiled), allowing flavors to mingle. Pa taught me to cook slowly to bring out the best flavors.

Stewing is suitable for the least tender cuts of meat to become tender and juicy with the slow, moist-heat method. This makes it popular in low-cost cooking. Cuts having a certain amount of marbling and gelatinous connective tissue give moist, juicy stews, while lean meat may easily become dry.

We were all a part of God's mixture and his plan. From a back door of the kitchen we shared a sandwich. From the wonderful gift of our playground supervisors, we enjoyed a Mulligan stew. From the Goodfellows of Christmas we gained a new winter coat, a pair of mittens or buckle overshoes worn to school with pride—to be lined up in the "cloak room" with those of others.

There were some poor people in our midst.

We were a Mulligan stew of people—a simmered dish thrown together for mutual survival. When someone fell, someone else picked him or her up. We played Saturday basketball in the school gymnasium without parental supervision. Dodgeball and tetherball were played on the playground. Solely, either Max Molock or Bubby Hargesheimer coordinated baseball in the city summer league. They lifted us up.

We were valued and included. Everyone had a skill and was appreciated.

We shared a cup of water from the same tin cup. We were an amalgam, a bonded collection of haves and have-nots. No one cared. We just did the best we could and knew that we could grow and become as good as anyone. Max and our teachers encouraged us, neighbors cared and adults treated us with respect—as we did them.

Our parents stayed out of the way to let us grow as trusted, resourceful people.

Oh, for the days of Mulligan Stew!

The Circus Comes to Town: A 100-Year History of Fun

Somewhere there's a story about the circus coming to Winona.

It needs to be told. As one who waited for the circus trains for hours in the dark of summer mornings in the 1950s, I can attest to the thrill, the anticipation of it all.

The arrival of the circus to Winona was an annual event for many of the years from 1870 to the 1950s. The circus of P.T. Barnum may have made it to Winona after Phineas Taylor (P.T.) started it in 1870, but there's no evidence. Most certainly the Barnum and Bailey Circus, created in 1888, dropped by with its eighty-five railroad cars. It was a circus that had been "taken to new heights" by James Bailey after Barnum's passing in 1891.

Under an "old rag carpet" borrowed from their mother, Marie, the Ringling boys (at first just five of them) of Baraboo, Wisconsin, started a penny circus in their backyard in 1874. Al, Otto, Alf, Charles and John showed early interest in the circus at their birthplace of McGregor, Iowa. In 1872, they moved to Prairie du Chien and then on to Baraboo, where they founded their first commercial circus. Their father, August Ringling (from the German Ru-engling), may have stopped off in Winona for a bit in the 1870s to work as a harness maker, his second vocation after farming.

Gus and Henry joined their brothers and the circus in the late 1880s. Their sister Ida, the youngest, married Harry Whitestone North, who worked the rails for C&NW from Baraboo to Winona as his regular route. He was forty-four and Ida twenty-six when they married in 1902. Their sons, John Ringling North and Henry Ringling North, were second-generation leaders of the combined circuses.

When the first-generation boys had gained eight dollars in Baraboo, they sewed a tent of sheeting, created a panorama on brown wallpaper and gained a Mexican pony to add to the family goat, fife, drum and Mom's plates. Soon they were drawing crowds and charging five cents.

The pony (Ringling's' first circus horse) led the parade, performed in the ring and tossed off one or the other of the Ringling boys to add to the excitement. Mom's plates got broken when the boys did their plate spinning. It was one of the featured acts, which included the goat act, clown song, tumbling by the boys, fife and drum, a trapeze bar, bending through a hoop and more falling off the pony to bring good, clean fun.

Their original (and long) name was "Ringling Brothers United Monster Shows, Great Double Circus, Royal European Menagerie, Museum, Caravan and Congress of Trained Animals." As the boys got older (ages fourteen to twenty-three), they took to the road with a wagon, three horses and the name "Ringling Brothers Classic and Comic Concert Co."

They visited the small towns of Wisconsin, performed a bit as a musical group at an opera house or two and created "entertainment of mirth and merriment." The boys gave "glorious processional amazement" in each of the villages in which they marched. In their single year together with him, they were taught by experienced circus man "Yankee" Robinson. He said they must "keep moving" and "create a reputation strong and true." Yankee died within the year, but not before stating that the Ringlings were to become world circus leaders.

Within ten years, the five Ringling brothers had a full-fledged circus of 1,000 employees, 350 horses, chariots, fifty musicians, three large rings, "millions of yards of canvas," and four large trains of railroad cars, all to arrive in Winona on June 18, 1894. The Chicago and Milwaukee trains had left Mason City the night before and would head to Sparta upon completion of festivities in Winona.

The Ringlings insisted on cleaning up a bad reputation of some of the "hangers-on" who followed the circus—those creating disreputable and dishonest dealings. In the Ringling Circus, they banned the use of profanity. When the train arrived in Winona in 1894, there was a full-time superintendent of Pinkerton Detectives who cared for "style, morals and character of the show."

As an editor of the Winona newspaper stated at the time, the story of the Ringlings "teems with lessons of patience, perseverance and honest effort." He suggested that, "Alexander may have conquered the world, but the Ringling Bros. pleased it."

All were pleased with the show. The Ringling Bros. Route Book of 1894 states the night house at Winona was "the largest night business in the State of Minnesota this year."

I wasn't there for the trains of 1894, but did wait with the crowd in the early morning of July 26, 1951, to greet "The Greatest Show on Earth" as it arrived in all its glory. The combined shows of the early leaders had debuted in Madison Square Garden in 1919, as "Ringling Bros. and Barnum & Bailey Circus." In 1929, they added Sells-Floto, Hagenbeck-Walace, Robinson, Sparks, Buffalo Bill and the Al G. Barnes circuses "to own every traveling circus in America." They were known worldwide for skill, thrill and integrity—and they came to Winona. Wow!

The thrill was in being present for the arrival of the circus—"to hear the rumble of the incoming trains." It was *Music Man*, *Quo Vadis*, and Frank Buck's *Bring 'Em Back Alive* animal adventure show all rolled into one (at 5:00 a.m. on Second Street). And we could get up close and persona, as part of the "enhancement of the glorious procession." Once organized, we walked with performers and animals to the circus site at Goodview, some several miles west.

With animals, performers, trainers and a large gathering of parade observers along Fifth Street to cheer us on, we headed west to the opportunity of a morning's work setting up the tents—and the promise of a free ticket for our effort. We longed to "see the wonder and astonishment of its circuses." How much could our scrawny pre-teen bodies help these seasoned veterans, their elephants and the choreographed construction of a mammoth city under golden tarps?

One writer spoke wonderfully of the travel of elephants past the crowd on Broadway in 1949 when she offered: "As 23 elephants lumbered down the concrete street their big grey felt feet made a wonderful muted sound—'smish-smosh-smish-smosh-smish-smosh.'"

Following those elephants to circus grounds, she observed, "And the elephants—the lovely, shapeless, droll giants with their twinkling eyes and perpetual half-smiles. They stood in the animal tent swaying from foot to foot, spraying great trunkfuls of dirt over their backs. Sometimes they set down and let the dirt cascade blissfully down the vast slope of their backs."

She was there!

Once we were inside "the big top" with balloons, cotton candy, pink lemonade and peanuts for the elephants all in hands of 4,500 patrons, the ringmaster stepped forward in his tall hat, shiny and glorious long-waisted star-spangled suit, and black leather boots. He was captured in shimmering

The Ringling Bros.'s circus elephants unloading from the train. (Photo courtesy of Feld Enterprises.)

glory in the spotlight. In the darkened tent, with drum rolls and slow, booming voice came his well-known words from center ring:

"Ladies and Gentlemen, children of all ages, welcome to the Greatest Show on Earth!"

It sent quivers up your spine—soon to see elephants and tigers and Lipizzaner horses in grand procession. The music stunned our senses. Trapeze artists would "fly through the air with the greatest of ease."

Emmett Kelly, the world's greatest clown, would bring his wandering "Weary Willie" appearance into view throughout the tents and into the crowd. He was joined by a cadre of clowns who unloaded from a single-seat car—as if a stuffed telephone booth of people were unloading.

A little person or two always joined the fray. Tigers stood on individual piers when a crack of the safari master's whip sent them from one place to another—with power, majestic beauty and obedience. Lipizzaners circled with bareback riders standing atop. Elephants bounded, rolled over, kneeled in place, and soon raised stunning circus beauties perched on their heads to their full height. Oh, the beauty of it all!

The ringmaster created the mood and energy. He led us through an ever-heightening process. With quiet, darkened lights and suspense, the raising of cannon and huge net on opposite sides of the tent—and *silence*—he

Emmett Kelly, the world's greatest clown. (Photo courtesy of Feld Enterprises.).

brought us to the firing of the human missile (male or female) from the Zac-chini Cannon.

The cannon was invented by Ildebrando Zacchini in the 1920s, after being inspired by Jules Verne. His "human cannonball" (son Hugo was the first) flew 200 feet across the circus tent to land in the net—and walk away. We could barely hold our seats as the cannon boomed and the flyer flew!

The pace continued for two hours.

From its start in 1871, Winonans fell in love with circus. Older's Circus appeared as "Museum, Circus and Menagerie" on June 17 of that year. With baby elephant, sea cow, gymnast, petrified giant and double-humped camels— all for fifty cents, children tewnty-five cents—activities were "enlivened by Prof. Good's New York Silver Cornet Band."

The Great Trans-Atlantic Expedition appeared in 1873, with "500 living wild animals." Howe's Great London Circus came in 1876, 1879, and

1916 (Emmett Kelly joined them in 1920.) Lent's New York Circus thrilled our grandparents in 1876. Cole's brought their show in 1878 to the old circus grounds next to the Milwaukee Railroad tracks. Lemon Brothers came for a first time in 1895, following up in 1897, with Barnum and Bailey closely behind them in same year ("not being here for several years").

Many deserving mention include Hummell and Hamilton (1897), Gentry's (1900), Hagenbeck (1918, 1927, 1935—to be absorbed by Ringling in 1935), Robbins Bros. (1928, 1930 at the West End Circus Grounds—with Buck Owens, film star), Sell-Floto brought Tom Mix and his famous horse "Tony" to the show of 1930 at the West End fields, followed by Al G. Barnes Circus (1931) and Russell Bros (1935). An indoor circus was held in 1941 at the Armory, conducted by the Moneli Bros.

Clyde Beatty and his circus met the sheriff in 1948 at their grounds on Second and Liberty over some money owed to Olmstead County. The Shrine Circus at Gabrych Park of the same year featured "Big Bill" Bloomberg of Wabasha as ringmaster—with forty years in "nearly every noted circus." Dailey Bros. came to the old airport grounds with five rings in 1950.

Ringling Bros. Circus was a regular in 1893, 1894, 1896, 1899, 1904, and 1916—when they brought forty-seven rail cars to town. The Sells Brothers were there to compete in 1894. The circus of 1896 brought a "crowd of bums," apparently attracted by the circus and crowds. Forthwith, they were locked up—all forty-one of them—until Tuesday. The police chief felt it best to "keep these hard characters in limbo."

The "Big One" for Winona was the combined Ringling Bros. shows delighting "thousands of people in town" in 1926, 1937 ("27,000 attended!"), 1939, 1940, 1949, 1951 and 1954. The "Greatest Show on Earth" had made it to the greatest city of America. Its "streamlined show" of 1939, with innovations of a new "Big Top," Caterpillar tractors instead of horses, and air conditioning of the big top was under the direction of new leader John Ringling North. The thirty-six-year-old nephew of John Ringling greeted the folks at the circus site on East Sanborn and Jefferson.

Henry Ringling North, the vice president of the operation, stated in *Billboard Magazine* that the greatest innovation—number four—came when he and John saw the Burlington railroad's bullet-like silver train (the Zephyr) at a crossing while in Winona.

John declared, "Come next spring there will be no more Pullman coaches—the whole circus train will be silver." True to his word, the circus of 1940 arrived in Winona in the "streamlined train." Having worked with new designer Norman Bel Geddes over the winter; "It rained blueprints."

His next promise was to bring air conditioning to the coaches of the train and to "streamline all the flies out of the cookhouse." His brother offered that John's ambition to do the final act "seems a lot like trifling with the Almighty."

The show of 1949 arrived for its "first performance in Winona in ten years" from Madison, Wisconsin, with four trains and a total eighty-nine cars. Included with the usual elephants, bareback equestrians and high wire artists were "Clausson's Acrobatic Bears" for "their first time in America." Did they know it was their first trip?

That 1949 show also brought Cecil B. DeMille, Hollywood's greatest director. He was observing and creating substance for the four million dollar *Greatest Show on Earth* movie that would open for Winonans at the State Theatre in 1952. Starring James Stewart as clown, Cornel Wilde as trapeze artist and Betty Hutton as aerialist, the show was a big hit across the nation—in stunning Technicolor.

DeMille stated of his weeklong visit on the circus tour, "The most amazing thing about this circus is the precision of production…it's precision, precision, precision."

The Greatest Show on Earth traveled the rails under the guidance of the Ringling Bros. A visit to their winter headquarters at Sarasota, Florida, recently allowed us to view the Ringling Mansion and Art Museum displaying a massive, worldwide collection of artifacts gathered by Mabel and John Nicholas Ringling. The busy state-owned museum, established in 1927, was left as legacy by "one of the richest men in the world." It is the site of extravagance, opulence and abundance for all to see.

A separate Circus Museum in Sarasota was created in 1948, with banners, artifacts and history, including "The Wisconsin," John and Mabel's separate, private Pullman car built in 1905.

On a recent visit to Circus World Museum at Baraboo, we again felt the ringmaster's power and majesty in a sample performance in the Ringling Bros. original home tent. While standing in the darkened tent or outside next to original circus equipment and wheeled cages on the property, we were drawn back to another era.

The rails were taken up in 1956. The *Daily News* offered the headline, "Ringling Circus Quits Big Top for Big Halls." The circus was sold, becoming wholly indoor. Emmett Kelly left the show to become the mascot for the Brooklyn Dodgers and a television and night show entertainer. Under new ownership and direction of the Feld family since 1957, today's circus is alive and well, with an abundance of performances throughout the nation (searchable by zip code on their terrific website.)

People can still see the circus either from the Red Tour (Fully Charged), Blue Tour (Dragons) or Gold Tour (Barnum Bash.) The closest performance for Winonans is in the United Center of Chicago, with twenty-one performances over a ten-day stand. Guess we'll need to ride the rails and reverse the process. The Dragons performance and its contested tribes offer all the "history of circus, with the addition of tribal myths and dragons" to create a new show.

It has been another journey for me through the history and records of Winona. I so enjoy the quest and the surprises. Confirmation has been achieved of the shared goodness and excitement by many of "Circus Day."

I am delighted to have been a part of the history and the sensate pleasure shared in 1939 by an editor of the *Republican-Herald* when he said:

> When the sophisticated say, "When you've seen one circus, you've seen 'em all," they forget that the greatest appeal to visiting the big top year after year is the association of memories. Many a businessman today remembers when he toiled, a hot and dusty boy, carrying a bucket that sloshed water on his trousers, to earn a free ticket from the elephant-keeper. His sense of enjoyment is no less keen when he sees the circus today, even though the elephants now quench their thirst from a motor-driven water wagon.
>
> Hope to see you in the "Big Top"—for "The Greatest Show on Earth.

Fast and Forte: The Music of the Circus

(This article about legendary Ringling Bros. and Barnum & Bailey® musical director
Merle Evans was published in 1962, in the *Ringling Bros. and Barnum & Bailey Circus
Magazine & Program*, celebrating the ninety-second edition of The Greatest Show
On Earth®. Used with permission of Feld Enterprises.) Title by Kent O. Stever.

During the nineteenth century, when Mendelssohn and Schumann and Franz
Liszt cracked the ice off music and gave it warmth and color and emotion in
what is referred to now as the romantic period, and then when Wagner came
along and made it louder and more emotional, the pattern was set for circus
music. It has reached its zenith under the baton of Merle Evans, who has directed music for Ringling Bros. and Barnum & Bailey for almost forty years.

Evans has been called the "Toscanini of the Circus," and James Fran-
cis Cook, editor of *Etude*, calls this homespun character "Will Rogers with a
horn." But the world knows him simply as the greatest exponent of solid circus
music in the whole spangle-studded history of this form of entertainment.

Throughout the country, in coliseums, auditoriums, and sports are-
nas, the new temples of the circus, Merle Evans' circus windjammers calmly
prepare to play two three-hour sessions (sometimes three), within the span
of thirteen hours. Before each show, Merle gives his musicians his standard
pep talk in gallop-time:

"It's-going-to-be-a-tough-day-on-the-lips-boys," he races. "Gotta-
sound-good-tonight-too-for-the-house-is-full-of-Circus-folks-and-their-kids.
Well-here-we-go-boys-hit-it-hard! 'Ringling Bros. Triumphal!'"

Musicians consider Merle Evans a remarkable guy. He was born in
Columbus, Kansas, and ran away from home to lead a carnival band when he
was only sixteen. After some years with shows of various kinds, he graduated
to the baton of The Greatest Show On Earth.

Merle's leading the Ringling Bros. and Barnum & Bailey band for so
many years is quite an achievement, but the Circus Toscanini never blows his
own horn. Modest to a fault, he prefers to let his record and the music speak
for itself—which it does—amidst a cascade of marches, gallops, schottisches,
tangos, rumbas, fox trots, waltzes, polkas, one-steps and cakewalks that do
the occasion like sequins in a giant animated mural. The music of the big
show is the loom upon which the thrill-studded tapestry of the performance
is threaded.

Evans's lads can meander right sweetly in the lacy dells of dulcet melodies, but the kind of music in which they really excel is fast and forte, with the brass section wide open and blowing its brains out and the snare-drummer's wrists moving like a crazy trip-hammer.

The notes pour out like beads strung on a spangled thread. The band starts to "straighten it out" (the circus equivalent for swingdom's "getting in the groove"), and if you were brought up like most Americans and cut your amusement molars on a circus teething ring, you can just close your eyes and see the big cats snarling, elephants doing their tricks, the faces of laughing clowns, and the beautiful precision of aerialists doing their stuff in the lofty reaches of the arena domes.

For good circus music can be felt as well as heard. From the pens of its composers flow the excitement and daredeviltry of the circus. The glory of open brass is there—loud enough to stir the ghosts of the departed Ringlings, Phineas T. Barnum, and James A. Bailey. And also, there, riding the bright crest of the music is the courage and tenacity of the troupers and the warmth engendered in the hearts of clowns who work to the added obbligato of children's laughter. It's all there—in the tunes played by circus windjammers.

Circus bands are taken for granted, like peanuts and pink lemonade, but the twelve labors of Hercules are a picnic compared to the circus wind-jammer's daily stint. Merle Evans' band plays upwards of 190 cues each performance and the circus season generally lasts from late January until the middle of December.

But have you ever heard a movie with the soundtrack missing? Well, then, you have an idea of what the Circus would be like without music. For music is the very pulse beat of The Greatest Show On Earth.

Glossary of Selected Cirucs Terms

Edited by Kent O. Stever, with thanks to Ringling Bros.

Acrobats—Circus stars that perform on the trampoline, trapeze, tight wire or tumbling mats.

Animals—Elephants, tigers, horses, dogs, llamas, alpacas and zebras—the performing partners of the circus.

Barnum, P.T.—A master showman who opened a circus in 1871, in Brooklyn, NY. He was a wizard at finding unusual acts that people had never seen.

Big Top—A large tent where the early circus was performed. It sometimes contained three rings at once—with 4,500 people in the tent for the show.

Catcher—A member of a trapeze act who catches the flyers.

Cherry pie—Extra work done by circus personnel for extra pay.

Equestrian—A horseback rider.

Flip-flaps—The trick of flipping from a standing position to the hands while riding bareback on a running horse.

Funambulist—A rope walker, taken from Latin roots *funis* meaning "rope" and *ambulare* meaning "to walk."

Gilly wagon—Extra small wagon or cart used to carry light pieces of equipment around the lot.

Grease paint—Makeup used by clowns.

Hair suspension act—An act in which ladies hang by their hair and perform tricks high above the arena.

Herald—Advertisements for the circus.

Hold your horses—Today this means to be patient. In earlier days, before cars, spectators came by horse to watch the circus parade. Sometimes the horses would be startled by the appearance of elephants, so a person would walk in the parade ahead of the elephants and say, "Hold your horses, here come the elephants."

Howdah—A seat or platform on the back of an elephant or camel used for riders.

Iron jaw act—An aerial stunt performance using a leather and metal apparatus which fits into the performer's mouth.

Jackpots—Tall tales about the circus.

Joey—Another term meaning "clown," in honor of the famous English clown Joseph Grimaldi.

Kazoo—a musical instrument frequently used by clowns.

Kiester—A circus wardrobe trunk.

Liberty—A horse act without riders, reins, or any restraints. Horses follow the spoken command of their trainer.

Menagerie—Backstage area where the circus animals are kept.

Michu—The smallest man in the Ringling Bros. circus (thirty-three inches tall.)

Mud show—A circus show that traveled over land in wagons; an outdoor circus show that plays on dirt lots that may be muddy after a rain.

Net—Used as a safety device in flying trapeze and other aerial acts.

Pachyderms—Another word for elephant. It means "thick-skinned" in Greek.

Pie Car—Train car where the chef prepares delicious food for the circus performers.

Riggers—Circus workers who set up all of the ropes and wires needed in the show.

Rigging—The apparatus used in high wire or aerial acts.

Ringling Bros.—The famous group of five brothers who created their own circus and later purchased the Barnum & Bailey Circus in 1907.

Ringmaster—The person who announces the circus acts.

Stunt—A daring act that takes courage and skill.

Train—P.T. Barnum used a train to move the circus from town to town; each Ringling Bros. circus train today has about fifty-three cars.

Under the Big Top—The tent where the early circus acts were performed.

Walkaround—A clown number in which clowns perform sight gags while continually moving around the hippodrome track.

Whiteface clown—Neatly dressed. This clown's face is mostly white, tending to be more serious.

Suzy's Apples

We were the real, "rag-tag," 1950s generation of children—coming from all walks of life.

I was in my element with other kids who called at my back door after supper to venture out for night activities. Some parents kept their more refined children indoors every night for safety and control. I was one of the many who had the freedom to bust out—with an expectation that whatever I did, I would behave. We weren't a "gang." Rather, we were a semi-leaderless mix of individuals with separate and appreciated strengths. Suzy was probably the closest thing we had to a leader.

She was a smart, cute, athletic kind of kid who could outrun a lot of the boys—and hold her own in a necessary "punch-out" session that sometimes occurred to settle an argument. There was an occasional bloody nose, usually not reported to parents. We had our own way of caring for one another. A swiped towel from a nearby clothesline, a turn of the water spigot on a neighbor's house and the injury was resolved.

On one night in our small, southern Minnesota valley town, Suzy led our gang of seven away from home territory and our usual turf of backyards, fences and escape routes. She heard that there were really big apples coming ripe in a yard on West Fifth Street—eight or ten blocks from home and just beyond the West End Theater.

We trusted that she knew what she was doing as we ventured with her through nine o'clock darkness of a late September evening. We knew our way around the neighborhood somewhat, since we had traveled the brick-covered Fifth Street for years on our way to baseball, skating, the "rec," and on Sunday paper routes. But we didn't know the layout of fences and gates and alleys. Suzy assured us that she knew the way.

Stealing apples was risky business. It had to be done under cover of night, since folks might be on their back porches until "lights out." During the day they mowed their yards with hand-powered push mowers, sprayed their apples or worked in vegetable gardens. In early evening they "sprinkled" the gardens with a garden hose and finally rested on their small, enclosed porches—away from mosquitoes and the burdens of the day. Once indoors for their final cup of coffee and the ten o'clock news with Cedric Adams on WCCO, the coast was clear. We were close to bedtime—theirs and ours.

Late summer sounds traveled across the still backyards as we took our first steps. We could hear the sound of a radio from a kitchen as well as the crunching of our feet on the crushed rock of the alley. Huddling down like a team getting signals from their coach, Suzy whispered instructions to stay down and limit apples to four each. We needed to be able to both carry our bounty and run like the wind.

Using hand signals, Suzy and the gang decided to enter the white-picket-fenced yard through a small gate in the alleyway next to the garage. Sheltered for the moment from sight by a garage and the prized tree, all that was needed was to slip quietly under the tree and begin the harvest.

I had just placed my two hands on apples high enough over my head to cause me to stand on tiptoes. Doing so, I felt a massive hand like Pa's reach the back of my neck and get a strong hold. I was nearly lifted off the ground. I knew the feeling from past experiences with Pa—not a welcome feeling!

Unbeknownst to us and to the homeowner, a neighbor had observed the gang on the prowl and made his way across the gate and into the yard as the eighth member of the raiding party. Having only two very large hands, our subjugator grabbed the most available and likely thieves and escorted us across the back yard. His other hand held a firm grip on the back of Suzy's neck. Fellow raiders scrambled out and over the gate and "headed for the hills."

Suzy and I were roughly placed together on the lighted steps of the back porch, a police-like flashlight now shining in our faces. We were scared beyond belief. The strong-armed man identified himself as one of the coaches of the high school football team. He had obviously dealt with miscreant youth before.

He told us to "Sit" and "Stay"—and we did! He went onto the porch to confer with the homeowner, a quiet, older gentleman who didn't deserve to have his life challenged by a gang of young hoodlums.

With names and phone numbers already taken, we knew we were in for it. Not only would the police haul us in, but we would get it at home, too. Only once before had I ridden in the back seat of a police car—to get a ride home from across the river when I participated in a rescue operation. Even though a non-threatening ride, the enclosure of the back seat by a heavy metal screen in front of me made it feel like a moving jail cell.

I wasn't looking forward to being locked up again. While waiting for our captor to return, we heard the phone ring. We expected it was the police calling to confirm where to pick up the thieves. We soon expected to hear the police siren.

As the screen door opened above us, we moved aside to let the coach and the homeowner come down the steps to face us. They had been in conference for a good while. We expected that they were waiting for the arrival of the police—as we were. Suzy's eyes grew big as the coach introduced himself as "Mr. Spence," and the homeowner as Mr. Einhorn.

Mr. Spence outlined the very personal threat that Mr. and Mrs. Einhorn felt from our marauding band invading their property. He told of the hard work and infinite care that Mr. Einhorn put into his garden and apples. Coach did his best to make us feel like lowlife human beings—and he succeeded.

Mr. Einhorn began to speak in a very gentle tone. He asked if we were hungry. Was this the reason for our theft? He obviously knew better. We were two of the strongest kids in the group. He wondered out loud why someone would steal another's personal property. We stammered a bit, but finally concluded that we weren't hardened criminals—just a gang "out for fun." It was the challenge of the hunt in the middle of the night that brought us to his backyard.

I got his drift, and soon apologized for violating his property and for stealing his apples. Suzy picked up on the theme and asked what we could do to make up for our inappropriate behavior. It appeared that Mr. Einhorn, not unlike our school principal, was a man who knew what life was about. He was asking us to solve the problem.

We were invited onto the back porch to continue our conversation. The coach put away his menacing flashlight and followed Mr. Einhorn's lead in attempting to resolve a problem. So far the police had not been mentioned. With an offered glass of Kool-Aid from Mrs. Einhorn, we relaxed a bit and began to breathe normally.

The plan evolved as Mr. Einhorn told us that our information was correct—the apples were at their prime. He fully intended to pick the several bushel baskets of apples in just days ahead. He shared his concern for climbing the ladder and his safety in picking the apples, as he had done over all the years. Mr. Spence volunteered to assist.

The opening was there and Suzy took it. She volunteered that the gang of seven would happily come and assist by climbing and picking. We hadn't done the job before, but I assured him that we would be as careful with his apples as we were in gently picking the tomatoes at home. With his guidance and Mr. Spence's assistance, we could make our wrong a bit more right, if he would allow us to assist.

Suzy assured him that all of the raiders would be present—fully prepared, contrite and cooperative. The listed seven gang members on the pad in the center of the porch table were to be in attendance at one o'clock on Saturday afternoon for the harvest.

We adjourned our late night meeting with an agreement and a feeling of responsibility for our actions. No mention was made of calls to parents or police. It was understood that all raiders would assume and resolve their own acts of contrition with parents. There would be no excuses allowed—nothing less than personal responsibility. Mr. Einhorn and the coach clearly expected that the mature handling of a serious personal matter could be accomplished by equally serious American youth. As in conversations with our school principal, Mr. Ellies, we were being taken to a higher plane.

Leaving the porch, we found the gang waiting in the brightness of a harvest moon on the school playground—as expected. It was the common assembly point understood by all. Hanging on swings and stretched out across the monkey bars, nervous team members listened as Suzy and I outlined the plan.

Each was to assume responsibility. Except for an outburst by Eddie that was quickly put down by others, all agreed to what seemed like a fair plan—including no jail time. The only sticking point was that each was to bring a parent-signed permission slip when they came to pick the apples. Mr. Einhorn and the coach expected our parents to know what they were doing. The "why" was up to each, as parents heard our explanations. When compared to a ride in the back of the black-and-white squad car, the permission slip was seen as the lesser of two evils.

On Saturday, we assembled on the school lot after lunch on a vibrant blue-sky day, riding our bikes and wearing tennis shoes for climbing. We weren't under the cover of night, but there was still fear of the outcome. We had each weathered the storm at home—and had the signed slip to prove it.

Parents felt very good about the solution. In their shared opinion, the homeowner and coach were being more than fair. Suzy led us across the back streets to arrive ahead of time. With Mr. Spence's help, we introduced ourselves and turned in the notes.

Materials had been laid out in the yard, with a tall wooden ladder, two stepladders, small mesh onion bags, bushel baskets and a long-handled mechanical apple picker. Mr. Einhorn had a plan to work our way down and around the tree, with a caution that all apples should be treated with greatest care. Coach would set the ladders up and detail the pickers to their spots in the tree.

We were to pick and place the apples in the onion bags and transfer filled bags down to a lower partner—being ever careful not to bump apples off as we passed. It soon became a dance in the tree, with ballet-like moves across branches. Bags were gently emptied into the baskets, with hand buffeting of apples for protection as they were poured in. Mr. Einhorn gently used his long pole to pick apples on the outward branches and lower them gently to the ground.

Within an hour the apples had all been picked, with nearly five bushels of gorgeous apples gleaming in the afternoon sunshine. Team members had all gained a new experience in climbing and in gentle handling of a beautiful, natural produce. It was soon evident that sincere appreciation for Mr. Einhorn and the coach was felt by team members; with friendly smiles and words of encouragement shared by all.

The next task was to sort apples, under the watchful eye of Mrs. Einhorn. With a steady smile and her clear direction, we sorted them onto a large multi-colored quilt she had set out on the lawn. She informed us that apples were to be stored in ordered baskets in the cool, dark fruit cellar next to the coal bin of their small basement.

Bumped or softer apples were first to be used for applesauce and baking. Gnarled apples or those with sunspots were next in line for peeling and general use, with remaining baskets to be filled with the top-quality eating apples—all covered and used throughout winter months ahead. Once complete, Mrs. Eihhorn selected, filled and set aside a small, apple-colored basket. In addition, she asked that we each select two of the very best apples to be placed in her special wooden bowl made from Vermont white oak.

Pairs of team members carried wire-handled bushel baskets filled to the brim to the orderly fruit cellar. They were set in order of use as directed.

Mrs. Einhorn gently covered the baskets with small towels she had made from colorful flour bags of the past. Closing the treasures behind the hand-made, slatted pine door of the fruit cellar, our mission was complete.

Gathered around the table on the porch with the small basket and bowl as centerpiece, we enjoyed a glass of Kool-Aid and a feeling of mutual accomplishment. Mr. Einhorn thanked us for our quality work. He expressed his appreciation for our strength, agility and gentle handling in gathering the crop. He also thanked us for the "gracious gift of coming to his home to assist."

He told of his high regard for young people. Whenever we were in the neighborhood we were invited to stop by to say hello. Mr. Spence told us that we were a real "team" and that he looked forward to coaching some of us when we got to the high school.

Suzy spoke for all when she apologized for our ungenerous act of attempting to steal the Einhorn apples. We hadn't considered their work, dedication or the wonderful nature of the homeowners when we had come in the dark. Our eyes had been opened. She thanked Mr. Spence and the Einhorns for "letting us learn a lesson."

Mrs. Einhorn took center stage and presented the small basket to Mr. Spence, thanking him for his help and for "introducing us to so many nice, young people." Drawing the wood bowl to her appliquéd, apple-covered apron, she invited each of us to take two of the apples—the very best of the crop.

Chapter Three

The School Patrol

It was cold this morning.

I looked out my ice-covered window to see the "Blue Moon" that I heard Pa talk about last night as he read from the paper while sitting by the woodstove. Knowing the snowplow had come through in the night, I took an extra twist in my tattered quilt to find the right adjustment in the bedcovers to keep warm for a few more minutes. I knew that I needed to get up shortly.

The plow had piled yesterday's snow up on the side of the street on top of the already huge mounds, upon which I often walked to school. In late afternoon, after chores were done, I sometimes skied on them with wood slats tied to my shoes with twine from the shed out back. For now, the cold of winter had arrived; the snow was over for the moment and the second full moon of the month shone brightly. I could see mounds next to sidewalks in the glistening light of the moon and soft touch of streetlights. There was a final cleanup in the neighborhood to be done before heading to school and safety patrol.

I had to get moving. Slipping on well-worn corduroy trousers I especially liked for cold days, I found a clean shirt in the small closet that Pa had created for me in my small attic room. Pa had singlehandedly converted the attic a few years ago into four bedrooms for five boys and a little sister, and built a staircase down to the first level from cast-off oak lumber from a construction job at the local teacher's college, where he was a summertime construction worker.

My wool hat, scarf, new buckle boots and trusty wool mackinaw hung in the little room at the foot of the stairs. I quickly dressed, splashed my face with water in the single bathroom off the middle room and pronounced myself ready for the day.

It was the start of a new week and a new year at school today—Christmas vacation was over. Before I headed out the door to my jobs, I needed to get the wood stove going from last night's embers. The potbelly stove was fed by wood piled on the back porch. My brothers and I dutifully split and sawed sections with the buck saw, stacked the pieces on our sled next to the old "Barn" and carefully moved the load to the porch.

Whoever was up first was responsible to shake the ashes and to fire up the stove for the day. Right now, I needed to remove some of yesterday's ashes to the metal bucket and grab an armful of wood to feed the fire.

Fire going, dressed for the day, I checked to see that my school patrol belt hanging from the clothesline in the middle room was dry. It hung next to those of two brothers. Together, we had washed and scrubbed our white canvas belts on the side of the kitchen sink last night with hand soap and a stiff brush. I would tend to it later, but first needed to head out the front door into the cold of morning.

I grabbed the metal shovel off the front porch and quickly cut a path through yesterday's snow down to the sidewalk, where I headed toward the corner with my shovel plowing a path in the center of our sidewalk. If I were lucky, one of my brothers would be up to clean the balance of the sidewalk and spread the ashes before I returned from my several shoveling jobs. If not, I would take care of it—but first, the paying customers.

My old reliable—the Brumbergs—was directly across the street. I would clear their walk first, then head across the street to our side where Mrs. Vater lived on the corner. The long corner lot took a lot of time, but the snow wasn't too heavy, so I could do it in jig time. Then I would finish out the Hicks's walkway and side drive, so they could get their 1932 Plymouth coupe out of the garage. It was early and I soon warmed in the still, cold morning. By the time I was on to the Vaters's driveway, I was fully warmed. I finished theirs and the Hicks's without any more noise than the scrapes of my single shovel.

I didn't hear anyone else out yet, but that wasn't unusual. I loved the quiet, the serenity and the joy of my work—and the potential profit. I might stop by the Brumbergs before I headed to school. Mrs. Brumberg was always up early and paid attention to my work. She greeted me cordially every time and paid the thirty-five or fifty cents that she decided upon.

Shoveling out the Vaters was a non-pay job. Pa simply expected that we would keep the way clear for the neighboring widow and her challenged daughter. It felt good to help out. The Hicks would see me after school and welcome me with a cup of cocoa and some friendly conversation. Their place was small and thirty-five cents was the norm, unless the snow was exceptionally heavy. I especially enjoyed the moments with Mr. Hicks in his little workshop in the warm, small basement with a furnace.

I was greeted at home with a clean sidewalk and ashes having been spread on the sidewalk for traction. Pa and brothers were all up and bustling around the little house—with six of us getting ready for school. There was goose grease in a bowl on the table from the goose dinner we all enjoyed on Christmas. Using the self-serve toaster with a side flipped down to take the bread, we could quickly warm (or char) our bread, depending upon how quick we were to notice. Spreading it with goose grease and a little salt—breakfast was served. Everyone was on his own—except for little sister, whom Pa cared for.

At lunchtime we scrambled home for a peanut butter and jelly sandwich or a cup of soup from a shared can with a brother. When Pa was working, sometimes Grandma would be there for a warm lunch for all of us. Little sister (now in first or second grade) came home and returned with us and somehow got fed. Pa was mostly laid off in the winter months. He made excellent suppers (often pancakes) that he served every evening at six o'clock. Except for occasional workdays on the farm with his brother, he was around home to care for us in the winter.

The School Patrol badge for the belt was circular and metal, with a sturdy pin clip on the back. My white badge was for the patrolman. A blue badge was for the captain and a red badge was for the chief. I had seen all the colors in our house over the years. My oldest brother began the process for us with his belt and badges—and the cleaning and drying (and folding) of his belt. My badge (and brothers' badges) were always set aside in a place of honor on the top of the bookcase of the middle room, where they were to be left—and respected—while belts were washed and dried.

It was seen as a great honor to be selected for the School Patrol, since teachers nominated names of boys (girls weren't included for some reason) to the principal and to the police officer who had charge of the citywide program. Every year, over 200 boys were appointed to the patrol of the various public and parochial elementary and junior high schools of the city and school district.

The goal was to be selected, to perform daily in all types of weather on the main streets of our community and to provide safe passage across busy city streets before and after school every day. In addition, there was noon patrol at the elementary schools, since kindergartners were to be escorted across streets between half-day sessions. The elementary schools had patrolmen and a chief, with the larger junior highs having captains, as well.

My brothers over time achieved rankings of captain and chief, yet I was proud to serve as patrolman for five years from fifth through ninth grades. The honor was to serve, to be responsible and to be counted upon to care for school and others.

Even though Pa wouldn't say it, he must have been proud to have had five boys serve others for five years each and to see their crisp, clean belts and colorful badges in our home over many years. The ultimate honor was to receive the five-year award, which included a visit to the state capitol in St. Paul and a meeting with the governor.

My job rotated by days and by time of day, with assignments made by the chief and our teacher advisor. The only equipment besides the belt and the badge was a wooden-handled flag, kept with others in a separate school patrol closet. Each would check his assignment, carefully put on the belt, grab a flag and head off well before school to an appointed corner a block or two away from school, depending upon assignment. The placement of patrols was strategic to the safety of children crossing the busiest streets.

At the end of the day, we were excused early from class to get to our posts before dismissal and hold the station until all children were safely across. At the busier corners (especially at the junior highs), a captain would be stationed on a corner with two patrolmen on opposing corners, with the captain or chief signaling "open" and "close" commands by whistle signals.

At normal corners, the two patrolmen would arrive and one or the other would shout commands across the street to stop the flow of traffic, with verbal "open" or "close" commands in all kinds of weather. For rainy days, we had yellow rubberized "slicker" coats that kept us warm and dry.

On this snowy day, taking my dry belt from the clothesline, I smoothed the belt and tried it on to make sure the fit was right. It needed to fit across the chest and over the shoulder, with the ends joining around the waist. Turning the matching metal clasps to join the ends around my waist, I was satisfied with the fit and inserted my badge in the proper position on my upper chest.

Taking the belt in hand, I began the folds of the belt in the fashion shown by my older brother—so that the completed belt was a stacked square with the badge on top. Wrapping a large rubber band around it, I carefully fitted it into my coat pocket.

Once at school, I would unravel the belt and hang it on the appropriate numbered peg in the patrol closet for easy daily access. Getting to school today was a breeze. After my morning warm-up, I was ready to challenge the mounds and the unshoveled walks in the few blocks to school. It was a comfortable route with greetings to friends and neighbors along the way.

Upon arrival, I looked at the schedule of patrol and found that I was to be on the corner of Broadway and Olmstead streets each morning all through the first week of the new year. I knew that today's fresh snow would be a challenge for both walkers and drivers, so I headed to my post a few minutes early. The mounds from the plows at the corners needed to be knocked down and paths made so kids could get through.

I was a big kid—strong enough to make a path for the little ones. With my partner we laid out the plan for the morning, assessed where we were to stand and observed the slick frozen snow on the street that would make it hard for drivers to stop quickly. Flags had to be up with plenty of time for drivers to stop—and positions had to be taken on the street side of the snow mounds without placing ourselves in danger.

We set about our business and soon had a comfortable rhythm of flag opening and closing that brought all safely across. Job done, we headed off to school and a warm cup of juice the school secretary made up for patrols as we came in on cold days.

This was my first year of patrol, but I felt like an "old-timer," having received tips from and observed older brothers on the job. Along with over 200 others in the city, I was appointed to my year of service in an official ceremony for all the patrol boys at the beginning of the school year. All the patrol boys were assembled for an induction ceremony hosted by the mayor, with the superintendent of schools and assorted city, police and school officials present at City Hall.

Every year, with some members leaving, some dropping and "newbies" appointed, the force held at over 200 since its start more than twenty years earlier. With sponsorship by the police, a full-time police officer coordinator for the city-wide program, local civic club interest and the support of the public, boys and program thrived. Supplies came from clubs and sponsors, with main fiscal support coming from the annual proceeds of the Policeman's Ball.

Boys, as leaders of the group, were invited to civic dinners and events. The total group was often invited to local athletic games and contests and events, with payment and supervision provided by local clubs. Certain few of the boys (approximately two per building) were selected to go to summer camp each year—paid for by the local Legion club.

It became obvious that the finest young men of the community were selected each year for the patrol—as evidenced by older brothers and by the team leaders at the high school who had served.

All—students, parents, teachers and community—held individual members of the School Patrol in high regard. They became examples and models of responsibility for younger boys to follow, as evidenced in my own household.

I was on my way to class and still warming fingers and toes when I spotted the pictures of last year's School Patrol in the showcase. Pictures of city school patrol, a separate picture of Madison School members, May picnic fun moments and others had been mounted carefully by Marilyn Neitzke, the school secretary.

On the day of the annual picnic—the greatest day of the year—all the patrol boys of the city were brought together on the Post Office steps downtown for a group picture. They lined up on the front steps of the granite-faced building for a group portrait. I admired the pictures and found my brothers.

I looked forward to my first picnic and the posting my own copy of this year's group on the wall next to my Winona Winhawks basketball schedule, over the library table in my small bedroom. It was my space for pictures of family and friends, good thoughts and possibilities for the future. The table, surroundings, and AM radio playing local music on KWNO while I did my homework brought me great comfort.

The picnic was held each year in mid-May at the Farmers Community Park, otherwise known as "The Arches" due to the circular overhead bulkheads of the railroad trestle that we passed under upon entry. The school buses would haul all of us out there with fun and expectation.

The park was a beautiful, trout stream valley with limestone hillsides and lots of room for exploration. There were ball fields and open spaces to run or gather. Most of us had been there for a church gathering or family picnic, so we knew the space. We had heard about past patrol picnics where games were played, prizes given, and most of all—a whole afternoon of all the hot dogs and ice cream that one could hope for.

Apparently one could continually cycle back to the pavilion where volunteers would dish out another hot dog or another ice cream cone over the countertop just above eye level—without question or payment—all afternoon long. Wow! What a deal!

I could hardly wait.

I arrived at class a few minutes later than the others, due to my early-morning responsibility and lingering at the showcase. Teachers recognized that we were early to school, and certainly not tardy. They were most understanding and always greeted us cordially, helping to bring us up to speed, if necessary. Having brothers before me in the school also helped my standing.

In a recent year, there had been four boys of our family in the school and their classes at the same time—grades six, four, two, and kindergarten. With responsibility learned from Pa and from a heritage of school patrol standards, the four of us set a record that won't be easily matched by another family. Each of the four was neither tardy nor absent in the entire year.

School Patrol built our personal assets and expectations. It was a pleasure to serve.

The Middle Room:
A Remembrance of Erika

On the morning before school on the day of her death, I snuggled into the small corner behind the wood stove in the middle room. I was soon on my way to kindergarten. I had brushed my teeth and splashed my face with cold water and combed back the cowlicks. As I sat in the corner between the wall and the stove I could look out through the small space and see her sitting quietly across the room in her small rocker. This was my mother—the object of my love in my first six years.

She was composed this morning and not wracked with the coughing spells that seemed to engulf her every waking moment. We had worked together the night before to create a crayon picture of our backyard that I would bring to school today for show and tell. It captured a scene of the two of us near the tall bushes in the side yard.

With Ma's pencil sketch and my crayon artistry, the blooms of flowers stood tall in the heat of that summer day. Berries of the bush showed as bright and colorful as the canary we were trying to capture. The small bird flitted back and forth between the cherry tree across the neighbor's back yard and into the protective bushes we faced. We were at the ready to throw our gauze netting over the bird.

We stood quietly in the same space with the hope that the bird would become accustomed to our presence. It had been a long time and a true team effort to try and to make just the right move at the right time to contain our prey. The small birdcage on a pedestal stood nearby. We had tried to put some seeds and berries in the cage with an open door in hopes of enticing the bird directly into the cage—but to no avail.

This was our last hope. We had tossed the netting over the bush a number of times, but the small bird either jumped to the innards of the bush or our netting got hung up in the outer branches as we cast it. When Ma felt good enough to be out in the yard, we would try our technique. These were moments to be remembered—a joint exercise in anticipation, partnership and futility.

The empty birdcage stood today in the old shed behind the house in the hope that we could try again this summer. Today, this seventeenth day of April, it felt like the cage would remain empty, as our colored drawing showed.

Gathering up my wool mackinaw and warm cap with earflaps, I buckled on my rubber boots. In my hand, along with my rolled drawing, was the small present for Wayne's birthday party I had picked out at the Woolworth store downtown. Ma had helped me wrap it with a piece of leftover Christmas wrapping. We tied a string around the small box and together tied a bow.

With treasured items secure, I headed out the door and ventured across the tops of snow banks now melting down as spring approached. The paths that we had made across the top of the mounds at the sides of the street had taken on a frozen, icy crust. My three-block trek to school was again an adventure across mountaintops, with the warmth of the kindergarten classroom beckoning at the end of my journey.

The first room on the right upon entering the back door of the school off the playground was Miss Kinzie. She was there at the door to greet me, as she was each day. A short, plump, and sparkly lady, her smile was infectious. She admired my picture and the gift box for Wayne. After putting them on the shelf above my coat hook in the cloakroom for safekeeping, I stepped into the warm and ever-inviting classroom.

Maple flooring had been well-worn by hundreds of children who had spent their half-days with Miss Kinzie over her many years. The piano stood in the center of the room to be used for our daily sing-a-long and to signal us when one activity or another was over and a new one was to begin.

Before class began, we had the freedom to use the small wooden slide in the classroom or go off to the corner reading area with the round rug to enjoy the warmth and comfort of the books, and the wonderful safety of our surroundings. The room was clean and meticulous, having been set up for the needs of children in the systematic way that Miss Kinzie had evolved over the years.

From the cloakroom to the cabinets, we found order. We knew where the paste jars were and where to put our projects when we were done. Each of our rest pads was carefully labeled, rolled and placed in the large open-front cabinet on the far wall. It was our home away from home. We were welcomed and comfortable.

The routine of the day was the Pledge of Allegiance, a song to warm us up, and then some activities to stimulate our bodies and souls. We waddled around the room like ducks for exercise, played circle games within our small groups and listened quietly as Miss Kinzie read another story to the class, with all thirty or so scattered across the floor at the feet of her high stool.

We listened to beautiful music on the large record player—a described sunrise over the desert, the ballads of the seasons or the soothing lullabies she played when we went down for our rest.

Just before our rest, Bill Groves, the school janitor, delivered a metal frame case of small glass milk bottles with cardboard tops to the room. Like Miss Kinzie, he was a fixture around the school. Like Miss Kinzie, he knew me because three of my brothers had been through this classroom before me. After our milk break and a rest on our personal mat, it was time for show and tell.

Each of us had a day for showing small parts of our life to classmates. We were encouraged by Miss Kinzie to do our best and be ourselves. Teasing and bantering were not allowed. With our teacher at our side, we could explain our story or show our item and know that no one would ever make fun of us.

With many of us being from the same kind of households where "hand-me-downs" were the standard, comments about our "coats of many colors" and the like were neither considered, nor expressed. For a class member who may have been better off, the rest of us would simply marvel at their new clothes and let them be who they were.

We were friends who excelled in different areas. We learned to appreciate one another's gifts through Miss Kinzie's careful guidance.

As I stood before the class in my black-and-white pinto flannel shirt and corduroy pants held up by a too-big belt passed down from one of my brothers, I was at ease. My picture brought many questions. Clipped to the teacher's big easel, I was proud of the colors and the artistic display enhanced by the large white paper background to which it was thumbtacked. Ma would be proud.

Other students presented their objects and received similar attention from classmates. Miss Kinzie always made a grand show of displaying the picture or object when the presentation was complete by placing them on the bulletin board or on the top of the tall table in the center of the room—the one she used for display and for her lesson books.

When all presentations were complete, the items remained on display until the end of the morning session. As pupils bundled up to leave, they would be claimed by their owners, with a special note of report and thanks attached for our parents from Miss Kinzie.

Lunch was not served in the school. Since the kindergarten was only for half a day, it wasn't necessary for us anyway. Kids bundled up in the cloakroom, awaited the signal to leave from our teacher and headed out the door at 11:30 a.m. Before I left, I was handed my picture by Miss Kinzie and told to put it in the cloakroom on the shelf once again, for I had a very special opportunity that none of the other kids enjoyed—to return for the afternoon session.

I was the only pupil in kindergarten to get two milks and two naps and to have two show and tell sessions in one day, due to the illness of my mother and the generosity of Miss Kinzie and the school. I re-crossed my steps on sidewalks and snow banks with my rubber-mittened hands unburdened, to be soon home for a sandwich and then to return at one o'clock for the afternoon session.

I was surprised to see Grandma (Pa's mother) in the kitchen when I came in the back door off the porch. As I came into the large kitchen the warm woodstove/range and Grandma were both beckoning welcome. She occasionally visited and cared for the two youngest, Billy and Janet, at home. Most often, one or the other of us transported them to Grandma's house in the east end via the city bus, bringing us there and back before school.

Ma's bedroom was the "front room," our small, combination living room and bedroom for Ma and Pa that was now a quiet zone for all of us in the house. With eight of us, it was a full house, with little bedrooms off to the side and a former pantry off the kitchen to sleep in for eldest brother, Frank. When Ma felt up to it, she was most often settled in the middle room near the potbelly stove.

Grandma told me she had learned that Ma had taken a turn for the worse this morning when the lady from church called. The nice lady from St. Matthew's Church would come by for a few hours each day to help out, check on Ma and sometimes make a sandwich for lunch for my two brothers and me as we hustled home from Madison School. Frank was in junior high and had stayed there at noon with his bag lunch the past few days.

Sitting quietly with the ladies at the oilcloth-covered pine kitchen table, they concluded that I could go and see Ma "for just a minute" before my brothers came in. I walked quietly from the kitchen, passing Ma's cactus collection in the window of the middle room, and stepped into her darkened room.

She was resting on her side, with the pillows and white chenille bedspread with small, tied red flowers brought gently around her. So often, on her good days, one or the other (or more) of us would lay with Ma on that bedspread and listen with her to the AM radio next to the bed or to the hand-crank Victrola seventy-eight rpm record player, or show her our progress at school.

She was immensely proud of our accomplishments and fully expected the best from everyone. Walking to the side of the bed next to the front door, I reached out and touched her forehead. She stirred, recognized me with a slight smile and closed her eyes again.

Knowing my limits, I told her how our picture had been well received by the class—and that I would bring her the note from Miss Kinzie after I returned from Wayne's party. I returned to the kitchen and found my two brothers being told that they could take their turns. My sandwich awaited—a nice slice of last night's meatloaf on Grandma's homemade bread.

After a few minutes on my bunk bed, I headed back to the school and playground, where I would hear the five-minute bell that signaled me and others back to class. It was cool outside, but the sun was out, so it was comfortable sliding across the city-built ice-skating rink with Davey and others from my class. With spring days now upon us, gaps of blacktop had begun to show through. Wayne soon arrived for the afternoon class and we all headed in to Miss Kinzie's room together.

Miss Kinzie was at the door to greet each one. As if I had not just left, she greeted me as brightly as one of the new arrivals to her afternoon class. The routine was the same in the afternoon as it had been in the morning—with warm-ups, story time and music to rest by. Bill Groves again came by with a milk bottle for each of us, and show and tell proceeded.

One of the kids showed off a shirt that his mom had made from the nylon of a parachute his father had used in the recent war. The light material was new for all of us, and the shirt a special hit in camouflage colors. My drawing brought "oohs" and "ahs" when I told about the "almost" capture of the bird. Again, Miss Kinzie spotlighted each of the presenters and set their items out for display. After a bit of number work and listening to the story of "Sambo" running around the tree and the tigers turning to butter, the day soon ended.

Several of us were headed off to Wayne's for the birthday party, so we gathered our materials, gifts and mackinaws and headed out the back door toward Belleview Street, where Wayne lived in a small house with his parents and four siblings. After assembling and running for a while around Wayne's small front yard, even-smaller barn and in and out of his dad's milk hauling truck, we headed into Wayne's middle room. With the oilburning stove in the dining room enhancing the wood stove in the kitchen, it was always toasty in his house.

We were greeted by his mom, who had special seats for each of the boys (only boys!) at the dining room table. There were treats in paper cups, a Kool-Aid drink and a large chocolate cake in the center. We played Pin the Tail on the Donkey by spinning something and pasting the parts of the donkey on the wall over the buffet. We had fun as Wayne opened his presents and blew out the candles on his cake. With a final treat of ice cream and cake (and coffee if we wanted it, since Wayne's mother always had coffee on the stove—and her kids drank it regularly!) we said thank you and good-bye and headed out the door.

I was anxious to get home and tell Ma about the party and give her the note from Miss Kinzie about our drawing. It had been a big day. I lived only three blocks or so from Wayne's—across the tracks and down a couple of blocks. I had taken the route a hundred times, both on my return trips from Wayne's and from the many times I accompanied a brother on the paper route as he collected on Saturdays.

Reaching the corner lot on our block, I noticed a number of cars that seemed to be gathered around the front of our house. Since we did not have a car, it was unusual to see so many there.

When I cut down the neighbor's dirt drive toward our back door, I went by our middle room window and saw a number of people inside. Entering the back door as I had only hours ago, I was met by Grandma, who told me that Ma had gone to heaven.

I later determined that one of the cars out front was a police car, another was a long, black car with shaded windows that reminded me of the grocery man's delivery truck, with canvas windows pulled down to cover the grocery boxes he delivered. Another car I knew was that of "Doc" Tweedy, the pleasant, round doctor who occasionally made house calls and cared for us. These people and others were all there to care for Ma.

While I sang "Happy Birthday" to Wayne and watched him blow out the candles of celebration, others were bringing Ma to her final place of rest—having passed away at 3:15 p.m.

I treasured the drawing until it got lost in one of my drawers. But my vision of our outdoor escapade has never been lost in all the years since kindergarten.

A Bus Rider's Story:
A 100-Year History of City
Transportation

I was a semi-regular shuttle rider of the maroon-and-cream Winona Transit buses, starting at the age of seven.

Holding on to the vertical chrome bar near the rubber-matted step up, I was off in the early morning for another big bus journey across town. I had a nickel for the fare. Kids got by for a nickel, with adults paying with stamped metal tokens available three-for-a-quarter from the driver's thumb-operated coin dispenser on his belt.

In the late 1940s and early 1950s, being a kid and being like most everyone else in town, I walked everywhere. When the snow thawed sufficiently to give way to spring rain puddles, I ventured out on my fenderless bike to feel the cold tire spray soaking my neck and back. The cold of my neck matched my red-raw, mittenless fingers as they gripped the too-cold handlebars on an imagined warm, early spring day. My leather-and-sheepskin cap kept my head warm.

The warmth of the bus beckoned on dark mornings as I saw its lights progress slowly toward me on Howard Street. I dropped the nickel in the Rube Goldberg-like receiver next to the driver to ding and twist down to the bottom, showing its circuitous route downward in the glass window. The warmest spot for my sister Janet, age two, and myself was about midway down the rows of the twenty-seven-passenger bus with green, firm leather seats.

Located under the selected seat was the blower unit to keep us toasty warm as we headed off to Grandma's for another day of her care. I kept one hand on the chrome bar of the seat ahead and the other around my little sister as she babbled her way down the west end, Lake Line bus route. We were moving toward downtown, where we offloaded to take a paper transfer from the driver and walk across Center Street to the waiting Main Line bus parked in front of Choate's Department Store, heading east. After school, I reversed the route to bring my sister home.

The beginnings of the Lake and Main Lines as community transportation in Winona came in the 1880s. In 1883, the city granted R.D. Cone and others a fifty-year right to create and maintain a street railway "from Winona Wagon Works (West Fifth Street) to macadamized road leading to Sugar Loaf Bluff (Mankato Avenue.)" The five-cent fare took one "over line." They stayed with the line until 1911, when it became Wisconsin Railway, Light and Power.

I followed the history of those streetcars (known as "the rattlers") as they tracked down the brick roadways on East Third Street and Sanborn Street toward downtown (Main Line). Later, in the 1950s, I drove my powerful Studebaker V-8 taxicab and rumbled its tires across the bricks, seeing vestiges of original rail tracks in the roadways of East Third and West Fifth Streets.

Once having left downtown, the Main Line (west) headed out the brick-covered West Fifth Street to the Wagon Works and the Jefferson turnaround. In the early days, the Lake Line crossed Lake Winona on Huff Street to bring Sunday picnickers to the cemetery and park.

In 1916, taxicab company owners Bert Beyerstedt and Mr. Mallery of Mallery's Livery were at a city council meeting to address concerns of their drivers' safety—possibly due in part to Mr. Mallery's running his taxicab into the side of a streetcar. Mr. Mallery's taxi was "of the new Ford model and presents an attractive appearance"—at least previous to the accident. In addition, a Safety Cab Company vehicle collided with a streetcar in 1930 at Fifth and Center streets. (Those darn streetcars!)

Buses replaced the rattlers of Winona in the 1930s, when ridership declined from a high of one-point-five million riders in 1926. The previous year, the Winona Trolley (officially known as Wisconsin Railway, Light and Power Company) had become a part of Mississippi Valley Public Service Co (MVPS). MVPS was formed in 1913, becoming the operating company of Eau Claire, LaCrosse and Winona electric power, and later, street railways.

With the expiration of the fifty-year contract with the city in 1933, MVPS created a one-year franchise that involved the demise of rail cars and the beginnings of bus service. The every-twelve-minute schedule of the streetcar became the every-twenty-minute schedule of buses on the Lake Line in 1934. Tokens were increased in 1934, to seven tokens for fifty cents.

Throughout the city, the rails were taken up and spaces filled. The car shop at 58 Johnson Street, next to the MVPS warehouse, was a service facility for rail cars, converted into a space for six buses carrying 2,000 riders per day. By 1938, rail cars were being dismantled and sold for "hamburger shops and summer cottage purposes." At five tons each, they were a challenge to move and place—and get over the High Wagon Bridge.

A final resting place for one of the streetcars (after fifty years of service) was as a coffee shop or bait shop of sorts. A weathered wood shanty when I knew it, it was located behind the small Hennessey's or Pomeroy's Grocery on Huff, between the tracks and Sarnia Street. I walked past the old car a hundred times on my way to the lake in the 1950s.

The Ray Fey family purchased the Eau Claire line in 1939, from Northern States Power. They purchased MVPS-Winona (with new fare boxes) in 1944 to create Winona Transit—adding new twenty-seven-passenger buses in 1946 and 1947 to serve twenty-two million riders. They added LaCrosse Transit bus service to their stable from MVPS in 1948, having seen the LaCrosse rail lines torn up in 1935, with bus service as replacement.

In the 1950s, bus service was extended to Goodview along the Main Line. Hours of service were from 6:00 a.m. to 8:00 p.m.—after the cutback from 10:00 p.m. due to higher operating costs and "excessive loss of summer revenue." Ridership had declined in 1952 by twenty-five percent, yet drivers were granted a union-approved raise of eight cents—to a dollar and twenty-eight cents per hour!

In 1955, Jack Blank, Superintendent, announced that new fare boxes were installed on all buses with separate deposited fares visible—with machines providing a musical offering. He said, "Electric machines give a distinctive bell or buzz sound for each coin fare deposited and registered. A quarter gives two chimes, a dime sounds two gongs, a nickel sounds one gong, a penny produces a buzz and a token makes a high chime." Drivers were removed from the financial equation—not being allowed (or required) to handle money by company policy. Mr. Blank stated, "The machine does all the work."

We rode those Winona Transit buses up and down Fifth Street in junior and senior high from the central schools to football practice and games at Jefferson practice fields. We had a warm ride down Fifth to get us home in time for supper—in the pre-Daylight Savings Time era and late-afternoon darkness. We didn't need a nickel, since the big slow-moving bus was our free alternative to a school bus. Buses operated every fifteen minutes, with admittance being a paper ticket or "bus pass" from the coach.

"Big Bertha" was the queen of the Winona Transit fleet.

Nicknamed after Bertha of the von Krupp family, who designed Germany's largest gun of World War I, this Greyhound-like monster, with her salubrious and genial driver Andy Kuklinski, ventured out to ball games in towns of the Big Nine Conference in all the seasons. Mostly we headed out west through Rochester on Highway 14 toward Owatonna, Austin, Albert Lea and others. On schedule, Red Wing called us up north on Highway 61.

Andy always greeted us with his charm. Seated right behind him was inveterate sports announcer Chuck Williams of KWNO. Across the aisle, the coaches generally studied their plays and newspapers and ignored the herd behind them.

A smallish, semi-pudgy and chatty redhead, Chuck was a graduate of St. Mary's, with an ever-smiling presence. A local legend as singular sports announcer, he covered virtually every home and away football and basketball game of St. Mary's, Winona State, and Winona High, with occasional tournament games of Cotter High School. In addition, exciting Winona Chiefs summertime baseball games came to us from all over the Southern Minny Conference, thanks to Chuck and KWNO.

When traveling west on Big Bertha, team members and coaches had the good fortune of having a late afternoon meal at Rochester's excellent Town House supper club. Greek owners Bill and Theoni Lecakis made us welcome to a sometimes buffet (two dollars for adults and one dollar and twenty-five cents for children.) Hopefully, a deal was negotiated by Athletic Director Vic Gislason for the forty or more starving players.

The ride home from afar was either celebratory or teenage moody, depending upon the outcome of the game. Regularly, too many verses of "Ninety-nine Bottles of Beer on the Wall" were sung, to the distress of coaches.

Over all the years, the buses and drivers of Winona served the populace admirably. Memories are positive and warm toward individual drivers like Andy, Frank, James, Jack and Bill, who greeted us like family. Swinging the big wheel away from the curb with ease, they watched out for our safety and warmth throughout a cross-town or highway journey. Some, like H. Glenn Berry with forty-three years of service, started as motormen on the streetcars of the 1920s, and served as drivers into the 1960s.

Hal Boyle asked in the Republican Herald of 1952, "Why not a National Bus Driver Day to honor the guy who all year long gets us in one piece to wherever we want to go?"

Fare enough?

The only complaint about new buses in 1938 seemed to be that the shop workers from the railroad shops on Marion Street often got the cloth seats dirty. A Winona matron, who didn't wish to get her frock dirty, suggested leather.

Tokens needed the higher status of their own chime, since they had risen in cost to twenty-two cents each by 1970. With a new (used) bus garage on West Third Street in 1962, lower revenues and higher operating costs continued to strain the efficient and service-oriented Fey Company operation. The handwriting was on the wall.

A run to the hospital and Vo-Tech was offered on a trial basis. Efforts to meet merchants' challenges against necessary bus zones for the safe drop-off of riders began to show the conflict of social and economic challenges of merchant and bus operator. Mr. Fey was heard to say in 1961, "Every time they open a new parking lot or add a few more meters (for downtown parking), we get a decrease in riding."

Individual choice changed bus ridership. With more personal freedom, a car in nearly every household and a robust economy, the former bus rider was now in the driver's seat—to head off to the highway shopping center. Sunday bus service was eliminated in 1965, when losses reached $4,000.00 per month.

Mr. Fey reported, "for every fifty-seven cents of mile-driven expense, there is only thirty-four cents of income." By 1971, the welcoming, unfolding bus doors became solid, closed two-part panels—not to fold or open again. Under Fey's ownership, Jack Blank's leadership and a total commitment to employees and riders since 1944, it was no longer doable. There was no profit to be had. Winona Transit went out of business in 1971, due to "cutbacks that cost Winona its transit system."

Attempts were made with the bus-taxi combinations of Star Transit (an offshoot of Yellow Cab), but even this lesser company was back again and again for subsidies from Goodview and Winona councils.

Today's routes for Winona bus riders are available, albeit limited. The Jefferson commercial line carries passengers from city to city, SEMCAC (a non-profit social service agency) provides busing to Altura, Lewiston and St. Charles on a reservation basis and Winona Transit Services continues to operate out of the garage at 260 West Third Street. With several sleek, modern mini-buses operating a route from the east end to Goodview, they continue a tradition of service started eighty years ago.

My rides on the maroon-and-cream buses of the 1950s allow me to hang onto memories of quality service and exemplary drivers. As I hung onto a chrome bar upon entrance or exit, or pulled the cord over the seat to signal my stop in the next block, I was building a tactile remembrance of supreme customer service to last a lifetime.

The author traveled the Lake Line and Main Line from Grand Street to Mankato Avenue, from downtown to Goodview, from Jefferson Field to home on darkening autumn eves— and sang enthusiastically in the dark night from the back seat of Big Bertha.

Route 42:
A Boy and His Paper Route

The backyard of the small yellow house faced the railroad tracks at Mark and Grand Streets.

The Burbachs weren't auspicious customers in any way, but their little house happened to be the first drop on my paper route, route 42. Whoever set up the routes so many years ago must have favored this starting point at Grand and Mark streets. With the *Republican-Herald* in existence for over 100 years and virtually every household in the nine-square-block route area a customer, there must have been a lot of "starts" at the Burbach corner.

The only bad thing about the starting point was that there was no entry point on the corner to the sidewalk except over the standard-sized city curb. With a large basket full of folded papers in my canvas mailbag, it was dangerous to bump up the curb on my bike as I often did when unloaded. I needed to head up to the tracks and cut in the driveway access to their old shed by the tracks and head back to the corner for a left turn. From there on, I was flying.

I would head toward Olmstead Street, past the Hoover house that was loaded with kids who needed a face wash. Their place always reminded me of the Ma and Pa Kettle movies I saw on Saturday afternoons at the State Theater for twelve cents. There were kids everywhere.

Shooting past my friend "Army's" house, I cut the drive in the back of the next corner house, crossed the street and began a new block and cycle. Waving at friends and customers in yards or on porches, I was all business of ride and grab and sail and connect.

Reaching into the bag at each home, I grabbed a pre-folded paper that I had folded only moments ago on the front porch of home. I used the fold-and-pack system I had learned from my brothers to stuff my official *Re-*

publican-Herald canvas bag. The "paper guy" had dropped the bundle of papers at the curb. I hustled the bundle onto the porch and began the routine. When the papers were large, I needed to cut the twine on the bundles to make two trips to the porch with the approximately 100 papers.

From years of practice "subbing" on Route 42 for an older brother or three, I had learned the route, perfect bike balance and how to fold papers and sail them accurately toward the front stoop. A strong fold was the key. They didn't need to land on the top step, but it was a special treat if they did. I never let an unfolded paper be delivered, unless it was a rainy or snowy day when I tucked each carefully into the door threshold.

After covering Mark Street, my daily, exhilarating ride continued in the blocks bounded by Sioux and Grand, Mark and King streets. The small houses on sixty-foot lots varied in style and appearance. In them were the real people of our small river town who worked in the bakeries, railroad shops, beauty shops, meat processing plant or flax processing factory.

They lived mostly in small clapboard or asphalt-covered, brick-patterned homes maintained with richness and integrity. Here and there a gingerbread-and-brick house sat on a lush green lot, giving a sense of fortress to the neighborhood. Across the route, there seemed to be a lot of white houses.

The Giel house, a small white house on Sioux Street, was the home of everyone's hero, University of Minnesota All-American Paul Giel. And he was on my route! The very small lot was covered mostly with an equally small house. The porch was nearly to the front sidewalk—an easy drop for the paper. The sidewalk on the side hugged the house on the "shotgun" size lot.

Thank goodness for the wonderful parks and play lots of the community where Paul could exercise his many skills. The only early play area for this two-sport All-American in his yard was in an area stretching from the alley to the back of the house. In the sixty-foot strip, Paul could back up, wind up and pitch his fastball toward the wooden clapboard siding—or a catcher if he had one. He had to hit the streets if he wanted to fire a long football pass.

About the time I reached the Giel home I seemed to be distracted. My friend Joanie lived in the house across the street. She was not on my route. Sighting her house nevertheless caused my attention to business to waver— and my heart to skip a beat.

The Einhorn, Pelowski, and Arntsen white, single-story homes were interspersed in the blocks. They were immaculate and consistent with the personal appearances of the chief of Municipal Works, the foreman of the

Swift Meat Company and the captain of the Winona Fire Department. It was obvious they had pride about self and home, carried from garden to porch to workplace. They were but a few of the many, but especially well remembered for their pleasant tone and beautiful homes.

The occasional two- or three-story homes appeared on larger corner lots along Howard Street. Company owners, bankers or attorneys seemed to live in these houses. Beautifully maintained by the artisans and workers of our small city, the homes offered cold stature to an otherwise working-class environment. Over all the years of wandering the neighborhood and delivering the papers, I don't recall seeing one of these owners in a garden—or even answering the door.

They seemed to stay inside their houses by the light of their lamps in comfortable chairs smoking their pipes, while someone else was designated to answer the door. They may have even pre-paid their accounts to the *Republican-Herald* with a check to the office, so as to not be involved mixing with delivery boys.

Mr. and Mrs. Kline were the exception. A pudgy, balding man in a white shirt and spectacles who continually smoked a cigar, he owned a very successful electrical company. Well-dressed and always at home when I collected on Saturday mornings, he not only greeted me and paid the bill, but insisted that I come into their beautiful home on West Howard Street and see Mrs. Kline, who always seemed to have a fresh-baked item from the oven. Together, we would sit at their kitchen table in the most luxurious of Winona's homes and share a quiet moment. These were genuine "rich" people who especially enriched the life of a paperboy.

Around the corner and across the block I saw the O'Deas, the Ziebells, the Kings, the Blanks and the Kammerers. One ran a theater, one was a police officer, one a carpenter, one a worker at Wingold Flour. Along with the others, each had a story to tell. I spent moments on their front porches—or simply said "hi" a hundred times as I passed their house on my bike—but somehow we made a connection. As years went on, I worked small jobs for several of them and went to school with the kids of the households. From the Kings I dragged home a large console radio that had small colored lights on the dial that I slowly turned to pick up ships at sea and foreign countries via the short-wave band.

There were the Dondlingers, the Rihs, Rolbeckies, Schneider and Pomeroy families—all grand folks in their small houses of the early 1950s. One of those houses was simply not a pleasure at which to collect. The mother and father were nice folks, but they seemed to have been overwhelmed by the number of kids in their large family—especially the babies running around in diapers. The smell was overwhelming. My eyes almost watered from the pungent urine smell, as I held my breath and tried to conduct business in collection of the thirty-five cents per week subscription.

For each customer collection, I punched "Paid" in my collection book with a metal paper punch about the size of a good, western cap gun. I felt like a quick-draw artist when I pulled it out of my rear pocket to punch the appropriate page of the green, cloth-covered hard cardboard book. In addition to handling the paper route's duties and collection, I learned my multiplication tables quickly as I multiplied thirty-five cents times the number of weeks paid.

Route 42 had been ours for at least ten years. Five boys of the family took a turn in folding the papers, delivering daily in all kinds of weather and checking in with the office every Saturday for an accounting. The payoff was immediate as each turned in the collected cash—to realize about seven dollars per week of profit and pay. When people paid ahead a few weeks, it increased the money in the pot for that week. But we had to be careful to turn it all in, or we would get caught short in each of the weeks ahead. Like my brothers before me, I was totally responsible for the duties of the day. And I enjoyed every moment.

The only largesse we received in the year was at Christmastime, when the paper gave us small calendars to place in the hands of each customer as we collected. It was their single opportunity to reward our quality service throughout the year with a "tip" payment for the calendar and for services rendered. It was a windfall that allowed me to buy a few Christmas presents for teachers, Grandma and Pa—and to help Pa out if he was "short" of funds during wintertime unemployment.

Pa's Christmas present was easy—a carton of Raleigh cigarettes for two dollars. He smoked so many of them that we counted the coupons enclosed in each pack and sent fifty or a hundred in for an item shown in the catalogue. The more he smoked, the bigger the prize! We never thought of the outcome. As one of the magazine ads of the times stated: "More doctors smoke Camels than any other brand."

Paperboys were a part of the social fabric of our small town in the 1950s. We made a daily impact upon the neighborhood as watchful eyes. A strange car in our nine-square-block area was easily identified, and the information was shared with Pa. If something were out of the ordinary, Pa would suggest that we mention it to a police officer. A couple of officers lived on the route, but squads regularly trolled the neighborhood and were easily accessible.

Likewise, the buildup of more than three of four papers on the front step was a cause for wonder and possible concern. If people were to be gone for an extended time period, they would either cancel or let us know they were off for a vacation or visit, and ask that we tuck the papers inside the door. There were customers who were single and elderly and occasionally needed looking after. In winter, when it was obvious that snow was built up around their front steps, I would grab the shovel off the porch and open the entryway for them.

Experiences as a paperboy taught me skills and responsibility that carried me into a strong future. I learned multiplication, accounting, diligence and personal ownership for a "missed" paper. Daily sharing in the lives of a hundred households left a strong impression on me as I observed how I was treated by people—and learned how I was to treat people in return.

I haven't folded and tossed in a number of years, but I am daily touched by (and thankful for) the memories of the wonderful people on Route 42.

Frozen Fun
at the Skating Rinks

High banks of snow encircled the rink created by the city worker. With the plow of his tractor, first rounds of the day pressed the fresh snowfall outward to add to ever-larger piles at rink-side. Then the power of the tractor and the sweep of the whirling broom on the front swirled a mini-snowstorm into the sterling morning sky. Nearly hidden by the powder, the tractor operator guided the machine around the rink.

He was kept warm by the heat of the engine captured in the weathered, cracked plastic-and-tarp cab. When plowing and buffing was complete, the tractor was shut down. In snow-encrusted bib overalls and military surplus leather and sheepskin mittens reaching nearly to his elbows, the burly worker stepped out to guide a large fire-hose from the rear of a city water truck to add a fresh layer of water to the surface.

Sub-freezing temperature and the calm of morning sunlight caused a steamy mist to rise from the ice—leaving a sparkle and sheen to the surface. All was ready for another day of activity at Lakeside Rink in the small southern Minnesota town nestled in the hills of the Hiawatha Valley.

Once the task at Lakeside was complete, the operator, truck and equipment moved on to the next park or playground. Behind virtually every elementary school, a rink was created. The cycle continued from snowfall to snowfall, from rink to rink, all through the frigid temperatures of December through March.

Lakeside was the largest rink, thanks to the natural freeze of the lake's surface and the ambition and pride of the plow operator. It was the jewel of our rink system—a place for gliding and racing for young and old alike.

The elementary school rink in our part of town was constructed on the blacktopped surface of the playground. By scraping down the first layer of snow and ice, followed by alternate plowing, buffing and water truck applications, the rink soon took form. After-school race-a-bouts and mini-hockey games were played, with rest periods taken on our back sides on snow banks created by the plow.

With snow pants over school pants, rubber mittens lined with flannel and wool scarves that protected our appendages, we stayed dry and warm on our after-school forays—without the benefit of a warming house. As the day wound down to sunset at 4:30 p.m., we headed home in the near-dark with skates hanging off our shoulders.

Walking home, adventure and challenge were found as we traversed the mountainous snow banks on either side of the street. Created by city plows in the dark of night—with whirling blue lights and the sound of thunder—they pushed snowfall after snowfall up and over the curb. Travel to school twice a day by kids of the neighborhood compressed footpaths over and around the tops of the mounds.

Sidewalks were the choice of summer and spring—even though most were kept clear by neighbors in winter. In summer, bikes of every form zoomed in and out of driveways and sidewalks as city blocks took us places in a hurry. In wintertime we traveled the hilltops at street-side on foot, or occasionally hitched a ride on the back of a city bus.

If we successfully hid ourselves from the bus driver, we could grab the bumper as he started from the corner stop and be pulled at fifteen miles per hour down an ice-encrusted street. A fresh snow on a dark night helped the slide and kept us hidden from the driver.

Our home for summer baseball games, the West End Recreation Center or "Rec," had a small rink laid over one of our ball diamonds. This general rink was lighted and fun for night skating—an intimate setting for just a few—when the lake rink seemed too large. Walking to the west end of town, we picked up a friend or two on the way, skated for a while and stopped by the West End Soda Shoppe upon return to share a cherry coke. For a hard-earned nickel we received a friendly greeting, two straws and a coke in a paper cone held by a metal holder.

We seated ourselves at a small glass table in the old ice cream shop and looked out on the busy brick Fifth Street. It was our pathway for travels on paper routes, to baseball games, toward church on Sunday or running the streets in the dark of night as we raided apples from neighborhood trees in late summer.

The wooden-framed rec center served as a shared warming house for general skaters and as a team locker room for members of the home and visiting teams who challenged one another on the hockey rink. It was the home hockey rink for the local high school hockey team and the semi-professional Winona Hornets. The Hornets played their home games there on Sunday afternoons—only an errant puck's flight away from our rink. It was the place to be on Sunday afternoons.

The hockey rink was not for general use, being reserved for team games and practices. It was bounded on all sides by a permanent wood post-and-board fence that took the shock waves of players as they collided. It also protected the observers from some harm. The fence was about four feet tall, with sturdy posts every ten feet or so to support the bouncing slats.

In clearing the rink, snow was tossed over the boards by the shovelful to give stability to the fence and to form a bank on which observers stood. The ice on the rink was thick and smooth and alluring—maintained on a daily basis by rec center workers, coaches and players. With early morning watering, hand shoveling and buffing by a spinning broom driven by a small engine, the surface absolutely gleamed for Sunday games.

Ah! The Winona Hornets—"Popeye" Wychra and "Moose" Benson, Roger Neitzke, "Hoot" Noeske, Eddie Ratajczyk and flying pucks. Their blue-and-gold jerseys shimmered in the sunlight as they took their warm-ups.

The visiting Mustangs from Rochester were adorned in red and black. They looked fierce and quick and ready to engulf our team of locals. Even though they had full adornment of complete hockey uniforms and a swagger of those who had practices in a heated indoor arena in a more cultured city, our guys had the strength of the small town hills and farms on their side.

Roger was the leading scorer of the league, Moose the meanest and toughest defenseman of any, Hoot his partner, and Eddie at wing absolutely flew! Popeye was a steady force in the nets—ably backed by Jimmy, one of the neighborhood kids who made good on the hockey rink.

They were a formidable team of ruffians who had grown up on the lake and shot pucks at one another since the age of five. With a few missing teeth and a scar or two as evidence of their collisions and their resolve to fight on, they were our team.

On cold, crisp Sundays, young and old alike lined up on the snow banks at rink side. Each observer took his life into his own hands, since body checks into the boards were a constant. Players, sticks and flying pucks were often dumped into the crowd.

Roger would come through again with his "hat trick"—the scoring of three goals in a game. Moose or Hoot would block out the charging herd. Popeye or Jimmy would put in another stellar performance and make over fifty saves. Fights and spilled blood on the ice surface were a part of the game.

Between periods, the players retired to the warming house. At the beginning of the third period, a couple of volunteers would walk the banks of the rink perimeter and "pass the hat" in lieu of paid admission.

For each of us, the bitter weather was a challenge to the toes. We kicked at the boards to try to get back some circulation. If there was space in the small warming house, we ventured into the sweat-laden environment for an occasional respite in front of the wood-burning stove. Team members huddled in the corners making adjustments in their equipment and game plan and were soon on the ice for the next period.

If we were lucky, we were able to have a word of conversation with a player or two as they exited down the wooden slat incline at the entrance to the warming house. They were fired up—and so were we! They were our hometown heroes of winter. On any particular Sunday they gave their very best in the final period and worked hard to bring home another victory.

Every so often we would leave the rec and west end to head down to The East End Recreation Center. Since it was a long walk from home to the East End—and unfamiliar territory—we didn't get there but once a year or so. It is almost a foreign country to us, since the Polish people dominated the East End.

They kept to their own and so did we. There was a Polish church and a meat market and an Athletic Club on Mankato Avenue. The club served as a separate province of the Polish people—particularly the men. We saw some of them in the summertime when teams from the East End dominated the men's softball league.

We had some of them on our boys' teams in summer baseball. Even then, the makeup of teams got separated by east and west ends. In elementary schools, we remained separated by neighborhood, but later years of schooling brought us all together. We then learned how to spell the hard Polish names and find new friends across the geographic and social divisions.

Every winter one weekend was taken up by the Winter Carnival—a unifying activity of the community. Kicked off by a massive parade in the downtown area with bands and floats and celebrities, we ventured from place to place to be a part of toboggan races, an outdoor cook-off, picnic and competitions of every sort.

At the East End Rec, a skating competition and demonstrations of visiting skaters from out of town were held. Hundreds of people stood around in the afternoon cold to view close-up the pair skating, ice waltzes and pirouettes of accomplished figure skaters. It was a sight to behold for those of us who could barely accomplish a crossover step in ill-fitting hockey skates while making our loops on the various rinks

Our favorite spot for nighttime skating was at Lakeside. The extensive rink, outdoor music, abundance of friends and the luxurious nature of the large warming house provided us with hours of entertainment. The usual gaggle of junior high kids in neck scarves and mittens played crack-the-whip while a well-dressed older gentleman in a black wool coat and matching top hat spun and smiled and glided with the greatest of ease. He had obviously been a superb figure skater in his youth and loved every moment of his turns around the rink.

Big metal loudspeakers on the front of the warming house at Lakeside brought melodies of the day—with skaters' waltzes in the cool evening. Skaters were warmed by their movement, by friends and by the warm stone building with its real furnace.

We twisted and turned and chased around the rink. When we truly wanted to venture beyond, we simply stepped over the snow bank of the rink and headed out on the frozen lake. In a light snow or when the moon was full, we glided across the lake to the other side to start a small fire from the reeds on the shoreline. Friends would gather, songs were sung and another night was complete.

Thoughts of friends gathered in the cool spaces of ice rinks warm our hearts today. A slow crossover waltz, the rush of the Hornets front line, the crack of the whip in our playground rink or just sitting on a snow bank with a special friend remain sparkling treasures of our winter youth. Impressed upon our senses today is the idyllic life of fun and joy and safety we enjoyed in a manner unheard of today.

We existed without parental supervision, continuous monitoring or rides to every place we visited. We simply stated our destination, headed out and returned at the expected time.

Trudging through the snow with skates slung over our shoulders, the welcoming rinks of our youth were just ahead.

King of the Moutain

We were pumped!

With school out, we were free for vacation fun, continuous snow and ice skating day and night. On snowy nights, we raced to the frosty front windows of our little home on Grand Street to see flashing blue lights and hear the roaring motors of huge street department plows as they stacked snow ever higher on the sides of streets.

Each day of winter, school day or not, we traversed the trails on top of the mounded snow with skills gained through years of practice. Going back and forth twice per day from school (home for lunch), we soon had trails stomped down on top of huge snow mounds to give us an ever-higher view of the world.

By mid-season we could be walking on piles that looked down on passing cars. We had a view of the world that adults could only wish for. To hurry up one side and down the other, to dive into the fresh snow or to ski down the side of a mountain-like lode was the essence of alpine adventure. We ran the tops like mountain goats.

When off the trails, we made "belly-whomper" runs and dives on the frozen street on our well-worn but trusty Flexible Flyer sleds. We stole rides on the back of city buses by grabbing the bumpers and hunkering down to slide along newly frosted streets. With some snowfalls, a combination of deep snow and slow buses made for rides all over town on the heels of our shoes or boots.

Day and night we found new ways to enjoy the spirit of the season and the release of Christmas vacation. At home with a shovel and busy hands, piles soon became forts of snow near the street. With every snowstorm and snowplow passing, our design and facility changed. We proceeded to cut channels and create warm spaces for scarves, mittens and stored items of importance. Lying inside, we would plan forays out into the neighborhood.

As we continued planning the labyrinth, fortress and private space, we also planned for warfare and bombardment procedures.

If snow from the plow heaped in on us, our only loss in the fort might be frozen snowballs previously made and piled up in pyramid fashion in the fort for a next bombardment of passing motorists or kids on the other side of the street.

The only personal danger for us was to be ensconced in the fort when the plow was doing its job. With years of experience we kept our eyes and ears open and had figured it out. Getting dumped on didn't bother us as much as the need to be on the lookout for our too-tipsy neighbor lady as she weaved her car back into her driveway after an afternoon at the club. She could easily run us over if we built anywhere near her landing zone.

On a cold Saturday afternoon before Christmas, we climbed snow banks on the way to Christmas play practice at the Lutheran church. With four-buckle overshoes clanking on each step, we followed the route to good intentions toward the annual church pageant, crossing driveways and hilltops, deep drifts and icy peaks.

We were distracted from our target about midway by a huge snow pile near the Baptist church. The plow had made a series of long runs in clearing the Y-junction roadway at the intersection of Wabasha and Eighth Streets. In so doing, the driver took a run straight at the church and heaped the snow into a glorious mound.

It was an opportunity and challenge to sway even the most committed religious from their task at the local church. What could a few minutes of playing king of the mountain hurt?

Kids from the other side of the West End were already on the hill, but they knew the rules. Whoever could dethrone the other through a combination of shoves, rushes, protective moves and wrestling matches became the momentary champion of the hill—appropriately named "King of the Mountain."

Sessions didn't last long, but seemed so. You fought for your life. Impacted snow entered every crevice and opening of your clothes and body. To be "King" was a fleeting achievement, but a position of honor nevertheless. It was like scoring the final bucket at the close of a basketball game—a memory to be treasured and resurrected for years to come. We fought hard and long. Finally exhausted, we headed up the last few blocks to church.

We knew our lines for the hour-long practice. The annual, multi-voiced, memorized production was a part of our being. Our individual pageant parts switched each year. But with our background and conditioned response imposed by the same Germanic Wisconsin Synod minister since kindergarten, linemaking was a breeze.

On our way home, we cruised the high hills around the hospital, cut through a few alleys, crossed the school rink and enjoyed the gift of another fresh snow.

Arriving at the front door, we were ready for the warmth of our kitchen wood stove and a cup of cocoa. With another day of winter in our pocket and having climbed the high snow pile, we felt like kings of the mountain.

Wild for Hornets Hockey:
A History of Semi-Pro Hockey
in Winona

Radiating westward from Winona on the Mississippi River are the most beautiful limestone bluffs and verdant valleys of Minnesota. Captured between the bluffs is Lake Winona, the favored ice of local boys—known as the neighborhood gang. It's the place where hockey began for me. Today we can look out on those frozen acres of Lake Winona, close our eyes and remember the real heroes at play—these Lakeside ruffians. The hometown champions gave their all for the sport, the community and for one another. They brought to all the most significant quarter-century of exciting sport the town had ever seen.

I was invited to share my thoughts on the subject of hockey.

Someone must have known that I had grown up with the game of hockey—and that I was out there waiting to share my facts and feelings. Like a goalie thumping his stick on the ice before game time, I've been champing at the bit to do so, for hockey has been a part of this young man's fancy since earliest days.

Growing up in the 1950s, I was the true hockey fan—in the time of paper routes, wood stoves, outdoor ice and rugged men who played for love of the game. I neither played the game nor carried a hockey stick, but memories are vivid of every flash on ice that happened on cold winter Sundays with my hometown team—the Winona Hornets.

Living near the lake, these ruffians grew up playing "shinny" stick hockey. In darkening winter afternoons they went after one another on the natural ice as their predecessors had done in the Middle Ages when playing a game called "colf," using curved bats and a ball. "Puc," a Gaelic word meaning "to poke" related to "the blow given by a hurler to the ball with his caman or hurley—always called a puck."

The boys didn't know a caman from a hurley, but they knew how to pass and block and intimidate as brothers of the ice. In the winter, it's what they did, creating an outdoor mystique of David's strength and a firebrand pond-hockey mentality in southern Minnesota.

In the early 1930s, these hometown boys took over the action. With homemade sticks, a battered puck and an overload of energy, they made their own warmth in after-school forays playing early, informal ice hockey. Hockey was played in areas sufficiently cold enough for natural, reliable, seasoned ice. Their rink on Lake Winona qualified as an appropriate setting. Toes were warmed only by fast action and a small fire of reeds pulled from the side of the lake.

The names of earlier superstars are yet alive in my mind and the memories of Winonans—Harders and Hittner, Bambenek and Dorn, Noeske and Wychgram, Hajicek and Hoover, Breza and Boland, Sievers and Neitzke were but a few of the many. They were a cross-section of descendants of early European settlers who had worked the lumber mills, flourmills, railroads and meat packing plants which sustained our community of 25,000.

Each had a puck in his pocket, a stick over his shoulder and sharp skates that swung dangerously as the boys hustled off toward practice and continual play. These were the real boys of winter who made for the legend of southern Minnesota hockey. In the hotbed of Winona Hornets hockey of the 1940s and 1950s, they took off and continuously led the tri-state Interstate League or the Southern Minnesota League in goals and hat tricks.

Sunday afternoons were alive on the ice at Athletic Park, where I was happy to be a face in the crowd. I saw games of action, fisticuffs and spilled blood, and real heroes—for whatever coin I might be able to draw out of my corduroys. As the hat was passed between periods around the wood board rink, I put in my nickel or dime. In the days of personal financial responsibility, long before "allowance" became fashionable, these hometown heroes gave me lessons on life for pennies on the dollar—memorable and invaluable today.

I saw them on the streets each day and on the rink for Sunday afternoon games. They grew bigger, and soon moved on to regional competition. In leather-and-sheepskin helmets, these boys started Winona on a path from lakeside to stardom. Organized a bit as the Winona Hockey Club, they may have bought their supplies at the local Out-Dor Store on East Third Street, where

"The Fastest Game in the World"

Hockey - Saturday - 2:30
ATHLETIC PARK RINK

An ad for a neighborhood hockey game, circa 1940. (Courtesy of the Winona Newspaper Project, Winona State University.)

hockey skates were four dollars and ninety-five cents; sticks were twenty-five, forty-nine or seventy-five cents; and pucks cost twenty-five cents. With proper equipment, they were soon off on a run.

Without a major sponsor, the Winona team played as the Hurry Back (Pool Parlor) Team for the championship on Lake Winona in February, 1933. They were in extremely "home" territory as they played for the prize on the lake where they had grown up. With used jerseys from the Winona Merchants basketball team and loaned equipment from St. Mary's College, these pretentious youngsters went on to face both the St. Olaf and St. Thomas college teams.

Playing at the lake rink, members of this rag-tag team were then politely known as the Lake Side Vicinity Hockey Team. They became "Irv Gappa's Team," the Lakeside Vultures and the Owl Motor Co. (Ford) team along the way—winning the regional hockey title as the *Republican-Herald* Team. Max Wolfe, formerly of Dartmouth, bolstered the team at one time. In their new sponsor-emblazoned maroon jerseys with matching socks, they played on rinks constructed at Lake and Athletic Park sites as a part of Winona's WPA project of the 1930s.

Now changed into young men supplied with the "real" stuff of hockey, this gang of lakesiders played in the Interstate Hockey League from 1936 to 1940. The boys of the lake were undefeated in games across the region, including Iowa cities and against the Marines team of Chippewa Falls, Wisconsin. They won one of the games eight to zero, with only six players on their team!

The 1940 team arrived in new scarlet uniforms and spun out a colorful whirl of hockey moves to confound their opponents. They finished the season with eight wins and zero losses, scoring forty-six goals to their opponents' twelve. In February of 1940, the team and forty fans traveled by bus to Waterloo, Iowa, for a tournament where Winona faced off against Cedar Rapids. The admission for four games was twenty-five cents. Upon their return, they played the undefeated North Mankato Vikings at home. For home games, the "ice on Lake Winona was in fine condition."

Sponsorship was irregular and often gone, yet the "neighborhood gang of south-side boys" continued the action to bring amateur hockey to the hearts of Winonans. From 1933 to 1941, the local team had a record of thirty-three wins, three losses and three ties—with twenty-seven straight victories from 1936-1941! Playing in the Interstate League between Wisconsin, Iowa, and Minnesota, they regularly beat the best of LaCrosse, Eau Claire and Waterloo teams. War years intervened, but they continued the pattern.

By the 1950-1951 season, the Winona Hornets (preceded by sponsorship as the Boland Blues) buzzed to the Southern Minnesota League championship for a third time. With a cumulative record over the years of sixty-two wins and eight losses, they held "the most outstanding hockey record in the state."

Dazzling in my time frame at age ten or so was Roger—"the Winona Flash." Helmetless, with a continuous smile and a flash in his eyes, he gained another faceoff, dug his skates into outdoor ice of the hometown rink and took off for places unknown to score multiple hat tricks. Similarly dazzling was his fellow lakesider—lanky, teenage "Popeye" who came along in 1947, as goalie (at age fifteen) to stare down and stop the goals of grizzled war veterans from Mankato or Rochester or Austin. The lakeside boys made it happen.

Roger and Popeye exemplified then (and now) the homegrown nature and special spirit of the hundred or so Hiawatha Valley players who gave their all to the team over the years. Roger and Popeye represent the tradition and effort of lakeside boys. They followed the lead of Jim Bambenek (the "original" superstar) to lead and score and dig some more. They were leaders of southern Minnesota hockey in the late 1940s and 1950s. Now retired to their favored hometown, their memories are rich of the days on the ice of Lake Winona and Athletic Park. Competition was fierce, but memories are clear.

One of Winona's early hockey observers said, "Hockey, with its speed, its thrills and its excitement appeals to every lover of red-blooded spectacular sport. It is the fastest game played by civilized men—quickly becoming one of the most popular sports of the day."

It whirls today in my mind. How right he was.

The Winona Hornets team picture, circa 1940. (Photo courtesy of the Winona Newspaper Project, Winona State University.)

A Saturday Save
(A Semi-Fictitious Tale)

S aturday morning was washday.

One or the other of us was the wringer, another the hanger and general clean-up person. Bringing in the old Sears wringer-washer that spent most of its life on the back porch, we heated some hot water on the wood-fired kitchen stove. Filling the aging gray washer with suds and hot water, we proceeded with the day's chore in the warmth of our good-sized kitchen. We then made up two washtubs of rinse water (one cold, one hot).

Following our simple process of wash/agitate, wring, rinse, rinse, and final wring-out, we soon accomplished the task the best that eight- and ten-year-old brothers could. On warm days in spring and summer, it was a simpler task to achieve, unhampered by weather. On cold days in December, however, our fingers quickly became as frozen as the clothes on the backyard lines.

Necessaries like underwear and socks were hung in the middle room, giving humidity to the house air—a task usually accomplished by an old metal pot filled with water sitting on top of the potbelly wood stove. As clothes quickly dried indoors, we rotated the clothes in from the outside over the next day or so. The singlemost, major job in the process was carrying the full rinse tubs out to the backyard for emptying—a two-man job.

With an early start we would be done in time to meet Pa at the 12:00 p.m. city bus at the corner. His weekly trip to the meat market and bakery on Saturday morning found him laden with fresh-baked bread and various cold meats that made the Saturday noon lunch a feast to behold.

Homemade sausages of various types—summer sausage, headcheese, liver sausage, homemade wieners, blood sausage and other wonders of the German butcher—delighted all of us on that special day. These specialties, along with assorted beef roasts, hamburger and chicken, would last our family of seven through a week or more.

Following our sumptuous lunch and having completed the chores of the day, we were free to do as we pleased. I often headed off to Davey's house, where we set off on another trip to the Army-Navy Surplus Store. A windfall caused by a recent garage cleaning effort made each of us semi-flush, with a couple of dollars to think about investing in new military garb and equipment.

We had to think carefully about our expenditures, since it was a long time between paychecks for us. Winter could be pretty good for income, depending upon the frequency and quantity of snow, of course. Snow shoveling paid off handsomely if you knocked on enough doors and cleaned enough sidewalks, but you didn't know when the next snow might hit.

On this early spring day we were in a bit of a lull, with temperatures around freezing most of the time and little sunlight to warm the hearts and gardens of neighbors who needed the brawn of tough pre-teens to help accomplish the chores. We were basically unemployed.

Summer was better, what with the house cleanings, outdoor chores of garage cleaning and garden turning and our entrepreneurial effort of gathering and selling rags and paper and metal to the "sheenie." We made out pretty good sometimes. Newspapers and rags gathered from neighbors, found metal (including crushed tin cans) and assorted castoffs could be sold for prices from pennies to fifty cents per pound to the local recycler, otherwise known as the junk man. We were the ultimate recyclers, long before it became fashionable.

On the way through the park on our way to our favorite retail outlet downtown on Second Street, we ran across Jesse and his gang. As gangs go today, it wasn't much. Could have been. It's just that Jesse wasn't exactly a leader of men, yet he somehow was able to surround himself with a ragtag collection of little warts whose noses always seemed to be running.

With about eight of these also-rans accompanying him, Jesse gained a bravado that was unlike his everyday appearance in the halls and caverns of good old Madison School. The greatest threat that he offered at school was to the janitor, since Jesse sort of brought a mess with him wherever he went.

We accepted Jesse for who he was and knew that we could almost single-handedly overpower his gang with a shout and a step forward. But there was always the potential of eight little buggers throwing rocks or snowballs at us at the same time.

We counseled with Jesse and his tribe under the massive budding elms in the park on that cool day in April. His plan was to head over to the boathouses across the river and forage for goodies in the summer residences of Mississippi River boat people. Break-ins to these half-house, half-boat garage facilities were common throughout the winter.

It seemed like there was a police officer visiting our school on a weekly basis to find the culprits. The worst that had occurred was the total burning down of two of the boathouses by two of our fifth graders—big-time criminals in our estimation. These two classmates were sent "up the river" for a time to the state boys' school.

From their experience we learned the allowable limits of pranks and boathouse visits. A bottle of pop and a pack of cigarettes taken might not cause an investigation, but a broken window or theft of a radio could bring the gendarmes to school and home. Jesse and his roving gang also knew the limits.

They also knew the dangerous side of such forays. Sometimes the boathouse owners would be there for an afternoon or evening of fishing through the ice. With electricity usually off in the winter, there were few visible signs or sounds of occupancy to alert young ears to dangers ahead. More than a few times, footraces occurred across snow and ice with fleet-footed ten-year-olds in the lead and angry residents in hot pursuit. Such was the challenge of the day.

The warm interior of the surplus store and the smell of cosmalene greeted us as we entered from a still, brisk day outside. Knowing the path through the store, we ventured past the knife cases near the front of the store, between the stacks of used but clean and pressed khakis at the mid-point, on to the barrels and compartments of bargains located on the back wall.

We didn't have a special need in mind this day, but knew there would be new items of adventure to greet us. It took little time to recognize the bargain of the day—a fifty-foot piece of Manila hemp rope for two dollars and ninety-eight cents. With three dollars between us and thoughts of how a sturdy rope could aid us at future campsites, we were soon on our way. With two cents and high hopes, we decided to take a brief hike across the river to the boathouse area.

The wax-impregnated half-inch rope was the stuff of real war surplus. As we headed down Second Street toward the high bridge across the Mississippi River, we considered the rope's former use as either tie-off to a Navy ship docking in England or as a towrope for a Jeep on Iwo Jima.

In any case, the strong young men of the United States military had made use of it. We were meant to carry on the tradition of firm hands and purposeful accomplishment. Just carrying our fifty-foot section reminded us that men had to be strong.

Our venture across the river showed us a bit of the beginning spring thaw. Large sheets of ice were headed down the river, surrounded by black, icy water. Occasionally we would see a large log floating by, part of the runoff from the valleys and creeks that fed the tumultuous river in springtime. It was definitely not a good idea to be on the river today.

Floating on warming breezes, hawks and eagles glided overhead, looking for prey in the fields and waters of the river valley. After what seemed like months of snow, ice and overcast skies, the sun was finally beginning to show itself a bit these days. Hawks, eagles, fishermen and ten-year-olds were all looking forward to the new season coming up.

We got to the bottom of the bridge on the Wisconsin side, cut down the hill and were soon on the dirt road to the public bathhouse and boathouse row. It was a fifteen to twenty minute walk from here to home. In the summer we could cut the time in half on our bikes, but most often we enjoyed walking, since there were new options open at every turn.

Bikes were great, but they didn't get us up and down hills or in or out of backyards and wooded spaces with the speed or inconspicuousness that we felt was needed. In the summer, our ventures across the bridge to the bathhouse and public beach on the river were daily. Then, speed was the order of the day, since we moved from chores to playground to beach with the fewest wasted minutes possible.

If it was a good day at the beach we might also need to hightail it home in time for supper. One-speed bikes on the uphill side of the interstate bridge were impossible to ride. We pushed them up the sidewalk between the road and the side of the bridge. The downhill side, once achieved, gave us a rush to the bathhouse on the way over or past the YMCA on our way home. Today the walk was slow. We were not in a hurry. We were also weighted down with our newfound treasure.

As we neared the old bridge past the bathhouse we heard loud voices. It was safe to assume that Jesse and his gang were up to no good. With boathouse row on our left and the voices on the right, we were confused. A deserted road shot off to the right. There usually wasn't anyone off to the right—except for some early morning fishermen or some late night high school kids drinking beer.

As we understood it, this was an entry road to the old bridge that brought farmers from western Wisconsin farms to the market across the river in the late 1800s, until today's bridge-and-dike roadway was built in the 1940s.

Today the bridge entry was overgrown, yet fishermen and students seeking solitude still used the path. We turned to head off that way, not understanding what was going on.

After passing the first few trees at the riverside, it was easy to spot Jesse's excited group standing on the shore, waving, hollering and gesticulating to each other. Their concentration was focused on the slough shooting out from under the old bridge that we had just crossed. Getting closer, we understood their excitement and apparent concern.

Hanging on to a piece of ice over fifteen feet from shore was Jesse! Somehow he had fallen through the ice. Fortunately, he was able to hang on to a large, fixed piece of ice. According to accounts gathered quickly from gang members, he had been hanging on for nearly ten minutes. From the distance, we could see Jesse resting on an ice slab with his head on his arm, while the rest of his body was underwater.

There was no way to get to him, all boats in the area having been put up for the winter. The freezing water rushing by headed directly toward the open river. There was one hope. With Davey in tow, I headed back up the path to the old bridge.

Hanging off the rickety side of the old bridge and securing the end of our rope to a side cement balustrade of the bridge, I attempted to toss the too-heavy rope exactly the right way. There was a chance that we could pull Jesse back toward the bridge, where others from the clan could stand on pier supports and reach out for him. Davey hung onto me. I tossed the rope again and again. Using the current of the river in the open water, we were finally able to float the rope directly past Jesse.

He grabbed ahold! Davey and I hung over the side of the bridge, pulling on the rope and getting Jesse to the safety of his friends below. Knowing from past experience that one of the boathouses was unlocked, several of the younger ones were sent off to get a blanket and any clothing they could find. The older ones were sent over the bridge to get to the YMCA and call the police.

Our immediate need was to get a fire going. From his pocket, Davey pulled out his trusty military-issue, waterproof match container. He soon had twigs blazing from his "farmer matches." With a quick search of the area, gang members found enough dry wood to get a real bonfire going.

Blankets and clothing having arrived, Jesse was held upright, wrapped and rubbed to get his circulation moving. He was very cold to the touch, had blue lips and was nearly unconscious. Yet we rubbed. Within what seemed like minutes, the police and ambulance arrived.

The ambulance had just left with Jesse, when along came "One-Shot Kelly," photographer for the local newspaper. We had seen him before at basketball games and gruesome train-auto accidents and knew that his reputation was well-deserved. In this case he took several shots, however. He wanted all of us together, then Davey and me on the bridge, and then a couple of shots around the bonfire. With the fire out, the police gathered all and took us home.

It was a quiet and special time at my house that night—a time of reflection and personal silence caused by too much adventure. Home was the place to be. Our rope hung in the middle room over the clothesline with the morning wash. The tale was told and retold as neighbors stopped by to get a first-hand account.

The next morning the Sunday paper arrived early, since my older brother had a paper route and the bundle of papers was delivered to the house. Along with the route supply, we always had a few extras that allowed Pa and brothers to read the first page story and view the pictures that One-Shot had taken at the same time. We were featured as heroes in a story entitled "A Saturday Save." It was the first time that any of us had our picture in the paper.

Davey and I rested on our laurels and accepted the acknowledgements and accolades that came our way as we returned to school on Monday morning. We placed our special rope in a place of honor in his basement cellar where we kept most of our military paraphernalia. It served us in all of our campouts for tying up gear and in the building of structures.

We even created a rope swing from a tree at the edge of the lake to serve the two of us, neighborhood kids—and Jesse and his ragtag collection—for the rest of the summer.

Chapter Five

After School

It's interesting how powerful we felt walking around Winona.

We knew that time in the woods, walking up and down the limestone river valley bluffs on a regular basis or riding bikes everywhere built us up physically for our future missions. Physical fitness wasn't something that a physical education teacher taught us. We didn't have one.

We found physical fitness on our own—like traipsing off to the Swap Shop, a second-hand store on the main drag of downtown, on a moment's notice or heading out in the hills on our bikes when the weather was amenable.

Like our heroes of World War II and Korean War Army combat movies and G.I. Joe comics, we knew that hard work and constant training would prepare us to be physically fit in time of national need. It was something that was just known.

Physical education consisted of kickball on the blacktopped playground at school recess under the supervision of one or more of our female old maid teachers. It was augmented by our once per week indoor basketball sessions after school. During these moments of shooting buckets and running drills established by Ev, a sixth grade teacher and coach, we envisioned ourselves as future superstars of basketball.

Our knowledge of superstars came from watching the high school team, with "H-Bomb" Heinz, on Friday nights, through an occasional visit to the floor of the local teachers college to watch a Saturday morning basketball team scrimmage, or by seeing the likes of the Phillips 66ers or the Holy Cross team members in the shiny pages of *Sport Magazine*. We were able to try out our techniques all week long after school on the tarred playground lot, with its steel-poled basketball "bang-board" with metal netting.

From Davey's bedroom window facing the asphalt of the playground, we were able to keep an eye on the space and the competition for use of the court for the hours we needed. We gained our slot in time without shivering on the sidelines as others finished their game. Temperature, darkness or the draw of an eight-cent Pepsi at Deilke's Grocery across the street helped determine the length of our sessions.

Shooting a ball with icy patches imprinted on it from each bounce one late spring day, we decided that enough was enough. You can't shoot a ball with gloves on. You also can't shoot a ball bare-handed for endless hours on a barely thawing day in April without getting frozen joints and ice on your fingertips.

The impediments of weather messed with our accuracy toward the steel-webbed net. Maybe that's why the best ball players come from Los Angeles or Atlanta or French Lick, Indiana. They can shoot until the cows come home—and have warm fingers.

On this particular day it was definitely time to move on. Since homework was somewhere between slim and none for mental giants like us, we decided to leave the court and head over the tracks to visit our buddy, Wayne. His house was always a good spot to visit in the late afternoon. His ma was forever cooking something on the wood stove whenever we came by, and she always made us welcome. It seems like the coffee pot never left the top of the stove, to serve guests and family at any time of night or day.

It was still a shock for us to sit with Wayne, his brothers, ma, or pa, the milk hauler, at the kitchen table and be drinking coffee. Why Wayne's family, with his father a milk hauler, had such a dedication to coffee is a mystery yet today. Some of us were still novices at the game of understanding pungent adult liquids, yet we imbibed.

We were raised in the state that boasted Princess Kay of the Milky Way, the annual queen of June's Dairy Month. Dairy products seemed to be everywhere. Even though dollars were short in our house most of the time, the milkman made his every-other-day stop at our house (and everyone else's) to deliver glass bottles of milk to the back porch.

It was milk for growing bodies and minds. As much as we went without other things, milk flowed throughout the years. Pa's milk bill never did get below the one hundred dollar level. We went to the corner grocery to pick up two-pound rolls of butter wrapped in waxed paper—or if dollars were very short, to get the plastic packet of oleomargarine with the push-button-yellow blob that we kneaded into what seemed like semi-yellow-white lard. We never did get quite used to it.

In Wayne's room, an extension of the small house across a small porch, we sat around like three small soldiers in a bunkroom. And no wonder—beds were U.S. Army issue, with "USA" stamped on the footboards.

A small, self-contained kerosene stove kept the room warm on a chilly day while creating a permanent smell of kerosene that stung our noses upon entry. The room and furnishings may have been sparse and utilitarian, but Wayne's comic book collection drew our attention and masked any discomfort. His assortment was stupendous—a resident horde of comic books over a foot high. The assortment included *G.I. Joe, Captain Marvel, Superman, Lash LaRue, Dick Tracy, Archie*, and what seemed like a hundred more.

We may not have been the most excited readers of American history or the dusty novels from the school library, but we were voracious in appetite for good comics.

As with marbles, the greater your stock, the choicer the opportunity for trading. The routine, of course, was to get together with others and with their stacks to trade one-for-one or two-for-one, if necessary, to both expand one's literary awareness and the quality of your stock.

Our friend, Bruce, was the only one of the gang who had a "controlled" stock. His father, the Sunday school supervisor and the junior high principal, was the resident censor in his house.

The rest of us seemed to be control-free, since our parents likely had read most of the comics themselves (or didn't care). The most common remark overheard from parents was, "at least they're reading."

David, the neighbor kid a few years older than us, had a good stock of comics, but we didn't engage in trading with him. His mother, a single parent with a strong Catholic background, saw that all of his comics were stamped with the seal of approval of the Catholic Church. Their subject matter just didn't have the "mass market" appeal of blood and guts and glory that we all sought.

After our "confab" in Wayne's room, we decided to head off on a comic book trading mission. On the way from Wayne's, we stopped by my house and Davey's to grab our stacks of comics. Dragging our stacks over our shoulder in cloth bags, we headed off to the Swap Shop.

It was only a couple of miles, so we could make it down and back before suppertime. With a few nickels in hand, we might even purchase an item of Edson's comic stock for half the listed price. If we chose to trade with him, the standard policy was "two for one"—that is, two of ours for each one of his.

But his shelves were loaded with adventures new and old, so we were ready to trade.

Comics, playground and home visits filled our after-school time span. We would walk to Wayne's or Johnny's or Bruce's (or my house)—or any one of twenty other destinations. Playmates were those with whom we went to school. All seemed to be within a ten block radius, as if someone had defined our perimeter of socialization. In fact, the school had created the boundaries. Since kindergarten, our circle of friends and range of our wanderings held pretty close to these defined boundaries.

In most cases parents were at home, but there was the occasion or two when we were left on our own to make hot cocoa or peanut butter sandwiches. There was the time when we got on the telephone and called names in the book at random to ask the answering party if their radio was on. If they said "yes," then we asked them how it fit and quickly hung up. It was good for a few yuks. Pranks were relatively harmless.

We occasionally tossed a few snowballs at cars and ran like the wind across backyards to our hiding places in the neighborhood. Only Jim and Eddie were more adventurous. They went off one day to the boathouses down by the frozen river and burned one of them to the ground (or the ice). They were found out and met their due with the police at school the next day and with some long-term counseling and guidance of "Pus-Eye," the county probation officer.

It's hard to remember someone new coming into our midst. There were a few, but like the new neighbors of today, they had a hard time breaking into the routine of relationships that had been established.

Little Marsh was an exception. He was a little guy who came into our midst for a few years, beginning around third grade. He was just too pretty. He had slicked-down hair, new corduroys on nearly every day and a house that was just too nice. I don't remember ever seeing him messed up or dirty.

We liked to visit his place. It had so many of the things that were absent in our little houses—like television, a forced-air furnace for whole house heating, new toys of the best quality and even a separate room for toys, comics and playthings.

In the living room, his parents had a brand-new Zenith floor model radio that was the world's best (or so we were told). It was wooden, shiny and effective. With it, one had the capability to bring in frequencies that ranged from our local radio station, KWNO, with its everyday happenings, to police frequencies and airline chatter, as well as "short wave"—a magical wonder that took us around the world.

We could listen for hours while very slowly turning the colored, lighted short wave dial. French, Japanese, and other stations were received with what seemed like hundreds of dialects we couldn't understand.

Marsh's every cap pistol, comic and toy—from electric football set to beautiful Lionel train—was shiny and new. We enjoyed them all.

With all of the things around him it was always a quiet house, nevertheless. His parents must have been successful. We hardly ever saw them.

He wasn't a bad kid, either.

Baseball Immortals

I was just over to school for an afternoon session of knocking the tennis ball around with the guys. We were pounding the ball off the back side of the old elementary school, taking turns tossing the ball at one another, aimed toward the marked-off strike zone we had drawn in chalk on the cement foundation.

The batter's box was to the left side of the rear school steps. There was just enough room between the ground and the lowest row of brick to draw a two-foot-by-three-foot rectangle on the cement base. Quarters were close for the batter, but the space couldn't have been better for a batter's box.

With soft dirt at our feet, the space seemed to have been designed into the building as a batter's box, not as a flower garden, as intended. Pitching one foot further to the left and we would have been aiming at that funny looking turn-handle on the water outlet. It was one of those that only the school janitor could open with his key.

The back side of the box was defined by the heavy cement steps which we entered upon arrival to school or when returning from recess. The steps were just tall enough, with a height that made you feel as if you were really stepping into a batter's cage. The space seemed to fit a ten-year-old body as we stepped up to the plate. It felt just right. Fortunately, there were not any windows in the nearby wall space; just row upon row of aging, reddish brick.

For our weekly baseball games in the city recreation league, there was no such thing as a formal, organized practice. These sessions at school and in aiming the ball at the back wall at home were the only practices that had application to the grounders and fly balls and pitching styles that we were to experience in the games to be played in the summer league at the West End Recreation Field or Gabrych Park, home of the Winona Chiefs.

With neither coaches nor parent involvement, we were on our own to bike to the park, get there on time and be ready to go when Max Molock blew the whistle. Max was the local, experienced college baseball coach who single-handedly coordinated the summer schedule, games and uniforms.

The league was organized by showing up at the small city recreation department room in City Hall. Filled with bats and balls and bases and a small wooden desk overshadowed by Max's rotund frame, Max decided the teams, distributed the jerseys and caps and handed us a schedule. We knew that we were duty-bound to show up at all games—or Max would remember.

There was no pre-arrangement of teams by adults, that unfortunately exists in today's world of children's recreation leagues. Max was the sole determiner and the arbiter of any complaints or differences. His goal was to see that all kids with an interest got to play. He didn't have favorites, but he knew the capabilities of the players from his vast experience with the kids and families in town.

Our unofficial pre-game practices were accomplished by tossing the ball at the wall at school, as we had devised. Hurling toward one another, we practiced our curves and fastballs with a whistling tennis ball to improve our control. Swinging our homemade bat or a borrowed Louisville Slugger, we tried hard to blast the ball out of the park.

We envisioned ourselves as home run sluggers, or better yet, pitchers. One of us was certain to become the next Bob Feller or Warren Spahn, but at game time, there just wasn't enough room on the field for more than one pitcher at a time. So, in our warm-ups at the school, one would bat while the other would pitch.

If we were lucky, there would be a third guy along to play the outfield and recover the long balls before they ran through the sparse bushes defining the blacktopped playground, down the worn grass and into the gutter, soon to disappear through the grate in the city sewer opening at the corner. Once it hit the drain, the ball was gone and the game was over. It didn't take long for us to figure out the value of the ball (or the outfielder).

It was fun to be the outfielder. A tennis fly ball aimed our direction offered real practice with a certain safety margin, for in the actual game there was the ever-present fear of missing the fly ball and getting bonked on the head by a hard-hit baseball—all in the company of friends and opposing team members. It wasn't the error or the pain or the fear that mattered as much as the hoots and the embarrassment that seemed to linger forever.

The major fear in going back for the fly ball on the school grounds was that you could smash your body on the steel pole that held the tetherball or on the steel uprights of the circular merry-go-round. School architects hadn't envisioned that they were locating these pain-filled targets in our center field.

With school closed for the summer and the playground shut down for the day, we had the whole place to ourselves. On the warmest of days we tried every conceivable way to break into the water spigot—to no avail. Bill Groves, the school janitor, was the only one who had the magic key. He wasn't around when we most needed him.

If we were flush with the necessary eight cents to buy a bottle of Pepsi, we could head across the street to Deilke's Grocery. We could make a Pepsi or a five-cent Popsicle last for a long time on a warm day.

The games were across town, but we easily reached them on bikes that seemed to have continuing issues of chain slippage, brake repair and flat tires. That's what summer was all about in our small town—fixing our bikes, doing our home chores and then setting off for the big game with our mitt hanging from the handlebar.

The jerseys were wool and so were the hats. By the time we reached our game destination, we were "warmed up" and ready to go. There were no pre-game calisthenics. We tossed the ball back and forth and waited for the previous game to reach completion. Then we charged onto the field. The decision of who played which position was determined by our own interest and by Max's careful observation of how the game was being played. There were times when we may have played three positions in the same game, but there were also stalwarts who held certain positions.

We knew full well that when we played certain teams that we could look forward to facing "Fireball" or "Big Gene" on the mound. The plumber's son, Mike, was behind the plate. Other athletically endowed kids would usually be found at shortstop or second base. The rest of us rotated around positions until we found our niche (sometimes a semi-permanent assignment to right field).

The games were exciting. Any at-bat against Big Gene was a moment of exhilaration and anticipation. On the rare occasion when we could get a hit off of him, we were thrilled. Other times we were happy to just have made it through the experience of living through a fastball or curve powered by technique and his 200-pound frame.

Even though he was our age, he was a very large person to face. Mild-mannered off the field, he was a force to be reckoned with from the batter's box. Fireball was similarly menacing. He was a year or so older, but had already achieved a hardened look and image from his escapades into the world of juvenile crime and from having served at least one term in the State Home for Boys at Red Wing.

We didn't know of the term "juvenile delinquents" at the time, but he must have been one. His nickname came from both his combination of blazing speed and wild throws. When he was on, you were smoked by this lefty in the fashion of Robin Roberts of the Phillies or by our submarine-throwing local hero, Hugh Orphan, of the semi-pro Winona Chiefs of the Southern Minny League.

Our tennis ball practice sessions behind the elementary school were beneficial in sharpening the eye for our games between the Fire Department Team and the United Commercial Travelers (whoever they were), or the Wingold team verses the Marigold Dairy, or any combination of other town sponsored teams.

When we ventured from the city's West End playing field to the home plate of Gabrych Park (in the East End and home of the Chiefs). we were in our glory. We could test our skills in the very place where our heroes played. This morning a walk across the mound, tonight a vision from the stands as hurlers and heroes chucked the ball at speeds we could only imagine.

On one special morning, we were on our way to the home of the Chiefs, with baseball mitts hanging from handlebars and favorite bats sticking out somewhere from bike frames like extra appendages. We envisioned a slaughter from our West End rivals, the West End Merchants. With Big Gene on the mound, Hauge at shortstop and Rollie Kratz at first base, the team was truly a formidable force.

They could hit, pitch and field. We could hope that they would have a bad day and that we could get in a few lucky hits and strikeouts of Woody or Mikey T., their lesser players. There was always hope that by a combination of luck, lineup change due to illness or no-shows—or a possible off-day for Gene—we could score a few runs and hold on for a meager victory.

As pitcher, I was in control of some of our destiny. My skills had been honed solely through daily sessions with the tennis ball against the back of the house and not from practice with a coach or guide. The occasional article in *Sport* magazine showed me how to hold the ball for a curve.

Mostly, I was pleased that Pa didn't holler at me for what must have seemed like endless hours of repetitious thud against the house or garage. My talents weren't that great, but I was consistent. I was able to keep it inside the box I had marked off on the back of the house.

The black uniforms of the West End Merchants made Big Gene and crew all the more menacing, as if they needed another piece to shake us up. With our so-so record as representatives of the City Fire Department, our reputation as nice guys who finished last seemed to fit. Our white wool uniforms with black socks seemed to be too clean.

It was like facing off the Brooklyn Dodgers against the local high school team. Their first batter was Rummy. He was a short, caustic, towheaded kid from the West End who was known for his personal veracity. We had faced him many times in basketball, football and baseball games. He was always a competitor who could drill you for a strong double on the first pitch or worm his way through the crowd with seconds left in a basketball game to score the winning basket.

I was resolved to strike him out today. With cheers from my fellow Firemen, I did just that. One-two-three, and he was out of there. What a thrill!

This was a game made in heaven. Everything went right that day. Big Gene was wild. My curve ball actually curved and the Firemen came through. We had hits that plooped over tall Rollie's head at first, stolen bases by Eddie the Rat, and a big bomb in the fourth inning from Kenny, the new kid from Wisconsin, who drove in three runs.

The Merchants were bigger, more ferocious and talented. But the bigger they were, the harder they fell. Rich caught a long bomb to center in the bottom of the sixth just as it was headed for the piles of flax in the neighboring Archer-Daniels Milling Company. His lefty saunter back to the dugout to end the inning and save us from at least two runs was a swagger that represented the frosting on the cake.

With cheers of support from team and Max, who never took sides, we finished them off. Two more hits and a run put us ahead six to one My only job was to control three more Merchant batters (if I were lucky). And I was (lucky, that is). We slid by two strikeouts to Rummy and Donald. A fizzly grounder off the end of the bat to first by Eugene himself ended the game.

We were pleased with ourselves as we rode our bikes back to the West End. It was a perfect sunshine-filled day for baseball, good friends and the ride down Seventh Street. We were bursting with pride as we re-lived the moments of the big game.

Rollie had been contained. Rummy had two strikeouts. And Big Gene was put down with a fizzly grounder handled ably by Kenny at shortstop and Digger at first. I knew that my pitching was "on." Maybe I would make it to the big leagues after all.

Parents and friends heard our re-telling of the story for months to come. The three short lines in the sports section of the local paper told the world and our competitors that we were a force with whom to be reckoned. That seven-inning exploit was enough for us to establish a place in local summer baseball history and to live the lives of immortals for weeks to come.

Success was ours. We didn't win many more games, but our steel baseball cleats were always just a bit sharper and our uniforms a bit less clean from that day forward.

Bouncing the ball off the side of the school seemed to have left its mark.

The Winona Chiefs:
A History of Semi-Pro Baseball
in Winona

Summer adventure for boys in our small town of the 1950s revolved around home and neighborhood. We had chores to do, freedom to wander, playground activities, bike hikes, ball games, BB guns and supper at six. Without permission, if chores were done, we could head out to the hills for a campout, zip off to the playground on a makeshift bike for games or quickly organize a bike hike to the country and neighboring small towns with a supply of peanut butter sandwiches and Ritz crackers in a bike basket.

An evening at the local park as fans of our hometown semi-professional baseball team, the Chiefs, was the highlight of any week. On bikes as a semi-gang or sitting on freshly cleaned milk cans in the darkened back end of Mr. Valentine's milk hauling truck, we arrived fired up to see our heroes.

Locals "Big George" Vondrashek, Chet Wieczorek, Lambert Kowaleski, All-American Paul Giel and Norm Snyder had their chance at the majors and initially or ultimately (after time in the majors) played with the Chiefs. These were guys from Winona, Rollingstone, Arcadia, Pepin or other little burgs around the Hiawatha Valley. We had seen most of them at Sunday afternoon pickup games at the "West End Rec" Field—the initial home of the Winona Braves—as they took the stepping stone to the Chiefs lineup.

We watched competing players Bill "Moose" Skowron and Johnny Blanchard before they hit the New York Yankees. Johnny Van Cuyk of the Rochester team and of Little Chute, Wisconsin, joined the Brooklyn Dodgers in 1947, with Jackie Robinson. Other players were either "going up" to the AAA team or "coming down" from their experiences in the major leagues. Van Cuyk, for example, played in two World Series, then stayed with the Rochester Royals after his time in the majors to live out his life nearby.

We were pleased to watch them pass through as members of visiting teams from Albert Lea, Austin, Rochester, Waseca or other small cities of the

Southern Minny League. There was Haake Mehli of Faribault and Sam "Sad Sam," "Red," "Toothpick" Jones, one of the first Negro players seen in Winona by way of the Rochester Royals, and the first black to pitch a no-hitter in major league baseball—for the Chicago Cubs. Our special import to the hometown Chiefs was Hugh Orphan of Fort Wayne, Indiana (a "submarine ball" pitcher).

Oh!—The names, the stars, the fun of it all.

These were evenings to remember. Thousands of local townspeople and neighboring farmers crowded into Gabrych Park, a high-ceilinged structure built on gifted land in memory of a war hero from the East End neighborhood. It was a monument to the ambition and dedication of Polish-Americans who had settled on their "shotgun," forty-foot lots in the 1870s—not far from the Mississippi River and the logging industry that brought them here. Along with their immense and marvelous St. Stanislaus Polish-Catholic Church a few blocks away, this field of dreams was a major source of pride to all.

They were sawyers, hostlers, roustabouts and mechanics that built the industry and the town. If not employed by one of the lumberyards that lined the river, they were locomotive mechanics or members of the line crew for the many railroads of the area.

In 1876, they organized their first baseball team, The Clippers, to win the state tournament. One of the East Enders, Julian Wera—"The Winona Flash"—left his meat-cutting job at the Interstate Packing Plant in 1927, to play thirty-eight games at third base for the New York Yankees, as they went on to win 110 fames and to wallop the Pirates in four games of the World Series. Wow! To play alongside Lou Gehrig and Babe Ruth!

Somewhere near the end of the 1940s, the PNA (Polish National Alliance) team that was competing in the Southern Minnesota League changed from an East End model to a more global "Chiefs" brand—and proceeded to fill the stands to capacity. On a first-come, first-seated basis, over 2,000 fans arrived at the stands with intent to get one of the prime seats behind home plate.

There were many protected seats in the thirty-row deep (and tall) wood-framed enclosure between first and third bases. With a roof overhead and a chicken wire screen in front, early patrons enjoyed protection from the summer rains and the foul balls that didn't sail over the grandstand to clunk into a parked car.

The bleachers on the first and third base lines were also good places to be. Though not covered, there was usually action in the bullpen on either side of the field away from the grandstand view. The Chiefs were in the first base dugout and their bullpen just beyond. We often liked to be on the third base side to scope out visiting pitchers or make smart comments through the wire to them—as if they couldn't get to us if they wanted!

The third base side also drew more foul balls to keep our attention, with nothing like a zinger at your head when you were turned away from the game. Whether caught or bounced off a head, the balls were returned to the team. We could turn them in to the concession stand for a nickel's credit. Those in the stands had to crane their necks to get a look at what we saw up close and personal.

With a home and away schedule to play, there was at least one game at home each week, sometimes two. With the tremendous popularity of baseball, the town fathers needed to build a second set of bleachers in deep center field to house the hoards.

Every game, home and away, was broadcast live on our local radio station KWNO. When the Chiefs were away, we gathered around the stand-up radio in the front room to hear the exploits of our heroes broadcast from afar through the inveterate, enthusiastic commentary of Chuck Williams—a local folk hero in his own right. Chuck graduated from St. Mary's College and dedicated his life to Winona radio and local sports.

The Chiefs were our superstars and heroes of summer. They related to baseball-minded young boys, to wide-eyed local girls of all ages and to fathers and family members who plunked down the thirty-five-cent admission. A night at the ballpark was an escape from day jobs in the factories and processing plants with their ever-so-repetitious tasks. Some slugged cattle or hogs all day in the packing plant, while others watched the continuous welds of links of chain pass by their station in the excessive warmth of the riverside Peerless Chain Factory.

Games took some away from their too-warm frame houses for a cool summer evening in the open air. Farmers completed evening milking chores early and took a break from fields and chores that would again engage them at 5:00 a.m. the next morning—and every morning thereafter. At the home ballpark, with a nickel bottle of Coke and a high fastball coming, all was right on a summer's eve. On special occasions, the Winona Municipal Band played a pre-game concert.

The senses were keen for the sound of the collision of a fastball and the Louisville Slugger held in the hands of Norm, our clean-up batter, or a quick, choppy grounder hit by Gabby Horman, our country-singing, ever-dangerous catcher, who often placed his grounders between the first and second basemen. Gabby composed and recorded "Moon Over Sugar Loaf" while in Winona, but went on to fame as Nashville singer Webb Foley.

Each event was a game of excitement and entertainment. It was real life unfolding before us. Real people with names like Gabby or Stan or Norm made it happen. Tomorrow we could see them at their jobs in the stores and factories, or just walking down the street. Tonight they were our heroes in woolen white uniforms not unlike those of the New York Yankees pictured in the pages of *Sport* magazine.

Even their foul balls were exciting when hit up and over the multi-layered forest-green, painted grandstand. Flying high over the wood-beamed uprights and tar-papered roof into the star-filled sky, the errant ball more than likely landed with a *thud* on the hood or top of a patron's parked car. A long and fair fly ball headed toward the 350-foot sign brought everyone to their feet. A double play from third to shortstop to first base was a sight and sound to behold.

With an occasional standing ovation, there were cheers enough to shake the rooftops. Wild cheering ensued every night the Chiefs were in town. Games were won and games were lost, but the cheers continued either way. They could do no wrong.

These heroes of summer were heroes to us all. They were heroes who caused us to see ourselves, our potentials. They caused us to dream the dream. Players embodied the effort, the hope and the dreams that the people in our small midwestern town held for them. The war was over, the Great Depression not so very far behind. People were remembering and thankful for the bounty in their lives.

With battles over, most of the boys home, and the economy on a constant upswing, there was hope for jobs and a reason for joy, with an eye fixed on a safe and prosperous future. There was again time for celebration in continued and small ways—a church picnic, a night at the ballpark, a walk by the river levee, or fishing at lakefront with special friends and a "picnic" of beer on the table. It was enough. Who could ask for any more?

As the evening paper was delivered, as people came home from work, as front porches filled with family and friends to enjoy the cool at the end of the day, or as we turned the colored dial on the radio to *Fibber McGee and Molly* or *The Inner Sanctum*, parents, idling visitors and young listeners offered constant recap and re-hash of our heroes' exploits on the baseball diamond. The Chiefs's game and the players who made the news were on our daily menu of conversation and anticipation.

With every train from Chicago to Minneapolis or Minneapolis to Chicago going by our front door, we seemed to have new arrivals for the team from Indianapolis or Chicago or points east arriving on a weekly basis. Each new member of the team dazzled us with his hitting or fielding prowess, but each also fanned the flames of our perpetual hero worship. As ballplayers in our small town who might have been small town boys themselves, there was no doubt that they were "big time" in our eyes.

They weren't any bigger than the local iceman or the high school athletic star or the strapping farmer from across the bridge, but they were larger than life to everyone they met. They had traveled the country. They had experiences of which we could only dream. They were our connection to the future.

One of our favorites was Emil, a little bit of a guy who played shortstop. He probably didn't weigh more than 100 pounds. In the long shadows of late afternoon and early evening at the ballpark, his five-foot-two frame took on dimensions that were as long as the shadows cast. He was then as big as his actions. He was the playmaker of the team who fired everyone up, the "chatterbox" throughout nine innings who encouraged the pitcher, batters and his fellow fielders; as well as setting the tone for the hundreds, and sometimes thousands of fans.

We didn't need a speaker system to hear Emil. He was perpetually in celebration of the joy of living and his love for the game. Quick playmaking, double-play gyrations and positive spirit were his trademarks. When you met him on the street, he was whistling.

He had come from tryouts in the Chicago White Sox network and World War II Army baseball on Guadalcanal (although he was in the Navy) to find a home with us. Even though pursued by other teams, he chose to stay and become a backbone of the team and a mainstay in the town. He played several years against and with the greats of the 1940s. When other Chiefs like Norm Snyder and Stan Shargey hit the long ball, it was Emil who finessed his way into our hearts with his dips and saves and words of encouragement. At shortstop, he was a formidable challenge to the power of those who stepped to the plate.

From experience and reputation, opposing players knew that any ball hit within twenty-five feet of Emil was a costly out. Taking up the space of a moving billboard, he jumped, leaped, and dove for seemingly uncatchable line drives and "too-hot" grounders. A quick flip of the ball to first base, and the visitor's batting average was further diminished.

He was the leader, a David on a diamond filled with Goliaths. He not only knew how to play the ball, but the crowd as well. The momentum of the game could shift from one of sullen silence and a four-to-two fall-behind score to a stirring moment of hope when Emil performed. As leadoff batter, Emil ignited a spark with a tap from his bat.

More than once, his blooper hit to short center, the stolen base that followed and the long ball of Shargey or Norm placed him in scoring position at third. Hope was alive. A home run would send the devoted into ecstasy. From a near loss to a turnaround, Emil had again led the charge.

Emil's day job was at the Neville's Clothing Store (later St. Clair's)—a local haberdashery for the well-to-do and those who wished to be. As years went on, I worked for a while side-by-side with Emil, selling men's suits and clothing. In no way could I compete. He was the star of the show and the ultimate salesman and playmaker—greeting every customer with warmth, charm and recognition. What a guy! He could sell you a suit and all the trimmings and make you feel like you were the most important man in town.

He would tie together a new suit with the "specials"—the new Arrow shirt, tie, belt and socks to match. The top-quality suits of Hart, Shaffner and Marx were Emil's specialty—finished off with a Harris Tweed topcoat. It was top quality in a quality-conscious America after the war, all served up by the greatest ballplayer in town. Who could ask for anything more?

When one came to town to be fitted by a master like Emil, the new suit owner felt "like a million bucks," as Emil was wont to say. Having met Emil in the process was a special bonus, at least equal to having a signed baseball card of Phil Rizzuto or Warren Spahn.

While Emil was selling suits, his long-time compatriot in the infield, Stan Shargey, was hard at work at the Badger Machine Company on West Fifth Street. He was doing his part to create the newly patented HOPTO digger to be sold around the world for construction jobs—later under the Warner-Swasey brand.

A real bull-nose at third and at work, Stan stood five-foot-nine and weighed in at 180 pounds—all muscle and power. His shot from third burned the hand of the first baseman.

He was serious and deliberate and knew his way around both third base and around manufacturing, having previously served on an Army baseball team during the war and as a baseball team member and employee of the General Electric Voltmen of Fort Wayne, Indiana—the national semi-pro champions. In between times, he played AAA ball at Sacramento and Oklahoma City and the Rome Colonels. His teammate was Hugh Orphan, the Chiefs's manager.

Luck and friendship must have drawn Hugh, Stan, Emil and others to Winona. Many found the home they sought—for they gave up the wanderlust of pro ball and settled in for a lifetime of steady citizenry in Winona. I knew Stan at Warner-Swasey and found him to be a hard-working, fun-loving type of guy with a ready smile and a story a day that I could carry on to the next manufacturing spot on my vending route.

Hugh was a successful upholsterer in town for many years with his shop on East Broadway. When visiting my mother-in-law in 2000 at the Lake Winona Manor, I looked in on him shortly before his death. I told him of my Chiefs memories—a memorable moment.

Hugh started with the Wausau Timberjacks in 1940, winning twenty games each for a couple of years. He completed his professional circuit as a member of the AAA Sacramento Sunbeam Bread in 1948, where his record was less stellar. He still had it in the 1950s with the Chiefs—a red-hot fastball that came at you nearly underhanded.

Our parents were terrific, but ball playing was a kids' game. They walked their walk of hard work and the Protestant work ethic. Limits of hard work, church and heritage tended to remove fun from their lives. Their lives had begun with chores on the farm when they were four years of age and continued on a fast-forward march of work and doing from that day on.

They didn't seem opposed to our having fun with the games of baseball, kick the can, or hide-and-seek. It seemed that they just hadn't had the experience. In their quiet ways, they remained good observers and supporters of our actions and those of our real-life heroes, the Chiefs. They didn't put down our dreams and comments and moments of excitement.

It is so interesting to discover that Pa, in his time as a junior high youth of German-Lutheran heritage, was named one of the most outstanding athletes in the early part of the twentieth century on the playlot in the east end of town. There were about 1,800 kids who participated—and yet the newspaper story I discovered in the archives named my pa and our neighbor, Carl, as the two most promising of all.

To my knowledge, Pa never attended a Chiefs game. I never knew that we shared the talk or walked the walk.

We were a fortunate few to be fans of the 1950s. Baseball was fun. Pitches and catches in the big games of the Chiefs zip into our memories. Even the fish-fly invasion that covered the night and caused game lights at our riverside park to be shut off for a bit to dissuade the populace of creatures was an event.

Having heroes of the Chiefs's hardball in our midst was a treasure. We learned about curve balls and bonks on the head. Even more, memories of a comfortable childhood of work and play linger. We learned that dreams are achievable.

We learned that life is meant to be good.

One-Sentence Fun

This is an attempt to tell a story—actually, five of them—each in one sentence. There is no specified form for this style of writing. It's just for fun. I gave myself permission.

Snaps Down the Front

My favorite jacket of all time was a black wool three-quarter length that I had in junior high with white piping on the sleeves and white snap buttons down the front that easily snapped to enclose the heat of my body on cold Minnesota days and nights or unsnapped in a flash by giving a quick yank from top to bottom for a quick escape when I needed to get out quick or toss it on the chair when I got home from school or the Y where I seemed to spend most evenings after supper watching TV, shooting hoops and drinking nickel Cokes from the machine in the vestibule near the pool table room where I learned to shoot "eight ball" that I often watched at the Hurry Back Pool Parlor where the best of the shooters in town spent their evenings and racked them up just below the Keglers Klub Bowling Alley on Third Street where "Jukes" Biesanz and other small boys of town set the pins by hand in the tiny enclosed areas behind the pins that were flying everywhere as I left to walk the mile or more home in the sub-zero night with my jacket and matching black wool cap to keep me warm as my corduroy pants legs rubbed against one another to give a musical tone to my walk over frozen ground that gave off its own creaking sound to break the calm of the still night that seemed to settle over our town from early December through the Ides of March when I could toss off my winter covering and move to the red nylon jacket that sufficed as cover in the spring and autumn days before I entered high school when I graduated to a worn-out leather bomber jacket with sheepskin lining passed down from my eldest brother to take me through the winters of high school with a woolen scarf and no hat since I was now "cool" and didn't need a hat since I drove a car of my own that usually started in the winter when the temperature was above twenty degrees and had a comfort of its own to rival my black wool jacket with snaps down the front.

Playing in the Backyard

David was a lanky kid who lived next door and couldn't eat popcorn because it affected his ulcer, only one of the unique things about him, along with his dedication to reading only Catholic comic books, a requirement of his mother Millie, the nurse, who made sure he went to Catholic school and went to church on all the holy days that we didn't know about in the German Lutheran church where we were more afraid of the minister than the ultimate truths of the church that were to guide us to salvation where David was headed the day that he played in our backyard with my brother and me and brought out a single bullet (a 38?) which he had in his collection he got from his brother Richard who was in the service to place it on the top of the old metal vise attached to our open-air workbench next to the shed where we kept all manner of tools, squashed tin cans in a barrel for the post-war effort and slotted spaces along the wall which, when emptied, became sleeping bunks for our youthful group of marauders when we "slept out" and went on evening apple and pear tree raids that were within the six-block area that surrounded our house that was right next to David's—separated only by large lilac bushes next to huge elms that were just a toss away from Millie's garden, from which Millie came running when David decided to "drop the hammer" (a real hammer) on the bullet and have it explode and drive nicely up his arm where he has a ten-inch scar to remember our playing together in the backyard of 467 Grand Street.

A Bike Ride

After enjoying the Sunday noon meal of roast beef and mashed potatoes with gravy that Pa had prepared for the seven of us while listening to the "real" polka music of Ernie Reck and the Country Playboys on KWNO radio from their extended studio in Arcadia, Wisconsin, we cleaned the kitchen to head out the back door on a beautiful summer day to hear David next door whistle

his call and motion us over to see the new bike he received for his birthday
that we celebrated with him yesterday with cupcakes in paper and a scoop of
ice cream his mother Millie provided on paper plates on the painted white
picnic table just outside the porch entry where David found his new bike upon
return from Mass just moments ago when we were scarfing down our wonderful dinner to be served again tonight by Pa as beef hash flavored with
cider vinegar and followed up with boiled rice, milk, cinnamon and sugar
covered with hot prunes that Millie had dried on her sun porch where David
constructed beautiful model airplanes out of balsa wood that he carefully cut
and glued together to make all manner of planes that he fastidiously decorated
with glorious colors and decals he sent off upon completion on flaming flying
missions caused by lighting them after dousing the planes in lighter fluid that
he got from his father Adrian's storage of tobacco, cigarette papers and smoking paraphernalia he enjoyed every day after work in his kerosene-laden, dirt-
floored workshop behind the house where we now watched him make final
adjustments on David's new bike which he soon headed off down the dirt
drive to the street where he made a few fancy turns, a "no-hands" run and a
few loops from street to sidewalk using neighbors' driveway entrances to show
the handling capabilities of rider and bike soon offered to my older brother
and to me to "take a spin," which I gladly did, to mimic David's marveling of
the bike's exceptional handling ability with a few twists and turns followed
by my own "no hands" technique as I headed past David's house in the sunlight to suddenly receive a bolt to my smiling front teeth that nearly knocked
me off the bike that I somehow controlled to a landing at the curb without
running into Pa's huge construction truck he had home for the weekend which
soon became an emergency vehicle for me as I was taken by Pa to a dentist
whom we seldom visited except to remove another tooth since we didn't go
there for check-ups and general care, only extraction, which is what Dr. Earsley
did when I arrived at his office on Fourth Street where I lost my smile for all
the years ahead, since my front tooth and smile had been shot out with a peb-
ble fired by David's slingshot and never completely replaced until I became a
teacher with a new tooth who learned how to smile once again.

Swimming Lessons

Everything happened on the street in front of my house—football games, bike
riding, playing hide-and-seek, greeting the iceman, building snow forts and

wading in the flooded streets and corners after a summer rainstorm let loose over our small town in the valley of the Mississippi River after the oppressive heat of a July day raised the corn stalks to new heights in neighboring farm fields allowing us to get out our skimpy swim trunks with string ties and float our boats of weaved popsicle sticks in the minor current from the middle of the block toward the slow-moving sewer drains at the corner where we gathered in the deepest spot and largest puddle when David shot off his CO_2-powered boat to take off like a jet and crash head-on into the curb over which we bounced our bikes on sunny days as we headed to the bathing beach across the river bridge and to the bathhouse with its small baskets for clothes and shoes that we stepped back into after a cold water shower in the wood-walled enclosure after we had risked life and limb once again by going outside the wooden walkway surrounding the "safe" area that we non-swimmers remained in until we had finished our seventh grade swimming lessons with Mr. Spencer during which we all swam "bare-ass" together and learned to float and paddle and sometimes breathe at the appropriate moment to assist us in making it to the diving platform over twenty yards and a lightyear away from Spencer's ritualistic punishment of errant class members who needed to walk the gauntlet and get swiped by all class members to become members of the "red-hand club"—named after the imprint of thirty seventh grade swatters.

Christmas Fun

This Christmas I decided to see if I could make it through a whole year in one sentence as I have been doing in some of the writings that I have piled up on my computer that no one else accesses except for the grandkids who occasionally visit and leave me automatic hookups to web sites that continue to show up for weeks thereafter with their glorious pop-up interventions at quiet times when I am working on another story to add to the dozen or so that I recently compiled into a book as a Christmas gift for our four children who all can read like the dickens since they attended the terrific Lakeville High School at which I am a sub a couple of days a week in the cold days before Janet and I head off to Mexico for a short January reprieve from frigid air while yearning for the springtime weather of Minnesota when we take up the planting of tiny seeds hardly discernable to one's eye to emerge as bounteous crops to grace our summertime table at which we give thanks every day for our good health and the fortunes of our four kids and eight grandkids who excel in all they do at home and schools that range from nursery to college for the two oldest ones who embarked upon learning and challenge that we earlier enjoyed to bring us to the cusp of retirement in which we will someday settle for a long winter's nap and dream of the goodness of life and friends and God's blessings that are truly the spirit of Christmas which we wish to share with you on these glorious days of remembering good times Janet and I shared with you in the backyard of our lake home of thirty-five years, or Texas or Arizona or places hither and yon where your smiles and offerings of friendship enriched us.

Merry Christmas!

Chapter Six

A *Thunk* in the Woods
(A Semi-Fictitious Tale)

I t's summer vacation. The hills are calling!

Upon completion of today's household chores, Pa gave me permission to set out on an overnight in the hills. He understood about these things. He knew that summer vacation for boys was a mixture of chore accomplishment on the home front and personal accomplishment on the adventure front—essential components of youthful development.

It wasn't really a discussion point at all. If I had accomplished the tasks of Saturday "wash" chores, hoed the garden or painted the house as previously directed, I had earned my freedom. Without a mother around to question and ask the more constraining questions that mothers specialize in, a deal was struck between Pa and me. I knew the limits—my stated intents, a vague idea of where I would be in case I was needed, and the well-understood belief that I would be on my good behavior. Thus, freedom was accomplished.

Needless to say, it wasn't long after permission was given that I gathered supplies from meager stores in the pantry and icebox. A chunk of hamburger, a couple of hot dogs, an egg or two, a peanut butter sandwich in an old bread wrapper set aside for ease of packing. If all was well in the household and income was sufficient at the moment, Pa might even let me charge the cost of a can of beans, a bag of marshmallows or a small can of Vienna sausages at Kindt's grocery store.

From big brother Frank's Boy Scout gear, I was quick to gather the steel-framed backpack, a special hatchet, cooking kit, tarp, and sleeping bag. After supper I would pack my knapsack for an overnight to the woods. Visions of roasting hot dogs or tin-foiled hamburger and over-heated beans on the side of the campfire were like fuel in my tank as I dreamed my way to sleep. With my ever-present hunting knife at my side, I would be on my way in early morning.

At Davey's house, a similar scenario was playing out. He had convinced his ma that a night in the woods was a rite of youth in summer days. He really didn't argue philosophically—only loudly and convincingly. His mother was a special person who, like Pa, understood the needs of youthful self-development and exploration.

She was understanding and tolerant of his dreams, visions and the need for practical experience. If only she had been our teacher, rather than Miss Stubbs, who was short, squat and militaristic.

Ma had seen us so often in our after-school quasi-military meetings in Davey's room. With army-surplus blankets, tall bunk-bed structures and tent poles, we regularly created semblances of a military operations headquarters in a space usually reserved for sleeping. With the proper password, Davey's brother, Donald, was allowed to enter his own room; the one he shared with Davey.

Flashlights, hushed tones, field maps and secrecy were the order of the day. Ma was careful to interrupt our proceedings in headquarters only when supper was called. After all, General Eisenhower and General MacArthur might have been meeting in that small room just off the kitchen where the smells of supper cooking over the wood stove permeated the senses.

We had known that approval was forthcoming, since we had trust in our separate parents' good judgment. Even though our separate Pa and Ma had not met (to our knowledge, at least), they were seemingly tuned into the same wavelength. When our ideas were brought forward there was usually gentle exploration and consideration, with details and limitations worked out over our separate kitchen tables. In a word, we had their trust.

Davey's pa was around, but usually not involved in such discussions. After a day of hard labor on the road repair crew for the city, he was content to sit in his easy chair next to the Zenith radio and catch up on local and international happenings of the day. Ma was the decision-maker on the local scene.

The duties of our mutual planning assignments had been decided. With a more-than-adequate measure of pride and bravado, we had worked out our jobs for the mission weeks in advance, as we met in Davey's cellar and my backyard shed. With hours of planning and plotting our adventure, we had detailed the supplies necessary, routes to be taken, and operations to be achieved (all on military time, of course.)

Davey's task of supply was to gather those items, codebooks, and any homemade treasures (like Ma's icebox cookies) with which we might be gifted.

Our assemblage of field maps, treasured supplies of unsweetened chocolate and flashlight batteries had been carefully stored on the shelves of old fruit crates in our cellar "fort." With our pre-planning, the preparation for movement from home to field would take no more than fifteen minutes.

Precisely at 0800 (military time), we met under the catalpa tree by the Jones's house. Mr. Jones was not the kindest soul in the world, but somehow or other he recognized that our assembly point under his tree wasn't a cause for major disruption of his life. He allowed us to meet there and pick up and carry away a handful of the long green seeds that accumulated on his lawn.

They weren't good for much. But as we walked from one place to another, there were always a few of these fourteen-inch whips with us. For a neat sound, you could whip your corduroy pant leg with them as you headed out on a neighborhood errand or back to school after noon hour. There was a connection between boy and tree that was inexplicable.

We were honored by Mr. Jones's kindness. Maybe that was why we used the tree as our midway point for our rendezvous for daytime or late evening escapades. He understood and we appreciated. With stem-wound military watches in our pockets, we were on time and ready to go.

Looking like pint-sized Willie and Joe, we set out with *Joe Palooka* comic books in the back pockets of our too-large corduroy pants. Davey's "real" U.S. Navy surplus cloth belt held his canteen, his leather U.S. military shell box and his trusty-hunting knife. With an olive drab backpack, a German helmet on his head and a machete in hand, he looked as if he were ready for war, or at least a semi-military operation in nearby hills.

My white Navy cap (slightly grayed from too many cellar meetings) topped off my outfit of GI boots, oversized field pack and tent. At my side, attached to my authentic clothesline rope belt, hung my pride and joy; an authentic Boy Scout (BSA imprint) hatchet, properly encapsulated in its cloth belt carrier, to protect both hatchet edge and youthful carrier. Our most important tool, the hatchet would make a formidable impression on the wilds of the hardwood forest in which we would soon reside. It would also give us strength against nighttime creatures daring to venture into our campsite.

Davey was the acknowledged leader of our foray into woods and military. After all, it was his tent that we had used so often. We had camped out for years in his backyard. In the small backyard, we were, at first, adventurers within limits. The back door of his house was only seven large, measured steps away from our tent entrance.

We didn't question the proximity to house and security. We knew that we were roughing it. His cellar, as military headquarters, also entitled him to military honor and bearing. We even taught ourselves to salute one another. When one owns the command center, military deference comes easy. In all other areas, we were equals. I was the planner, designer and organizer of tactical procedures. I was better with lists, budgets and design—a fitting role for an operations officer.

Walking through the neighborhood on the way to the bridge across the lake and to our semi-secret trail into the woods, we came across schoolmates who were simultaneously inquisitive and awestruck. Since our mission was "secret," we could only share the vague details of our foray to freedom.

To tell one of our neighborhood friends where we were going was to tell the whole neighborhood. Nearly fifty kids our age lived in the ten-square-block neighborhood that we called ours. With the myriad of backyard trails around and through gardens and over fences with known low spots, and with the speed and agility of young legs to deliver a message of importance, the network of communications between neighborhood kids rivaled anything that Alexander Graham Bell might have created.

We knew that to enjoy our venture was to stick to secrecy. Even though their parents may not have let them far from home, we were concerned that one or more of the wayward youth might discover us during a daytime hike. Between the two of us, we did a masterful job of convincing the others that through Old Man Schumacher (the German butcher), we had been given a measure of military responsibility and "orders" to scout out a wilderness area for purposes that we were not at liberty to divulge.

Everyone acknowledged Schumacher as the leader of the wartime protection association within the neighborhood. We had all heard parents and teachers express their high regard for this very large, very German butcher who had done so much to protect life and limb in the neighborhood while so many of our dads had been overseas.

His billy club, issued by the town council to Area Protection Wardens, hung in a place of honor in Schumacher's Meat Market even today. Several years after the war, it was a symbol of strength in his place, smack-dab in the middle of our neighborhood. To invoke the support of Schumacher to our mission was to immediately authenticate our purposes. We went on our way.

It was hard to hold back the excitement we felt as we ventured off on this first-ever outreach to the woods. For this night in the dark woods surrounding our river valley hometown we would gladly give up a few extra hours of sleep or home time. It wasn't only the excitement of being trusted by our parents to be off on our own. It was the opportunity to prove our capabilities, as well.

We knew our way across the blocks, as we knew virtually every crack in the sidewalk on our path to the lake and across. Since our earliest days we had ventured to the lake for fishing and hanging out under the massive, ancient cottonwood trees on the shore.

We followed our dirt path along the lake to the bridge, crossed over the water and soon made footprints in the natural grasses at the foot of the bluff. Our goal was to get about halfway up the hillside to a flat spot we knew so very well. There we would establish our semi-secret beachhead. We could have found our way in the dark, having taken this route so many times as we ambled out for summer hikes.

Davey was anxious to get going. He was intent on getting started with chopping down small trees to begin our lean-to. It was to be adjacent to our tent site, a site out of the rain and hot sun where we could keep some of our important inventory—and would keep us out in the elements without retreating to the tent. The tent was for sleeping.

The sun was just too much to be endured in a tent on a hot July afternoon. Any rain was to be enjoyed. If our construction was as good as we envisioned, we would be able to sit outside in the worst of any summer weather we might come upon. Being confined to a tent was just too restrictive.

Traveling a hundred yards or so up the hillside, we found just the right size and quantity of small trees, a mixture of small oaks and other hardwoods. With our trusty hatchets soon in action, we chopped methodically for what seemed like hours in the steamy hot sunlight. The green wood we cut would give the right support to a roof on our improved lean-to, soon to be covered with branches and leaves.

Using leftover twine from a backyard garden project, we tied all the makings into a sturdy, shaded and dry environment for storage, with suitable protection from the elements. A well-cleared dirt floor was made smooth by a combination of gouging out rocks with our knives and smoothing the earthen floor with branches and flat rocks. In "jig time," our space was created.

We were interrupted in our morning chores by the sound of a tractor. Wary that our site might be discovered and that we would be told to leave the place, we snuffed out our small fire and ran for cover. Davey pulled out his trusty telescoping spyglass to survey the area.

Just across the small valley we saw a small, gray Ford tractor moving up the hill. The neighboring farmer, whom we knew to be Mr. Bergler, was moving up his side hill, pulling a wagon loaded partially with fence posts. We figured that he was on his way up to the top of the hill to a field that pastured some of his Holstein milk cows. From earlier forages around the vicinity in past years, we knew the lay of the land.

We often followed the cow path up to the top, past the field and to the cap of the limestone bluffs. From there we could see nearly the entire river valley, which stretched as far as the eye could see. We knew that these were exactly the places and precipices where Native Americans of the past had climbed to do their own surveys and to send smoke signals.

It was time for us to make the climb. With an eye on Mr. Bergler's old, squat tractor making the hill climb on his side of the valley, we carefully moved from tree to tree on our own path to the top. We arrived at the base of the limestone outcropping just as he emerged from the trail through the woods to enter the field.

It was beginning to really be a sun-filled, blue-sky "Cracker Jack" day. We waited until our farmer friend had set about his chores before slowly beginning our ascent up the back side of the limestone. There was no easy way. The stone was a combination of weathered rock, sand and sharp edges. We wondered to ourselves how the Native Americans had done it.

Skinned knees were a part of every trip up to the top. The Native Americans had nothing more than loincloths to protect them. We were well protected with official military shirts and corduroys, but were soon reminded that they weren't enough. With the height of the rock and pinnacle, the potential for slipping on the sand or the shale-like rock and the well-known fact that rattlesnakes liked to inhabit the area, especially on sunny days, we chose our steps carefully.

Even though we had not confronted a rattler personally, we knew that they were there. Almost to verify and further heighten our awareness, we found the skin of a snake, likely shed in recent days. We consulted about our next steps and decided that we should continue, but knives were to be at the ready.

With a long stick in hand and knives poised, we took on the additional role of rattlesnake hunters. We reviewed the possibility of rattlesnake for supper. We had heard that it was a delicacy. By creating a primitive frame structure of green wood branches lashed together over the campfire, we were mentally preparing the evening meal of roasted rattler sections.

Our attainment of the top was uneventful. We found a flat, dry surface that was just big enough for us to lay flat and still have enough room for a signal fire, if we felt the need. There wouldn't be snake supper, but we made the peak with few scrapes and a real sense of accomplishment. Even though we took to the top like real scouts, there were moments of fear and trepidation. Davey was the adventurer in every trip to the top. I was the cautious one. It was unsaid, but we both knew the capacities and capabilities of the other.

We watched our farmer friend begin to cut the hay in his field nearly a quarter mile away and knew that our hideout was safe for the moment. Being prepared, as good scouts were, we pulled out our old Bull Durham tobacco bag, a trusty packet of cigarette papers, and proceeded to roll our own.

Now and then we filched a few real cigarettes from home, but generally we produced our own from leftover butts that we found around the stores and street corners. By taking the old butts apart and shaking the tobacco into our Bull Durham bag, we soon had enough for our ventures out at night or into the field. We didn't think we were "cool." We just thought that having a rolled cigarette was a part of life, since we both were observers of that process in our homes for many years.

Lighting up, we laid back and looked at the blue sky and puffy clouds and proceeded to discuss world events. Somehow, those world events, beyond the world war and our next foray to the Army Surplus Store, began to be directed more and more to the girls we knew.

There was Diana, the talk of the fifth grade; Beth, the prettiest girl in the class; and Mary, who was simply intriguing. They each had something special to offer, whether it was the signal "I like you" or the way that one or the other came up to one of us on the playground or in the hallway. We knew there was something there, but we couldn't quite fathom what the message was. It was somehow different from the messages that we received from the guys, however.

After several serious moments of discussion, we knew from Native American lore and stories of patrols in G.I. Joe tales that it was time to move on. It was a sense that led us, not a wristwatch. Having had our smoke and observed the territory from its highest peak, we knew that all was safe in our environment as we headed down to the encampment.

The late morning sun arrived with full force. Tasks were several as we found water at a nearby spring, gathered rocks for the campfire boundary, and the necessary dry leaves and twigs to get the fire going at lunchtime. We had created a peaceful setting of home in the forest, with the advantage of a large tree limb overhang to cover most of our campsite as a first shelter from any hard rain.

Our site was just far enough out in the open to take advantage of the drying sun coming to us on this hot day in July. Lunch was done with ease as we framed our fire pit and overlaid it with a piece of metal screening found on the trail. Our U.S. Army mess kit flew into action to heat water for coffee and clean up. Schumacher's special homemade skin-on wieners sizzled on the grille. In the safety of open space on a sun-filled day, our thoughts of scary snipe hunts and creaky sounds in the night were behind us.

Our afternoon was occupied with a challenging hike up to Devil's Cave, just to the west of the cemetery. We passed around the cemetery where Ma was buried and followed a deer trail toward the cave. The limestone bluff rose nearly four hundred feet above the valley's floor and was particularly precipitous to climb. To get to the small entrance to the cave, we needed to get nearly to the top of the bluff and then take a downward path into the cave naturally formed in the limestone.

Scraping our fingers for handholds on rocky outcroppings, we made our way carefully. With the sunshine of the afternoon, we anticipated rattlesnakes sunning themselves on the ledges. Arriving in the shade of the cave front, we ventured in for a cool respite and spent some time with our trusty knives doing a bit of carving and sharpening of sticks for cooking over the fire.

From our perch, we could see the lake before us, find our homes and school and observe towboats passing on the river. There was the spire of St. Stan's Church on the east side, the flax mill on the west end and our downtown streets and stores in between. In traversing our small town of 25,000 people we never needed a map, since we had the total vision of our hometown domain clearly in mind.

We felt powerful walking down the hillside. We knew that our time in the woods, walking up and down the hills on a regular basis and riding our bikes everywhere was building us up physically for our future missions. Like our heroes in Army combat and through our *G.I. Joe* comics, we knew that hard work and constant training would prepare us to be physically fit in time of national need.

With wood gathering completed, we were ready for supper. For our evening meal, we had saved our chunk of hamburger to be prepared in an open fire. The fresh hamburger package of this quiet morning would soon be transfixed from its too-watery state into the type of hardy feast one can only envision. Hamburger in tin foil, salt and pepper, an onion brought from the home garden and a can of VanCamp's beans on the side; a feast was in the offing.

It was a succulent vision based upon our experience. We had tried our hand with campfire culinary creations many times. Backyard forays with speedy, sizzling hot dogs from Schumacher's Meat Market, over-boiled cans of cheese spaghetti and multi-hued, smoky toast created over an open flame had prepared us for this moment.

Later excursions had moved us into the world of potatoes, vegetables and meats wrapped in tin foil for baking in the coals. These experiences in the culinary arts told us that the current recipe was the best. We simply cut the onion (with the ever-handy hunting knife), mashed the hamburger into patties, added a chunk of cheese and threw the package in (or on) the fire. The key, of course, was to wrap it securely in tin foil to preserve all the special juices.

With salt and pepper and a little patience, the meal would soon be ready—a feast of culinary completeness fit for kings. What with tomorrow's hills to climb, caves to explore and commando techniques to perform, nourishment would be essential to fortify us. Breakfast planning, however, was not so complex. It was enough to just grab a peanut butter-and-jelly sandwich and head for the woods.

Settling in for the quiet of the evening, Davey and I sat by the fire and related ghost stories and stories of snipe hunting in these very woods. Only two weeks ago, we had the terrifying experience of a snipe hunt with "guidance" provided by my older brothers and a playground supervisor.

With them acting as leaders, a small and loosely organized group of neighborhood pre-teens (including Davey and me) was taken on a late afternoon picnic and bonfire to the nearby lake park. Upon completion of a Mulligan stew-type supper, we all joined in a sing-a-long, played counting games in chorus with verses dedicated to the number of bottles of beer on the wall, and, finally, listened to ghost stories around the campfire told by our eager elders.

As stories were told and the quiet of evening began to surround us, the campfire glowed with ever-softer dimness. The circle of listeners magically came as close together as the kernels on a cob of corn. The sense of silence and oneness with nature became profound. In a word, we were entranced. After all, my bigger brothers were held in high esteem. We were proud just to be there.

We didn't know that adventure was to overtake us. For, upon completion of the stories and with very limited preparation or explanation, our guides told us we were going on an evening hunt. Explanations as to hunting technique or reasons for the intended hunt in the first place were sketchy.

With little word of warning, we soon found ourselves strategically and individually placed in the now-darkened forest. Our sole weapons of the hunt consisted of a gunnysack and a stick. Apparently, the stick was for armament against and capture of the unknown "snipe." The snipe had been briefly described to us as a small bird that wandered nocturnally under the branches of small trees and bushes found in exactly the kind of habitat in which we were located.

The trail that led from the park to the forested heights of nearby bluffs contained much sign of the quarry, according to our more experienced leaders. From them, we learned that our job was to take up the appointed stations at 100-yard intervals, hold to near-perfect silence and await the passage of the slow, wandering bird. It seemed like little challenge, since we were skilled hunters, in our estimation, and the unseen snipe was slow and dumb.

All we needed to do was to drive the feathery bipeds into the sack with the stick, held ever-so-tightly, and then, upon capture, to make certain that the sack was held securely closed with a strong hand. Once we attained the greatest number possible, we were to await the return of our leaders—who would take us back to the park for the count and re-telling of the hunt's success.

With eerie evening sounds of the woods and a basketful of reminders of just-told campfire stories to heighten the jitters that we were feeling, each of us held to his individual perch, as directed. Remaining as quiet as possible to afford us the chance to gain the advantage on the hunted, it was soon easy to hear the rustle of leaves, the call of creatures near and far, and our own breathing.

It remains in memory as one of the few times that I heard my own heartbeat. Was it so very quiet in the woods that night, or was my heart beating at an exceptionally quick and loud rate? Since the snipe had exceptional hearing, one can surmise that he, too, heard the whispers in the trees, the movement of my shuffled foot in the leaves and my very heartbeat.

That night, the ever-elusive snipe did not appear to me (and, I later found out, to *any* of us). As we spent what seemed to be endless hours in our lonely quest for snipe and survival, the only thing that was seen were the stars above and the seeming movement of trees and shadows. It is remembered as a night of chattering teeth and endorphin-engaged wonder about the length of one's future.

The stars were our only friends. We were in a new world of sounds that represented our wildest imaginings of stories read and told about disappearances and maiming. We knew of bobcats that hunted by night in the woods. We had heard the stories of enraged farmers who were known to drive youthful vagrants off their land with pitchforks.

We also knew that there were people who had been lost in the woods, never to return. With larger than normal eyes and keener-than-ever sense of sound, each of us held to our appointed stations for what seemed like endless hours.

The trampling I heard coming through the underbrush was destined to be the worst possible ending to my short and generally well-behaved life. I would never admit this to another soul, but my corduroy pants developed a warm sensation on the inner part of both pant legs as nature took its course. Only then did I recognize the sound of big brother. His appearance is one of the most vivid remembrances I hold yet today of the meaning of family.

Upon arrival back to the campfire with brothers and friends, our higher-than-normal voices reported on the sightings of large mammal movement, the visions of semi-lit ghostlike creatures in the trees around us, and the mind-numbing and excruciating sounds heard and endured in our nocturnal stations on the hillside.

One of the hunters was so frightened by what he heard, saw or imagined that he arrived at home a full ten minutes ahead of our stop at his house to check up on him. Needless to say, as we walked homeward, our normal saunters down well-known sidewalks and backyard approaches toward places of home and parent were at world-record pace for ten-year-olds, who might have otherwise enjoyed and prolonged an evening adventure that allowed us to stay out after ten o'clock.

Who was to know that the snipe hunt was a gigantic ruse created solely to scare the "be-jeebies" out of young boys? Mission accomplished.

Back on the bluffs with Davey, peering out from within the pup tent, we wiped the sand from our eyes and overlooked our world. It was a world of our lean-to, morning-damp clothing strewn across nearby branches and the potential for *adventure*!

A new day was beginning. Morning dew hung heavily across the valley. A milky view of the nearby lake hazily presented itself in the early morning light. We gazed upon the day with wonder and delight. In this day was found the stuff that dreams were made of—for we both had spent many hours designing plans while we sat in Miss Stubbs's classroom last year.

She thought we were daydreaming, and we were frequently remanded to the custody and company of the school secretary, whose harsh looks were all it took to impale one or the other of us to the exceptionally hard oak bench outside the principal's office.

If only Miss Stubbs had tapped into the adventures that were in our minds, she probably could have earned a prize for creative teaching. She would need, of course, to have tapped into the secrets that had been shared in the quiet moments of planning by two adventurers.

Outside the tent, yet within reach of a long scrawny arm-stretch, stood our inventory of our wooded adventure. In line from careful organization of the previous evening stood flashlight, hatchet, U.S. Army stamped canteen and ditty bag (a World War II surplus item available at the surplus store, the habitue of youthful adventurers prone to defense of country.)

We kept our machete and knives at the ready inside the tent in case of intruders or attack by unknown forces. Not far off to the side stood food items of varied worth. Soggy potato chips, worm-filled apples and watery remains of our hamburger didn't look as nutritious in this early hour as they did just a day ago.

The sun was only now beginning to warm through the side of the tent. With the feel of a rock from the bumpy ground protruding into one's bony back, it was time to move—for the sake of personal comfort and for the call and allure of the ever-beckoning woods. There were forces in those woods that needed to be dealt with.

Davey's "up and at 'em" got things going for us on this hazy, lazy day of early July. We were fortunate to have spent a mostly sleep-filled night. The sounds of the owl and the whip-poor-will were like a lullaby for those of us hardened to war and night battles described in *Joe Palooka* comic books and from assorted reports of the victorious fighting adventures of our boys "over there."

We often envisioned tanks and jeeps of the enemy moving into our rural, small town setting in the hills and valleys of southern Minnesota, as we had seen the tanks and jeeps rolling into the cities and villages of France in the Sunday afternoon news before the main feature at the West End Theatre. We were filled with confidence and optimism gained from neighbor boys who had returned from the war. We knew that we could win any confrontation.

When we listened to "Two-Tone," the whistling ex-gyrene who was attending the local teachers college and playing halfback on the football team, talk about the strength of our armed forces, we were in awe. He was the epitome of the "All-American Boy." His self-confidence and strength showed through the nylon shirt that he wore, made from an actual Army Air Force parachute.

Merlin, another neighbor, now driving a cab as he attended the college, spoke more quietly. He, too, had been "over there." It was just different with him. He liked to talk about the woods and the hills of home, rather than the places in the remote South Pacific islands where he had fought the Japanese. We knew that he would be a good teacher.

His strength was there for us to draw upon. He greeted us daily as we crossed paths. We knew that with his able assistance, and that of Two-Tone and Captain Jim, another neighbor, who occasionally piloted his B29 bomber over the neighborhood to greet his folks, we would be able to defend the home territory.

Kenny right next door had done his part, too. He was a cook/baker in the Army. From him we could get the necessary directions on feeding the forces as we took to the woods. On this morning our reveille was slow, since we weren't "on alert."

Every day we were somehow engaged with the lives of national defense and personal self-sufficiency. Parents who lived through the Great Depression and soldiers who lived through the war prepared us. If we had a dollar or a moment after school, we were on our way to the Army/Navy Surplus Store to make the best bargain and equip ourselves.

Everything in the military store was very well packaged—in the fashion of the military establishment—to protect it in its shipment from the place of manufacture halfway across the world and now back—to reside in bins or hang on the walls of our local store. Most all of the goods were authentic.

The officer materials and decorations were more expensive than the enlisted non-commissioned soldier and sailor items. We could dress and rank ourselves depending upon size and our own dollar availability. We knew ourselves to be "troops" and never self-promoted ourselves beyond the rank of "Sarge." Therefore, we were generally within budget.

Some of the hardened items like knives, bayonets and machetes had apparently never been unwrapped from their date of manufacture. We were the first real warriors to hold them in our hands. The tents and tarps and ropes and shovels and helmets and waterproofed matches and containers were the "Real McCoy."

We could fairly well duplicate the scene of the military bivouac, right down to fire starter and military-issue flashlights. It was simply a matter of balancing the few dollars we had with the practicalities of how much we could carry. Even though there were reported to be military jeeps available for forty dollars (a story we heard throughout our lives, with the first yet to be seen), we were neither financially prepared nor state-allowed to participate in vehicular traffic. Whatever we possessed was to be carried on our back or rolled across town in our old wagon, a rather non-military type.

It was not a part of our awareness about the dangers, the true losses of life that would occur should the enemy invade our home territory. We knew only that our prior knowledge of the hills and valleys, reinforced by the stories of success of our troops and their very real support, would give us a substantial edge in any river valley battle that might come.

The only injured wartime returnee we knew was Mr. Gleason, who amiably rolled the sidewalks of our neighborhood. A veteran of World War I, his lost legs were likewise removed from our sense of reality. He had been a fixture in our neighborhood for all of our young lives. It had been thirty years since his return from another war over there, and his connectedness to real war and human maiming was distant from us. With our own visions of the glory of war and youthful tenderness, we didn't equate his gentleness and inability to go beyond the neighborhood for the rest of his life as an act of war. He was such a kind and gentle soul to each of us as he received his daily paper from an older brother or me.

Our first action of this second day of freedom was to gather up twigs and rotted wood pieces for our morning fire. There wasn't much need for the heat of the fire, since the July sun would soon show us who was boss in deciding the limits of our physical activities that day.

"Where's the matches?" Davey asked after a fruitless search of bags and supplies.

"They're right over there next to the potato chips." I replied.

"How come you left them out in the open? They won't be much good if the dew gets on them."

"I know that. That's why we got the waterproof type. They're in the match holder that I got from the surplus store. Take the top off. They'll be fine."

We were working out the first of our differences of the day. It seemed like we were always checking on one another's competencies. It was just a part of the natural flow that existed between us. We were able to check and depend upon one another quite a lot.

We could read one another, add just the right amount of encouragement or suggestion and keep the steady course. We were forever together in all sorts of ventures from the earliest of days. Kindergarten was the beginning. We probably collided at the bottom of the wooden slide, or wrestled for turns on the monkey bars.

Even though our life that year was spent on the well-worn and hardened maple floor of the classroom, we were able to learn softness and sharing that carried on for all the days of later life. In our matched pinto-like shirts that our parents found on sale at the same store, we began our days together. It was a sign, a special message that we were intended to be buddies.

For special programs and year-end school picture, you could find the pinto twins together. Our lives continued to mingle from church Sunday school, second grade recess, third grade softball and everywhere else—to our now wild venture into outdoor living.

We had moved on from pinto shirts to army fatigues with big G.I. pockets, but we were the same guys. The uniform of the day was suited to the action-oriented life of the woods and for our quasi-military venture. Peanut butter and jelly sandwiches were tossed into the bag to sustain us on the trail. The morning fire was going. With a can of beans heated over the coals, we had our sustenance. A plate of beans and a swig from our canteen got us started.

Our fires were always kept small, for we knew the Native Americans would have done it that way. From Saturday afternoon western movie experiences, we knew that their cooking fires were to be kept small. If the fires were too big, the smoke would be a dead give-away to the enemy.

The only time that fires needed to be larger was when smoke signals needed to be made to communicate from one side of the valley to the other. We would create such a fire only when we felt a need to let others know where we were. Morning breakfast was not one of those times. We just needed a start to our day.

With a kick from a too-large boot, we could put the fire out in an instant. It was the way that things were supposed to be done. We lived by the code of the woods, the code of the simple, the code of the quiet and natural.

We grabbed our knives, canteens and cans of Vienna sausage and headed over to the spring. After a splash on our faces from the small pool, we filled our canteens with fresh water and headed up. Our goal for the morning was to get over the hill and explore the back side of the ridge. Following a deer trail through the thick forest, we were soon at the top.

Turning our backs to the river, we could see for miles. Spread out before us were farm fields and the continuation of rolling hills and valleys deposited by glaciers so many years ago. Off to the right we observed an old farmstead. From past experience, we knew that buried treasure awaited us—where old farm implements sat there might be a bigger, adjacent dump. Farmers of the past seemed to get rid of old machines and bottles and household paraphernalia by dumping them in the woods at the edge of a field.

More often than not, a pile of rocks and a few metal pieces sticking up above the ground identified the spot. After plowing the fields, rocks were extracted by the farmer by hooking up a horse or tractor to a low homemade stone sled. The farmer then rolled the rocks onto the sled and removed them to the side of the field. In the springtime after fresh plowing, we would sometimes walk his furrows and find stone arrowheads that Native Americans of another century had used for their hunting. We had a special shelf in Davey's cellar for our collected Native American treasures.

As we headed toward the anticipated dump area, we walked through the field and kept our eyes open for arrowheads. Slanting off toward the dump, we saw deer tracks and kicked up a pheasant, but no arrowheads. With a little digging at our private archeological find with our knives, the tangled web of rocks and limbs and grapevines yielded our first object—a piece of broken bottle. We knew that we had arrived.

For the next couple of hours, we dug and pulled, shoved and lifted and looked for buried treasure. A metal strap or two from an old wagon helped us with our digging, since we had left our machete and military-issue folded shovel back at camp. Just about to give up, we moved one more rock and dug a little deeper. Beneath the rock's space, we were met with a *thunk* when we pounded our metal strap into the soft ground. It was too hard a thunk for a tin can and didn't feel like a rock. On hands and knees with knives working together, we carefully dug down.

Gently working the soil, we soon had it sufficiently loose to get in with fingers still sticky from Vienna sausages. We could feel something there and decided to dig around the object with our hands, and put away our knives. We used the metal slats to enlarge the hole and soon got the dimension of a medium-sized rock. A little careful scraping showed us a faint whitish piece of something. We took a break to figure out how to best do the job of removing what we concluded must be a ceramic pot. We decided to enlarge the hole and get underneath the object so that we could raise it as a whole, and not break the bowl or pot.

After getting our hole expanded and the soil softened, we again went back to carefully brushing away the dirt with our fingers and extraction of the object. After endless moments of great anticipation, we were able to get all four hands into the loam and move the object side to side. A little more digging and our two sets of hands were underneath. Using a squatting position, we worked together to nudge and push and, finally, hoist our treasure into the sunlight.

Moving to a rotting log that served as a bench, we began to carefully scrape the object to understand what it was. It was just too irregular for a pot or bowl. We figured that it must be broken, because we could insert our fingers into the side of the form. With more careful scraping and insertion of ten-year-old fingers into the form, we were shocked to make the discovery of our object at the same time. It was a skull!

We didn't know whether to run away or call the police. This was just too much for our young minds to comprehend. We could understand an old arrowhead or a broken pot left behind by the early settlers, but we just couldn't get our minds around the fact that we had a human skull in our hands. What would Miss Stubbs think now!

We decided to wrap the archeological find in grasses and grapevine and get back to camp. Excited wouldn't even begin to cover the way we felt. We were both so excited that we had to "take a leak" before we headed back across field and ridge to get down the hill to camp.

Our first task was to get a fire going so that we could get some hot water. We started the fire, gave our treasure a rinse in the spring's pool and set our skull on a rock in the sunlight overlooking the fire. While we had the fire going, we roasted hot dogs from Schumacher and enjoyed a peaceful lunch with our new friend. Once the water was hot, we proceeded to get out an S.O.S pad and some warm water and give him (or her) a bath.

We proceeded with camp cleanup, put out the fire and assembled our gear for the trip home. Davey wrapped our find in a towel and put it in his backpack. Our moves were quicker now. Our adventure in the woods had come to an end. Halfway home, we exchanged backpacks so that I, too, could carry the treasure.

Our goal was to get to Professor Einhardt's home. He was a long-term professor at the teachers college and lived right next door to Davey. We were well-acquainted, since he sometimes sat with us on his porch and discussed Native American lore and history. We also were intimate with his lush garden in the backyard, since we occasionally visited it at night (without his knowledge) to steal a few of his fresh kohlrabi.

Professor Einhardt was at home, since it was the summer term and he was teaching only one class. He was shocked and amazed that his two youthful friends had found such a treasure. He took us with him to his lab at the school where he did some measurements and additional cleaning of the skull with stinky chemicals.

Then he got out his books and samples and began to make identification. After what seemed to be endless moments, he drew a preliminary conclusion of the age of the skull and the possibilities of who it may have been. He wouldn't say, but in our hearts we believed that it was the head of a Native American chief who resided in these hills before the settlers.

He concluded that it was about 100 years old and that it would be necessary for others to research the find and the site of our discovery. Even though it was hard for us to give up our treasure, he notified the police chief and offered to coordinate further excavation and involve other learned researchers.

With our adventure concluded, we sat back on our laurels for the balance of the summer vacation. The newspaper article and the description of our find led to notoriety that we had never expected.

We were stopped at the store by neighbors and by strangers who wanted to know more about our exploits. The neighborhood kids' communication grapevine was working at highest efficiency. Everywhere we went for days afterward—at the playground or the ball field—kids wanted to know about our find and about the adventure.

We probably could have become tour leaders of campouts and excavations in farm fields. On quiet moments of rainy days, we relived our adventure in Davey's cellar or in the shed at home—sometimes with a rolled-up cigarette if Davey's Ma or my Pa happened to not be home.

The police kept the skull and set about the business of assessing the find. After a couple of months, the research by the professionals had been done at the site and in the lab with the actual specimen. From age marks and tooth structure, it was concluded that it was a Native American who lived in our beautiful valley in the 1800s.

No other body parts had been found in the search, but a few pieces of a Native American necklace were found. No criminal investigation would move forward. The artifacts were returned to us. We presented them to Miss Stubbs and the school. The artifacts are displayed in the main hallway of our old elementary school yet today—more than fifty years after our find.

Bill Groves, the custodian of the school, built a wood-and-glass showcase with a small brass plate on the front. Etched letters in the plate acknowledge our find, the date, and our names, along with the quotation provided by Miss Stubbs from Henry David Thoreau (a fellow walker of the woods) who said, "I wish so to live . . . as to derive my satisfaction and inspiration from the commonest events, everyday phenomenon."

Home and Hearth

Pa and my brothers were all up and bustling around the little house—with six of us getting ready for school.

There was goose grease in a bowl on the table from the goose dinner we had all enjoyed for Christmas. Using the self-serve toaster with sides that flipped down to take the bread, we could quickly warm (or char) our bread, depending upon how quick we were to notice. We spread it with goose grease and a little salt, and breakfast was served. Everyone was on his own for breakfast—except for our little sister, whom Pa cared for.

At lunchtime we scrambled home from school for a peanut butter and jelly sandwiches or a cup of soup from a shared can with a brother. When Pa was working, Grandma sometimes would be there with a warm lunch for all. Little sister (now in first or second grade) came home and returned with us, and somehow got fed. Pa was mostly laid off in the winter months. Except for occasional workdays on the farm with his brother, he was around home to care for us in the winter.

He made excellent suppers (often pancakes) that he served every evening at six o'clock. If you weren't there, then you missed it. No ifs, ands or buts. You just didn't eat that meal. It's hard to think of a supper that I ever missed, come to think of it.

After supper and after every meal, kitchen cleanup chores were completed on a schedule created by our big brother. We turned the single, cold-water spigot to fill a scale-encrusted aluminum pot to heat water on the gas burner. With warm water for washing and a second pot for rinsing, we accomplished our task in minutes.

Since our mother had died when we all were very little, the tasks of scheduling, head-wash checks and general first-sergeanting came to him by way of heritage and expectation. Six kids required a firm style and clear direction. There was never a problem.

Frank directed us under the watchful eye of Pa. Pa was always there after his hard days of construction work, manual labor in the mill, driving truck or at home, if winter unemployment reigned for him.

Supper was a variety including, in no particular order, goulash, pork chops, boiled potatoes, fried sunfish, pancakes, and leftovers—even donated leftovers from a neighboring chef at the Winona Hotel. We never knew quite what to expect, but we knew it was always the best that we could do on that day. And it was oh so very good!

Each of us was most capable of preparing his own food for the balance of the day. There was not a critical concern. We lived like the rest of the people, from day to day, from paycheck to paycheck, from summer garden produce to the largesse of wild game shot in the fall by an uncle.

We often had a goose from Grandpa's farm at Christmastime. A kitchen wood stove with side gas burners cooked it all. There was plenty of wood to feed that fire and the pot-belly stove in the middle room to heat our small house.

Even the simplest meal of salted goose grease on bread or a fresh tomato from the garden eaten outdoors on a hot summer day was a delight. The only thing I had trouble handling over the years were the chunks of strong onion that found their way into many of Pa's dishes. This could be overcome by separating them out and sliding them to the side of the plate—one of the few allowed leftovers of our meals.

Sunday was most special. After taking our nickel from Pa to Sunday School to continue our perfect attendance string, we hurried home to what we knew to be the meal of the week. At high noon, after hearing Ernie Reck and the Country Playboys play an assortment of polkas and schottishes live on the AM radio, dinner was served. There was always more than enough. Whether it was one of the large beef roasts that Pa bought at the meat market served with boiled potatoes and gravy or a coon-and-beans baked dinner, it was a feast fit for kings—and one never to be missed.

Like feeding fishes to the masses that we heard about at church, there was enough to feed seven (and an occasional guest or two) and still have enough for ground hash for supper and beef roast slices in our sandwiches for the week. How big were those roasts, anyhow?

The warmest spot in the house was the corner behind the potbelly wood stove in the middle room. We took turns in this special spot as the evenings of winter moved along. We did our homework on the floor nearby.

Pa would settle in his big chair in front of the stove after supper and into the evening to read the local paper and rest from his day's labors. Even though we all looked forward to checking on the daily comics, it was a simple and understood practice that the paper remained whole and in his possession for the evening. Between reading the paper, nodding off, feeding the fire and listening to the evening radio broadcast, his night passed by—and so did ours.

We were always dutiful about doing our homework, accomplishing the many chores of cleaning the house, doing the wash and maintaining the yard and house. Everything was kept "ship-shape" in our rooms, the yard and the shed behind the house. This was our domain and we were happy to have our space.

Somehow we were able to remain physically "ship-shape" as well, even though we didn't have a balanced diet of fruits and nature's necessities. Four of us in the same elementary school were nether tardy nor absent during an entire year—a record probably never surpassed. Doctors hardly ever came by. God seemed to watch over us all.

Except for Frank's major bout with diptheria (a life-threatening respiratory ailment now resolved by DPT vaccine) in his teenage years, illness was seemingly non-existent—other than the normal measles and chicken pox of youth. Six young ones did have a challenge with the "sentence" to house and yard for a week or more of quarantine by the city health department during Frank's illness, however.

Puzzles were ongoing in our house in those days and the many days of the cold winter. We had a board and table in the middle room next to Ma's cactuses, where she introduced us to puzzles, to canasta and to other card games. Without her there, we didn't have a lot of "team play" at our house. We built a puzzle alone or read a book or a comic or played with our friends, mostly outdoors.

Pa was always there to see that we did our homework and to generally supervise our comings and goings. We listened with him to evening radio broadcasts and shared the blackened popcorn and "old maids" that we made with the metal shaker over the kitchen burner. He sat at the kitchen table and was there for our occasional question—including late into the evening until each was home and in bed.

When it was our time to retire, it was a mad dash for a splash-rinse in the coldwater bathroom behind the green door to our U.S. Army cots in individual rooms upstairs. Pa had completed the rooms so that each of us had a personal space that lasted us through high school, early marriage or into a career start in the U.S. Air Force.

Saturday nights after Pa installed the shower, Frank was the inspector. He decided the degree of our cleanliness. If not sufficient, then back into the shower. A radio program and a layout of Sunday School clothes and we were off to bed.

A tattered quilt was carefully gathered around every bone and sinew to ward off the cold in our unheated attic rooms. Dreams were quick to come, centering on action-filled plots from comic book scenarios or the planning of adventures of the next day.

We were blessed to have a comfortable U.S. Army bed, a wonderful Pa and a safe home.

Commerce and Connection: The History of the High Wagon Bridge to Winona

I t was rickety when I knew it. Probably more rickety now—but oh, so beautiful! The Wagon Bridge just invited one to explore.

At age ten, taking my bike across the interstate bridge (with a tough uphill push) brought me down the other side and to the Latsch Bathing Beach road—home of summertime fun and the remains of the High Wagon Bridge. Whether out for a day of swimming at the beach or simply taking a bike hike to explore the wilds, I was in love with the space around that bridge.

We dived off the trail and ran down the river, or crossed the Wagon Bridge and fought our way into the brambles of Wisconsin. We always stopped to peer through the cement balustrades at the easy flow of the Mississippi—thinking of the horses, wagons and early auto occupants crossing the bridge so many years ago on their way toward the river span of the High Bridge of Winona.

It was truly a high bridge—seventy feet at the center. The horse "owned by the junk dealers on West Second Street" was forced to cross the span too many times. One December day in 1900, the unnamed horse collapsed near the top and needed to be shot by a police officer. No report of mistreatment to the Animal Humane Society was in evidence.

Professor Harry Harmon of California brought his talents as "celebrated bridge jumper" to Winona for a "successful jump" on May 15, 1895. He passed up Red Wing's newer and wider bridge opened the previous month. At 480 feet of span, it was the widest river span north of St. Louis—but only sixty-nine feet tall. Harry wanted height.

A wagon bridge was recognized as a necessity as early as 1857, when Winona was described as "a central city of commerce and bustling industry." Railroads were beginning to feed the western counties of Minnesota. The steamboat landing at Winona was vital, but insufficient. A Northwestern Railroad bridge was built in the 1870s, and another authorized in 1888, to be built by the Winona and Southwestern Railroad. Sample toll rates of Sioux City at the time were six dollars per locomotive, passengers twenty cents each, with charges for each railroad car attached, either passenger or freight.

Preceding any bridges, a ferry system to and from Winona was in operation for many years. The first was a steam ferry, followed by a cable ferry. By cutting away the ice of winter, the ferry continued to run.

In 1891, the High Wagon Bridge from Wisconsin to Winona was proposed to the City Council with a possible Center Street landing. With 100 pilings and the first span on the Wisconsin side in place by December, the 360-foot main channel span was soon completed.

On July 1, 1892, the "Bridge Opened Today" proclaimed the *Daily Republican*. Fee for travel across the bridge remained the same as it had been for the ferry—approximately five cents each way. The Wagon Bridge was located well south of the current Interstate Bridge and railroad bridge—as evidenced by a 1942 picture of the three bridges.

The Northern Light Hotel of 4,000 square feet, two stories, limestone walls, Georgia pine lumber and a bowling alley opened on the Wisconsin side of the bridge in October of 1894—in time to see the northern lights. John

The High Wagon Bridge in Winona, which opened in 1892. (Photo courtesy of the author.)

Rogers may have wished for more light as he left the hotel one evening a month or so later. He was held up by some of his drinking buddies while walking with them across the bridge to Winona from the Northern Light. In the company of several recognized Winonans of the past, these bad boys were investigated, with Alex George being charged for the theft and beating of John. John's four silver dollars, a couple of tens and a check to him for $1,100.00 (Wow!) were stolen. He could have gotten a room at the Northern Light and stayed safe.

By January of 1898, the bridge was proving its worth, with 829 teams of horses, wagons and other contrivances having crossed in one day. Receipts were nearing $100 per day on occasion, with annual receipts around $6,000. Interestingly, by 1900, the bridges of Red Wing, LaCrosse and Winona were reporting decreased revenues.

The bridge was big business—and needed careful monitoring. Fees needed to be collected, the official bell and register needed to be rung and recorded. Foot passengers and bicycle riders were to be charged a full five cents each. Unfortunately, T.E. Smith, bridge tender in 1897, was in the saloon while on duty and not ringing the bell nor charging those notorious bike riders when he was present.

He needed to be suspended for ten days, after only several months on the job. In addition, someone had been counterfeiting round-trip tickets, causing further concern for the bridge committee of the City Council. Oh, the challenges of bridge administration!

As the years went on, the foot traffic on the bridge was waning. Cattle, sheep and hogs were fewer (at five cents per head beyond ten—the same rate as walkers and bicyclists). People diverted across the river ice in January to avoid paying the toll. Upkeep of the bridge planks was a concern—and change was coming. After both LaCrosse and Red Wing declared their bridges to be "free bridges" by 1917, a headline of 1919 read, "Winona Businessmen Want Free River Bridge." Yet "record tolls" of 1920 kept the bridge as a fee bridge, having in part to do with "a greater debt than the original borrowed amount."

Horse-drawn vehicles were scarce by 1917. On one June day in 1925, more than 1,000 vehicles crossed the newly repaired tar and plank surface. After forty years, the "New High Steel Wagon Bridge" that had been celebrated with parade and fireworks on the Fourth of July, 1892, was being tested to its aging limits. A speed limit of fifteen miles per hour was imposed—with a six-ton weight limit necessary for safety.

For safety sake, $30,000.00 and forty tons of steel were added to the girders of the bridge in 1934. Yet, the fate was in the squeaks and rattles. The old bridge just couldn't sustain the load, as evidenced by the collapse of the LaCrosse Bridge of similar age. Winona Mayor A.H. Maze appointed a bridge committee in 1935, and the movement began. Transfer of the title of the bridge was made to the two states. With U.S. Senate and House approval in 1938, a new Winona Bridge was moving ahead. Funding was to be accomplished by the two states.

Gretchen Lamberton of the *Republican-Herald*, esteemed local journalist, offered in 1962, that when the old bridge was demolished the city received "an absurdly low bid." The bidder had checked the original engineering specifications and found that "piers had been set on huge white pine planks." He rescued and resold the planks for furniture making. Gretchen stated the yield was "a treasure of great white pine planks the likes of which hadn't been seen since the virgin forests were cut down."

The new 2525-foot Interstate Bridge didn't have wood supports, yet with two 125-foot cantilever sections, a 200-foot suspended truss span and a 130-foot height, it opened with fanfare on November 21, 1942—for a total cost of one-point-five million dollars. The governors were present for ribbon cutting and a dinner hosted by Winona Mayor Floyd R. Simon.

In contrast to the Wagon Bridge divers, the only high-diver to tackle the 130-foot high Interstate Bridge was not from Austin or Chicago or California. He lived under the bridge on Winona Street. Charles "Charlie" Buggs, age fourteen, climbed to the top of the bridge after sunset one evening in June, 1953, with his neighbor and a flashlight. There was no crowd gathered on the levee.

Charlie and James Stueve, sixteen, decided to either capture or spy on pigeons roosting at the peak of the bridge. They made the ascent, but Charlie lost his balance on the way down. He fell to the river below, miraculously missing the massive piers and abutments. Still clutching his flashlight, he swam to a pier, climbed a sheer ten-foot wooden wall and waited with flashlight still on until police rescued him—shivering and complaining of a headache.

As with the High Wagon Bridge, the Interstate Bridge has served its time—with spars yawning and creaking. A new bridge is again in our headlights. Load limits have again been set, and new steel will soon be ordered to repeat the cycle of seventy years ago.

During my childhood in the 1950s, we zipped past the then-new YMCA on Winona Street to twist our single-speed bikes and tawny bodies across the steel and cement bridge. We found our way across, seldom stopping but for a moment—due to the whiz and continuous flow of traffic right next to us on the semi-protected sidewalk. It was a structure that served—form following function—but left us with few tactile memories.

It was a way over and a bumpy limestone step down the bank on the other side that led us along the river's Latsch Road, toward the pleasing residue of the old bridge and to a marvelous bathing beach with bathhouse and showers.

In our teenage years, my buddies and I were there near the old bridge site on occasional dark summer nights—with a quart or two of Wisconsin beer purchased underage at a small bar on the Wisconsin hillside. We wandered down the trail, found the remnants of a cabin and long-forgotten picnic table to risk an evening fire and further enjoy the adventure. Truth be told, there were a few moments we didn't tell our buddies about—like when we brought one of the girls across the bridge for some late-night "spooning."

My teenage years also brought me to a life across the Wagon Bridge— at the boathouse of my best girl. Appropriately supervised by her mom and dad, we spent our seemingly endless summers at the Winona Boat Club harbor with family and friends. For years, we headed out from the boathouse to fishing, to the river sand islands for weekend picnics, to water skiing past towboats and barges of the river, and stayed on select weekends to enjoy celebrations of the boat club in all the seasons, including ice-fishing contests and an Hawaiian luau.

With her dad's beautiful mahogany Trojan *Day Cruiser*, we followed the waters under the Wagon Bridge at night, heading to the main channel and upriver to Wally's at Fountain City for an elegant dinner. We loved the moonlight cruise home.

Later and longer ventures in the *Jeffe III*, "Dad's" beautiful, dual-powered Johnson outboard motor cruiser, took us under the bridge again and on a heading to Lake City and Stillwater's historic Lowell Inn. After a day or two on the river, we were greeted to our reserved weekend stay at the prestigious Lowell Inn by the elegant and coiffed Nelle Palmer—former vaudevillian and matron-in-charge—in her Dolly Madison dress.

Not seeing me leaning over the cigar case next to her in the exquisite foyer, she offered a quietly murmured and overheard statement. As our gang of fourteen (adults, teenage kids and beaus) trudged into her grand "Mount Vernon of the West" in sand-gathered river garb, she asked no one in particular, "Who are these people?" We did spruce up nicely for the multi-course fondue and wine-laden evening dinner in the elegant Matterhorn Room, thank you. Memories will never fade of the joys of summer on the old bridge and its river surroundings.

A strong effort was created in recent years by Winonans to restore the remaining parts of the Old High Wagon Bridge—remnants to be enjoyed by yet another generation.

How Did They Get Across the River?

My personal research project took me into the history of Winona's first bridge—the High Wagon Bridge of 1892. It was a fun trip, but I had a nagging question: how did the trains cross the water?

One thing led to another in my new search. Before the bridge, there had been a steam ferry, and then a cable ferry that brought wagons, animals and people across.

As early as 1857, Winona was shown to be "a central city of commerce and bustling industry." Railroads beginning there began to feed western counties of Minnesota. There was need for a bridge to accommodate the rapidly increasing freight and passenger cars of the rails, as they wouldn't fit with the hogs and bicycle riders on the cable ferry.

The solution seemed to be a train ferry, designed to carry railway vehicles. The main level of the boat would be fitted with railway tracks. The vessel had a door at the front and/or rear to give access to a ramp or apron on shore. The slip also had a ramp or apron balanced by weights to connect the railway proper to the boat, allowing for the water level to rise and fall. Purpose-built train ferries were (and are) quickly loaded and unloaded by the roll-on/roll-off method. The ramps and doors could be stern-only, or bow and stern for quick loading.

Railroads were evolving—and rolling—with Winona as an epicenter to railroads and commerce. Commencing in 1854—only a few years after Winona's settlement in the shadow of Sugar Loaf—a charter was granted to prominent Winonans to create the Winona and St. Peter Railway. That railroad brought its first carload of wheat from Stockton to Winona in 1862. By 1864, they had reached Rochester; 1868, to Waseca; and by 1871, they had completed 165 miles to New Ulm—continuing on to the Black Hills of South Dakota. The Winona and St. Peter lasted until 1900, when it was subsumed by the Chicago and Northwestern Railroad.

Early incorporators of the Winona and Southwestern Railroad Railroad heading to LaCrescent were historic figures of Winona. R.D. Cone, A.B. Youmans, Henry Lamberton and William Windom, among others, were the lumber barons and early designers of the city. Windom went on to greater designs as Secretary of the Treasury of the United States. When the sparks were settled and the line was built in 1872, the president of the corporation had become local resident William Mitchell—of Minnesota law school fame.

Winona gained its "magnificent iron bridge" in 1872. It connected with the LaCrosse, Trempealeau, and Prescott Railroad. The folks at LaCrosse continued to ferry their freight cars across, until opening a railroad bridge in 1875. In the interim, all passenger trains passed through Winona—bypassing LaCrosse.

The Southwestern line continued into Iowa. By 1891, it had reached Osage, Iowa. Records show "the train left Winona at 3:40 p.m., arriving in Osage at 8:30. p.m." To return the next day, one "could board the 'mixed train' (hog and human) leaving at 7:00 a.m. to arrive in Winona by 5:45 p.m." Ah, for the joys of country travel!

By 1890, a replacement bridge was built over the Mississippi River in alliance with the Green Bay, Winona and St. Paul Railroad. Winona Bridge Railway Co. was formed to oversee bridge service to Winona until 1985. The bridge was dismantled in 1990, with any remaining partnership transferred to Canadian Pacific.

Finding My Way

The corner was turned at age ten.

I had lost my innocence—even though I may never have really had any.

We carried on upon the death of our mother. I was age six, with brothers (four of them) ages four to thirteen—and a little sister, age two. Home was a safe place; a secure, comfortable place. Yet there was little emotional involvement with family members. No one was there to discuss, guide, or assist the inevitable—the finding of our future. We became miniature adults—not because anyone told us we must, or counseled us to become—only because it was our reality.

Pa, a good hardworking laborer of German stock, did not allow us to be "cast to the wind." In spite of the suggestion that we all be distributed amongst requesting families, he answered with an emphatic "No!" He would do it, and he did—raising six kids by himself without resources other than his sturdy stock and Germanic resolve.

He guided us by setting a direction in which to travel, and by having expectations. There was no guidance or personalization. Each of us was to find his or her own way—intellectually, emotionally and spiritually. The gifts of our mother and father were interpolated through the experiences of the thirteen-year-old brother who became first sergeant and mentor to us all. He didn't tell us what to do. His examples of scholarship, leadership, personal responsibility and ownership were simply followed.

By age ten I had no one to blame other than myself. I found my own way to work, to achievement, to friends and future. I stumbled. I stopped. I restarted my move forward. Like others in the family, I supported myself through work and effort. Different in style from others in my family, I found what worked for me. I satisfied the basic tenets of Pa and the real world.

We each found our way. We were independent contractors in a loosely structured family where we paid our "room and board" when we were working. We joined the Boy Scouts, stayed in school to succeed and often lead. We stayed out of jail.

The softest point of my life was at school. Teachers and classmates were most caring. From the kindness of my kindergarten teacher and the principal, I was allowed to attend school for two half-day sessions during the time of the loss of my mother. As years have passed, I suggested that I was given a "leg-up" on others through this experience. I had two naps and two milks every day.

Teachers followed and encouraged in their own unique ways, one after another. My second grade teacher stayed with me throughout life; to be there upon the awarding of my Ph. D. In her nineties, I received a letter from her at Christmastime, remindful of our second grade big hand-printing, big tablet exercise. A twelfth grade teacher offered me a personally funded scholarship to Winona State.

A brother led the school orchestra. Another wrote poetry. Someone (or two) became National Merit Scholars. One of us had a good hook shot. A couple found their way to the military and succeeded at highest levels of non-commissioned officers, with decorations for exemplary worldwide service. Ten college degrees were earned along the way.

We built assets throughout early days to carry us into our futures.

Thanks to Ma, Pa, favored teachers and big brother for letting me find my way.

Chapter Seven

The Race for the Crown

The kids were lined up along the side of the street.

News had spread like wildfire that the race for the championship of Goodview was on the line. From surrounding blocks in the small village, kids all turned out—a ragtag collection of barefoot kids outfitted in the village mode of summer dress. Cutoff blue jean shorts, shirts sewn by their mothers from military apparel of fathers who had recently returned from World War II, and a few flowery dresses made from colorful flour bags made for a scene suited for a Norman Rockwell cover on *The Saturday Evening Post*.

This was the time of "Victory Gardens," of homegrown sustenance and survival for young parents who had risked their hard earned $100 to buy a lot on the sandy soil of the countryside. The emerging village was a step away from an adjoining town of 25,000 people at the side of the Mississippi River in the bluff country of southern Minnesota.

Streets were of crushed limestone from the bluffs that surrounded the town and village. As kids rode their bikes across the crushed rock, they occasionally spun out and ended up on the ground with stones impregnated into knees and hands. With a brush-off, they were back on their way. Barefoot or on bicycle, today they had all arrived.

Norbert, named after his father, had arrived in the village recently with the unlikely nickname of "Nubsie." In one regard, Nubsie fit in just fine, since all of the boys seemed to have a name like "Clarkie" or "Jimmey" or "Chuckie" or "Butchie." They were all there today, along with girls with more standard names—Barb and Molly and Judy and Nancy and Madeline and Karen.

One exception to the standard was a tyke of a girl who seemed to be more tomboy than little girl. Like the boys she most frequently played with, "Jannie" had a name and style that mimicked theirs. Jannie was as cute as a button and a favorite of the boys and girls alike.

She played dolls on the lawn of her new front yard with the girls as they divided their patchwork quilt into quadrants where each of the four girls could set up her own dolls and home nursery. They set up tea sets, visited one another's "homes" and performed the tasks of being mothers to their dolls. Playing the role of "Mrs. Gottrocks," Jannie would visit and chat with her supposed neighbors about the challenges of their households as their mothers so often did.

But truth be told, she would rather be off running with the boys. By age four she had already gained her new Schwinn bike, even though she had to grow a few inches and a few years to reach the seat. She was always chasing with the boys, barefoot or on her bike.

With the boys, Jannie ran and played ball. She was always the pitcher, a position of honor. As a small gang, they took off across streets and sandlots to a swimming hole, to the little neighborhood store or to meet under the streetlight after supper for a game of kick the can. They were always together—boys and dogs and Jannie. She wasn't the tag-along. She was an acknowledged leader in creating their ventures. She ran hard, biked easily at the lead of the pack and always could do "double-twists" that the boys couldn't even touch. And she ran.

Nubsie, on the other hand, was an unknown commodity. He had just arrived. A gawky stringbean of a kid, he always wore his long pants and leather shoes. He was easily accepted into the group, since he too liked to run and jump and play. Unlike Chuckie, there were probably a few germs on Nubsie's body. Chuckie, although an anxious player, had an overly anxious mother.

Chuckie was allowed to play, but always arrived squeaky clean and polished. It was rumored that Chuckie didn't have a germ on his body, thanks to his mother's fastidiousness. He couldn't come out after dark, didn't venture too far from home without Mom's permission, but always enjoyed the outings. At one time, Jannie had a slight case of impetigo. When she visited Chuckie's home, she played with Chuckie and his toys. Needless to say, when the play session was over, Chuckie's mother burned all the toys! But I digress. The race was on!

Jannie had fine-tuned her skills over years of running with the boys. She was fleet as the wind, able to beat every boy and girl in her age group. Then Nubsie showed up. He had demonstrated his skill in running with the boys in their outings. Rumors began to emerge that a new leader had joined the pack, since he was beating all the boys in their footraces. Today's meeting was inevitable.

Nubsie arrived at streetside on his fenderless bike. He was tall and smooth. Even though his appearance wasn't that of an athlete, he was always out front in his runs with the boys. He stood taller by a head than Jannie. She was barefoot. He was leather-shod. A more unlikely pairing couldn't have been created.

The meeting had been decided a few days ago as Jannie played marbles in the sandlot with the boys. The topic of speed and challenge came up. It seemed that the boys were beginning to favor Nubsie for his running prowess. Something needed to be settled. Even though Jannie lost her brother's marbles at the game, she wasn't about to give up *all* the marbles—especially her leadership as lead runner in Goodview.

The crowd was anxious. Like a group of sandlot kittenball players waiting to be chosen, they kicked at the stones and waited for the action to begin. The rules and the distance had been decided. The long block from Jannie's corner to the street of Mary's Little Store would be the distance, about a half-mile.

Mr. Swenson, an occasional tippler in the late afternoon, was chosen as the official starter. He was right next door—and could be counted upon for clarity in the morning sunshine. Besides, he happened to have a starter's gun.

At the finish line would be the head of the village activity group. Uncle Bill, as everyone knew him, was acceptable to all due to his position and his years of fairness to all the kids of the village. He just happened to be Jannie's uncle. Bill stood in the middle of the street at the finish line he had marked off. He was waving a red flag to indicate his readiness.

As runners took their mark in the gouged out limestone, parents began to emerge. With no bushes of any size yet in the new village, a clear view down the street showed a goodly number of onlookers from start to finish. This many people hadn't been seen on the street since the village constable closed it off for the annual picnic and barbecue.

The cheers began to rise. It was a decided clamor for the tomboy, but the voices of many boys shouted for Nubsie's victory—a seeming right in their minds.

Nubsie bent his beanpole frame to the ground as Mr. Swenson announced to participants that the start procedure would be a countdown of "Get Ready, Set, Go!" and the simultaneous firing of the starter's pistol. Jannie was in her crouch. She was determined to retain her crownless crown. With one final caution to the crowd for quiet, Mr. Swenson began his countdown.

The discharge of the small pistol went off like an M80 on the Fourth of July. The runners were off.

At the first fire hydrant some 100 yards out, Nubsie was in the lead. His gangly arms and legs were flailing as he dug those leathers into the street and set stones flying. Jannie had met her match. Her bare feet ran smoothly across the compressed stone, but his legs were just too long. By the midpoint at the alley next to Odegaard's, she was twenty yards behind. The crowd roared encouragement to both runners. By the time they crossed the second fire hydrant with 200 yards to go, Nubsie's smooth step faltered. He was running out of gas!

Jannie saw the opening and headed for daylight. Her smooth rhythm and years of experience in running the sandlots kicked in. With hardly a look at Nubsie or the cheering crowd, she aimed herself toward the paper roll stretched across the street. In a flash, she crossed the finish line with red flag waving. By now, Nubsie had slowed considerably. She beat him by a full ten yards!

Stories are told yet today of this young lady's accomplishment—her victory securing her a place in the legends of Goodview. She had beaten the best.

Her unofficial crown has remained in place for over fifty years. It has yet to show the first signs of tarnish.

Radio:
Reality and Wonderment

As a ten-year-old, it was hard to find the strength to hold on tight enough and simultaneously twist the small, metal on-off post of the old AM radio. Located as it was in a small space below the brass dial of the 1930s radio, it always hurt my fingers to make the twist. The post was supposed to have a plastic cover on it, but like many of the items of our limited-resources household of the 1950s, we just made do.

My brothers and I found a way to turn the knob on the Philco and get it to hum as it warmed up and soon emitted a high-pitched squeal. We then turned the dial from 530 to 1500—or somewhere in between—to locate stations near and far. Our favorites were WCCO-CBS at 830 Minneapolis, and Winona's KWNO, our local, homegrown station of the stars at 1230.

In the "front room" of our small home in southern Minnesota—before television and the multiple, plastic twisty toy transforming creatures of today— we found ways to imagine and entertain ourselves. We listened to the radio.

It created for us our own wonderful images. We "saw" *Big Jon and Sparkie* play out as we made our Saturday-morning chores even more fun by gathering around the worn and scarred console in the front room. We marched with Big Jon or with Don McNeil of the earlier *Breakfast Club*. Mr. McNeil, a suave and cultured host, had played to millions since the time when our radio had been new. He was a fixture.

I liked Big Jon and tolerated Don McNeil, but really looked forward to "King." He was the fierce lead dog who aimed his dog team in hot pursuit of bad guys on Saturday morning's *Sergeant Preston of the Yukon*. Characters and action were drawn into the corners of our minds as Royal Canadian Mounted Police Sergeant Preston and King mushed across the Yukon, dodged bullets and whirled through Arctic-force blizzards.

Having read Jack London's classic short story "To Build A Fire," I could feel the whistling wind of the Yukon coming over the radio. Personal backyard experience in Minnesota snow forts in the dead of winter assured me that I knew what Arctic cold was all about.

Radio was our life attachment to everyday reality—to suspense, comedy, sports and music. Our own wonderment created vivid pictures from the words and sounds floating to us across the airwaves. The sound of a creaking door and an ensuing mystery got our attention on *The Green Hornet* in a darkened-evening broadcast. Even though Pa was there with us for shared popcorn and security, the images were still sometimes scary.

We laughed again—for the hundredth time—at Fibber McGee's closet door opening to the sound of falling clutter and contents. Jack Benny and Rochester slowly drawled out their words on *Sunday Night NBC* and easily drew us into their long-winded scenes and images.

Bobby Benson of the B-Bar-B Ranch (and his Riders) came across airwaves in a fashion that was easily recognizable—even more so after Bobby and the Riders visited our town under sponsorship of Little Miss Sunbeam and the Federal Bakery. We saw them up close and personal—right before the pie-eating contest in the Armory Hall.

We never saw "Sky King," a 1940s and 1950s title character, but his American radio-adventure series was one of our favorites. Arizona rancher and aircraft pilot Schuyler (or Skyler) "Sky" King most likely portrayed Jack Cones, the flying constable of Twenty-Nine Palms, California—a true-life person of the 1930s. His personal plane was called the *Songbird*. Though he changed from one plane to another during the course of the series, the latest plane was never given a number. It was simply known as *Songbird*.

Max Conrad, a globe-circling, world-acclaimed and record-setting pilot, lived in our town. Between his small plane flights of new and uncharted routes to and from Europe and elsewhere, he voluntarily taught boys of the neighborhood how to fly. Max gave us the real presence of Sky King. Although Sky's show had strong cowboy show elements, King always used his plane to capture criminals, find lost hikers or even capture spies on the coast of California. Max did no less—as evidenced by his rescue flights of hunters over the Mississippi River in our home area during the Armistice Day snowstorm of 1940. The blizzard dropped up to twenty-seven inches of snow in a matter of hours and took the lives of forty-nine in Minnesota alone. Max, like Sky, made a real difference.

King and his niece, Penny (and sometimes his nephew, Clipper), lived on the Flying Crown Ranch near the (fictitious) town of Grover, Arizona. Penny and Clipper were also pilots. Relatively inexperienced, they looked to their uncle for guidance and mentoring. Penny was an accomplished air racer and a rated multiengine pilot whom Sky entrusted to fly the *Songbird*.

On many of the radio shows of our day, there were "radio premiums" offered to listeners. On November 2, 1947, in the episode entitled "Mountain Detour," the Sky King Secret Signalscope utilized on the show was offered to listeners. The Signalscope included a glow-in-the-dark signaling device, whistle, magnifying glass and Sky King's private code—along with the ability to see around corners and trees.

Each was advised to get their own for only fifteen cents—and the inner seal from a jar of Peter Pan Peanut Butter (produced by sponsor Derby Foods). I was always short of either the fifteen cents or the prescribed Peter Pan label, having instead a tin pail of generic peanut butter. In our house of Pa and six kids, essentials were most often packaged in tin pails, flour bags or burlap, rather than in more expensive jars like Peter Pan.

Premiums were innovative, such as the Sky King Spy-Detecto Writer, which had a "decoder" (cipher disk), magnifying glass, measuring scale, and printing mechanism in a single package slightly over two inches long. Other notable premiums included the Magni-Glo Writing Ring, which had a luminous element, a secret compartment, a magnifier, and a ballpoint pen all in the crownpiece of a "fits any finger" ring. Sometimes the offered rings turned your finger green. The radio show ran until 1954.

Another favorite, *Captain Midnight*, featured a veteran flyer of World War I who led a secret squadron doing espionage previous to World War II. His was an extremely popular radio show, with an audience of millions, over fifty percent of which were adults. It was updated after Pearl Harbor to include the introduction of Axis and Japanese enemies. Scripts depicted women being treated as equals, not just characters waiting to be rescued. Both Joyce Ryan of the secret squadron and Fury Shark, daughter of villain Ivan Shark, pulled their own weight in the adventures. Joyce went on Captain Midnight commando raids and became involved in aerial dogfights during World War II. I felt like I was in the seat behind her.

Using Code-O-Graphs decoders (also available with the proper coin and label), listeners were able to decipher encrypted messages previewing the next weekly episode, sponsored by Ovaltine. The badge-like decoder with a winged clock pointing to midnight was a true prize to have in hand with friends in a quiet room, listening for the next episode.

Broadcast messages were encrypted with relatively trivial mono-alphabetic substitution ciphers with word division—but as stimulating as Ovaltine to ten-year-olds. With continuing updates, the program even introduced us to jet fighters.

Pa's bed with the white chenille bedspread in the front room was the place to be for *Gillette Friday Night Fights* sponsored by Gillette Blue Blades. Lying on the bed with the radio speaker at the same height, I had up close and personal blow-by-blow coverage in a ringside (bedside?) seat. The action-packed nine o'clock fights brought us Joe Louis during the last days of his twelve-year world heavyweight boxing championship reign that ended in a gracious retirement in 1949.

The fights, with Howard Cosell at the mic, led us to Willie Pep, Kid Gavilan, Jake LaMotta, Sandy Saddler, Jersey Joe Walcott and Rocky Graziano—all scrappers with names that could only be destined for boxers. They battled into our hearts on their way to stardom, along with super-talents Rocky Marciano, Sugar Ray Robinson and Ezzard Charles.

In anticipation of the fights, the local *Republican-Herald* newspaper published competitors' heights, weights, arm and waist dimensions and other measurements to give us a full picture of favorites seen (heard) on the evening fights. Lying in the dark with the glow of the radio dial, I listened for the bell of every round of fifteen and truly saw a fight in action.

When the old radio was later moved to my small bedroom in the attic, and after a night of boxing or personal action, KWNO brought me the latest popular songs on a late-evening *Music 'Til Midnight* show, starting at 10:30 p.m.

Listening to some personal requests for records from kids I knew—or an occasional personal message the disk jockey might allow—this "heady" stuff caused me to slip off to dreamland. If I did not turn off the radio before falling asleep, I was wakened by the steady, loud hum of the radio coming back on the air at 6:00 a.m.

Saturday afternoons in the fall, Minnesota Gopher football games were broadcast through the open front door and windows of our house. From our front room's AM console radio, the boys of the neighborhood listened to the games on the porch. We were in our glory with winning Gopher teams.

Local All-American hero Paul Giel led the charge for the Gophers. With the sounds of the marvelous marching band to serenade us while we played football in the street at halftime, we captured the strong sounds of the Gopher Marching Band and the oft-repeated Minnesota rouser words, "Rah! Rah! Rah! For Ski-U-Mah!"

Advanced technology hit our house when I was about twelve. In personal charge of the family paper route controlled by brothers and me for the previous dozen years or so, I was doing my normal Saturday morning collection of weekly payments when I was offered the prize of a lifetime. One of my patrons on Olmstead Street was updating to a new radio and/or television. They graciously gifted me with their huge, stand-up radio console with all the bells and whistles.

Without question of Pa's approval—and without hesitancy of action—I was back in a flash with a brother and our trusty wagon on which we hauled old newspapers and collected scrap for the recycler at the end of the street. We pulled the wagon and shiny treasure home, careful to avoid curbs and known bumps in the sidewalk.

The fully wrapped, multi-toned woods of the gleaming mahogany cabinet surrounded a fascinating series of dials and buttons. We found a red light, a green light, an amber light and a sweeping range of radio bands—from ship-to-shore to police calls to the exciting worldwide reach of short wave.

In addition to the beautiful wooden finish and standard AM programs so enjoyed, we soon found that we could pick up pieces of a Mexican serenade, a conversation in Japanese, an Italian ship at sea or Christian messages from missionaries around the world.

An occasionally found program on BBC (British Broadcast System) was more than we could handle with their bland and droll commentators. The new radio found a special place in the middle room where Ernie Reck's polkas or the ramblings of *Amos and Andy* could be heard from the kitchen or the front room. Late at night, one or the other of us could be found sitting in the dark, slowly turning the colored bands that evidenced new cultures out there.

Sunday afternoon broadcasts of *The Bell Telephone Hour* were more settled in presentation, yet equally compelling. I felt I was there on stage with the symphonic works of Italian and German composers, with polished musicians of stage and Broadway, and with popular singers of the day. Each graced us with their gifts as the family clustered around the radio.

The studio orchestra performed the very best of music while supporting musicians and singers of the highest quality. We were honored to hear the likes of Marian Anderson, Bing Crosby, Dinah Shore, Jascha Heifetz, Yehudi

Menuhin, and Ezio Pinza, among others. There was little imagination required—just personal, quiet entertainment that stunned our senses.

As our teenage years progressed and cars came into our lives (like
the 1949 Mercury four-door I purchased for forty dollars), we had to have a
radio for Sunday rides in the country with our special girl, for local news and
games, for weather reports and for *Music 'Til Midnight*. The fragile radio tubes
were always going out, or some small solder job was necessary, which was
done by my friend Edson. With old cars and older batteries, it was a caution to
run the radio when the motor was not running (a typical teenage experience
when with one of the opposite sex.)

Marconi and McDermott and Armstrong and General Sarnoff have a
special place in the hearts of those of us who treasure our life with radio.
Marconi invented the concept of radio waves, McDermott created the vacuum
tube, Armstrong modified the signals and "the general" established a network
of broadcasts and stations that brought new and expanded life to virtually
every household and "front room" of America.

We learned, we laughed, we imagined. What a gift!

The Villains Come to Winona: Ruminations on Professional Wrestling

Actors and wrestlers in China have been notified that they can pursue their professions three years longer, after which they must follow more useful and honorable calling.

— "A Telegraphic Brevity," *Winona Daily Republican*, January 16, 1873.

Along with evenings spent at the Hurry Back Pool Hall and Billiards Parlor on Third Street where we watched semi-pros play "snooker," visiting Kegler's Klub Bowling Alley's upstairs to watch hand-set games of local bowling champs, or later "dragging the gut" of Third Street in a hot rod (or a parent's sedate old car) looking for night action, my early teen years were spent on one enterprising activity after another.

Wow! The characters I met, the action I saw along the way. There was never a dull moment in the 1950s of Winona.

I discovered professional wrestling at age ten.

Five hundred was a full house at the Wigwam. The atmosphere was electric (although the bulbs were dim) as we entered the large wooden doors of the second floor. Flashing capes and sweaty bodies overcame the darkness of winter nights. It was a world removed from the one we knew. An adjacent apartment gave residents a living-room view of the action. The balcony was filled.

Television was yet to enter our homes. We heard radio shows throughout the week with criminals being chased by the Green Hornet and J. Edgar Hoover. Gillette Blue Blade boxing matches on Friday nights held our attention through every bell of every round. We could only imagine the behemoths of the ring and crime. But here they were—up close and personal—in long hair and flashy tights. Some were good guys. Some were threatening. Like Abe Zvonkin, some were mild-mannered—but for him, "everything goes in the ring."

Today I'm rediscovering the names and the wild action of professional wrestling in Winona in its heyday. It is a newfound treasure. Professional wrestling! *Grrr!* This is too much fun.

The Winona Opera House was the "packed-house" setting of presidential speeches and "toss 'em out of the ring rassling action" for Winona's sports addicts. In April, 1911, scheduled wrestling had 167-pound Fred Beell taking on 180-pound Carl Bursch (the German) in the first documented start. Busch called Beell "the biggest little man that ever lived."

The action heated up that night and for fifty years thereafter. Before tackling the German, Beell had defeated World Champion Frank Gotch on December 1, 1906. Quite a claim to make; for Gotch, of Humboldt, Iowa, became undisputed champion from 1908 to 1913, "when the contests were largely legitimate." He was known as "The John L. Sullivan of Wrestling." Beell beat Busch in two falls. Local artist Lex Clayton was also on the match.

Clayton, a wrestler, retired to Winona and to taxidermy in 1904. When T.C. Norris of Los Angeles looked Clayton up for a grudge match at the Opera House in 1905, the newspaper stated that a "clean affair is promised." Lex staged several more matches in Winona in 1906, with one in LaCrosse in 1910. His brother, Mort Clayborne, was a competitor in the Winona workout. Physicians observed and examined Les and declared they had "never seen a man whose muscle is in such perfect condition." In two previous Winona events he had been known to "give a clean, scientific exhibition."

Stanislaus Zbyszko (five-foot-nine, 232 pounds, twenty-two-inch neck), the reigning 1921 National Champion, went on to 940 straight wins after being pinned by Frank Gotch in six seconds. Stanislaus, age forty-two, fought Joe Varga in February, 1923, at the Winona Armory in front of a "record crowd." He attributed his strength and success to "clean living"—possibly following the advice of an ad in the *Daily Republican* of August 1, 1883. The ad in question said, "'If weakness of brain or bodily powers.' Then get Allen's Brain Food. *Meno san in corpore sano*—A sound mind a sound body."

Wrestling was becoming a growing attraction and a serious money-making proposition. According to purists in 1931, it attracted "riff-raff" from the football and boxing worlds. One of those who apparently didn't have the pure spirit of wrestling was Primo Carnera, World Champion Heavyweight boxer in 1933. As a boxer, he lost his champion's slot to Max Baer—and was knocked out by Joe Louis. He continued on several more years in boxing. In 1946, he was attracted to "rassling" and won seventy straight matches.

At six-foot-five and 275 pounds, he was a formidable Italian force. He was known as the "Ambling Alp"—as boxer or wrestler. His presence and that of others caused a national outcry. People "go to wrestling matches to see wrestlers" after all—not boxers and football players. One of the "most notorious badmen" of Winona wrestling, Ivan Kamaroff, had wrestled Carnera to a draw.

Kamaroff, "The Riotous Russian," came out of New Haven, Connecticut, to take on Con Bruno, known as "Mr. New York City of 1940" in a match in Winona in February, 1951. Announced in the *Republican-Herald*, "The Villains Meet on Tuesday" at the Red Man Wigwam at the corner of Fourth and Franklin.

It was a formidable card, with Minnesota's "all-time great" Bronko Nagurski on the card at 242 pounds against 218-pound Canadian star Roy McClarity. Roy was a featured television performer on wrestling shows of the East Coast.

Stan Mayslack, a popular 248-pound Minneapolis wrestler often featured in Winona, met what promised to be the "roughest affair of the night" against Hans Hermann ("Hermann the German"), a mere 267 pounds.

The heat of the crowd rose as we awaited the toss of one or the other of these hulks into our laps. We surrounded the ring in hard-back wooden theatre chairs giving little protection to our ten-year-old bodies if the monsters broke loose. At one time, Hermann was mad. After being booed by the 356 fans who didn't like his illegal tactics against Mayslack, he told the audience: "Oh, shut up!"

Bronislau "Bronko" Nagurski, "The Nag," of Polish-Ukrainain descent, came from the Ontario of his birth and his International Falls residence to lead the University of Minnesota football team as an All-American tackle and fullback. Nagurski was discovered and signed by University of Minnesota head coach Clarence "Fats" Spears, who drove up to International Falls in 1926. Arriving, he watched Nagurski out plowing a field. According to legend, Spears asked directions to the nearest town, and Bronko lifted his plow and used it to point in the direction of town. He was signed on the spot to play for the Golden Gophers. Spears admitted he concocted the story on his long drive back to the University of Minnesota in St. Paul.

Bronko left Minnesota to play for the Chicago Bears football team in 1930, leading them to a national championship. He offered in 1933, "I prefer wrestling to football—if it's a matter of making a living—but as a game, I like football best." Coming to wrestling and Winona in 1934, he proceeded to win nearly all of his first 500 matches from that point on. He lost four; avenging three of those.

In May of 1950, he took on Ray Dunkel in Winona. Dunkel, a collegiate champ from Purdue, was opposing evidence to the populace that "wrestlers have (only) lots of muscle and hard heads." "It's a lie!" the newspaper shouted. Dunkel had a bachelor's degree and was working on a master's. Nothing was said of Bronko's college experience.

Dunkel was a Winona regular, taking on the "villainous" Hans Hermann the next time. Leo Nomellini of Italy and the University of Minnesota took on bearded favorite Stan Mayslack of "Nordeast" Minneapolis the same night. Nomellini, a former pro football player, was set up to become Nagurski's successor. The match of the 320-pound Zebra Kid and Frank Marconi, a 265-pound ruffian from Salem, Ohio, filled out the evening's bill.

Bronko became World Champion of the National Wrestling Alliance in 1939, and was fitted with the $10,000 diamond-studded belt. *Sports Illustrated* named Nagurski as one of the four greatest athletes in Minnesota state history. A Minnesota treasure, he brought joy and clean excitement to the boys of Winona, Duluth, Rochester, and Minneapolis.

He was re-signed to the Chicago Bears in 1943, was declared 4-F on his military physical in 1944, returned to wrestling in 1945, and continued to wrestle throughout the region into the 1950s. Interviewed in Winona in 1951, at age forty-two, he was tiring of travel. Saying said that he had lostfifteen to twenty times in eighteen years; he suggested, "by and large the best wrestler will win the match." He retired to a farm and a gas station in International Falls, where the high school team became known as "The Broncos." At one time, he played as a professional basketball player.

Tiny Mills, of Camrose, Canada—a six-foot-three, 276-pound giant—was in Winona in 1952, to go against the Black Panther of Omaha "for a one-hour time limit." He had earlier split in individual matches with Bronko. The original Henry Middlestadt, Tiny teamed with brother, Al, to become Canadian Tag Team winners. Coming to America, he teamed with Stan Kowalski of Minneapolis in the 1950s to win titles. With Al, the twosome had formed "Murder, Inc." With Kowalski, it was the second coming of Murder, Inc. Mills lost to NWA Champion Pat O'Connor singly, but later teamed with him to win the Tag Team title. He also won the Calgary regional title with Black Jack Daniels, of Minneapolis.

Stepping down into Ray's new Hudson, we found our way to the Wigwam after an early supper to gain "the best seats in the house"—which Ray always promised. He was Bill's dad, and a good friend to kids who needed to be out on a school night. Wow, what adventure! And safe, too!

Logan Clendenning, M.D., writing in the "Diet and Health" column in the local paper in 1937, stated that football was four times more dangerous to the player than "rassling" was to the wrestler. He suggested, "42% of football injuries are suffered by the tackler and 18% by the ball carrier." His study didn't cover injuries to patrons of wrestling matches.

Clendenning may not have considered all injuries resulting from the holds of wrestling—the stretches, arm locks, chokes, leg locks, drop kicks, scissor holds and undefined techniques of the well-versed world-wide competitors who tripped one another in the Red Man Wigwam ring. We watched for the "armpit claw," someone "skinning the cat," the "cobra clutch," and the ultimate, "Tree of Woe." One wrestler even used hidden pencils to stab opponents in the face. These were tough guys who may not have reported every "owie." Dislocated arms were pulled back into place—and the match continued.

Female wrestlers were also a regular part of the action at the Wigwam and the Armory, with sellout crowds predicted when women were on the ticket. They were "top contenders among the country's women performers in the grunt and groan game." A few were Dot Dotson of Tampa, June Byers of Houston, Texas, Bonnie Bartlett of Hollywood, Shirley Smith of Little Rock and Dolly Dalton of Chicago. They were often on the program, with the likes of the Purple Demon and Champ Killer Thomas.

The 1939 series sponsored by the American Legion (in support of Junior Legion baseball) brought to town the likes of "Dirty Dick" Raines and "Handsome Don" McIntyre, a Washburn College all-star. Raines, Hawaii champion of 1939, brought his skill set directly to Winona to finish off McIntyre, a popular Minneapolis area wrestler who was "second to Bronko as the most popular wrestler in Minneapolis." It wasn't only McIntyre's good looks. At 226 pounds, he was described as "fast, flashy, scientific—and a perfect sportsman inside and out of the ring." How could Dirty Dick even stand a chance against Superman?

The Opera House started the action in 1911, with the Winona Armory hosting many city events from the 1920s into the 1950s. Bobby Benson of the B-Bar-B (a cowboy radio personality) was there for me to see in the 1950s, but the Armory wrestlers of the 1920s had moved on, in the 1930s, to the Athletic Club and Catholic Recreation Center (600 fans were there for Nagurski in 1937).

3 BOUTS 8:15 p. m.

WRESTLING SHOW

TONIGHT!

DOT DOTSON
146 lbs., Tampa, Fla.
vs.
BEVERLY LEHMER
140 lbs., Council Bluffs, Iowa

Professional Women Wrestlers

OTHER BOUTS

STAN MAYSLACK
248 lbs., Minneapolis
vs.
JOE CORBETT
238 lbs., Boston

BUTCH LEVY
252 lbs., Minneapolis
vs.
JACK DILLON
250 lbs., Chattanooga

Sponsored by Leon J. Wetzel Post No. 9
American Legion

Red Men Wigwam, Winona, Minn.

Tonight: 8:15 Admission—$1.20

A wrestling advertisement in Winona, with female contenders topping th bill, circa the 1950s. (Courtesy of the Winona Newspaper Project, Winona State University.)

All soon settled into Winona's premier wrestling domicile—The Red Man's Wigwam—in the 1940s and 1950s. In May of 1952, promoters tried the outdoor Gabrych Park venue to benefit the Winona Chiefs. Only seventy-six fans appeared. Wrestlers refused to fight with such a small audience. The event was cancelled, and money refunded. The all-time record crowd occurred on April 10, 1952, when 814 rabid fans jammed into the Red Man Wigwam where the next day's headline was, "Girls and Tag Draw Record." Adults were a dollar and twenty cents for admission, children fifty cents.

On Wednesday nights, Alma, Wisconsin, attracted wrestling fans to the Riverview Hall. Playing on Saturday nights in the same ring was the Louis Schuh Orchestra of Winona.

To be expected, there were several Winonans who took to the professional mat. Lex Clayton, retired wrestler, led the way in 1906. Hippy Ross, 180 pounds, known as the "Winona Strong Man," debuted in 1935 versus Harvey Kahoe of St. Paul. Hippy had been trained by Spike Graham of Winona and was known to be "fast and powerful." Spike was also a referee.

Hometown favorite Walter "Sailor" Nappy left the waters to take on Charles Taylor of Des Moines, also in 1935. After early boxing success, Hank Olson, at 180 pounds, took on Dude Smith, 192 pounds, of Chicago at the Winona Armory in 1939. It is not learned whether these Winonans were successful on the circuit. We can only hope that they were given a second chance at Alma's Riverview Hall.

One of the frequent visitors to Winona as manager, promoter and referee was Wally Karbo of northeast Minneapolis. Wally's entourage often arrived and left in the same vehicle in Winona or Rochester or LaCrosse or Duluth—as witnessed by a disappointed youthful usher I interviewed for this story. He volunteered at the Duluth Shrine Auditorium wrestling shows in the 1950s. Previous to seeing the cheerful carload leaving the auditorium, he had thought all the hateful matchups were real.

Wally was a jack-of-all-trades and a master of all. He must have had a degree in mathematics in order to create the scribbled round-robin schedule of wrestlers and events and cities and non-repetitive matchups. Wally's acumen and ring control were legendary. He handled all of the wrestlers no matter what their size. But then, he probably signed their paychecks.

Wally and Vern Gagne founded and owned the American Wrestling Association from 1960 to 1991.

I was fortunate to be a part of this exciting time in Winona's history. The stories and names appear to be endless; with discovery of past memories amazing. I am satisfied that I have captured the essence and history of professional wrestling in Winona. In my search, I discovered the words of an esteemed writer for the *Republican-Herald* who visited the Red Men Wigwam in 1954. Her response is joyous and telling. Gretchen Lamberton reports:

> The other night I went to the most soul-satisfying show I've been to in years—a wrestling match at Red Men's Club. It was soul-satisfying because it was a great big dirty (and expert) fight plus a great big dramatic show with black villains against handsome virtuous heroes, and the audience could and did get into the act.

It's always fun to tell off a villain. At a baseball game it's quite satisfying to shout at the umpire, only you know in your heart that he's really not a villain and anyway he never shouts back at you. But these wrestling matches are a different kettle of fish. Usually a beefy dirty-wrestling villain is pitted against a big clean-cut hero. The crowd screams, threatens, curses him out and sometimes actually gets into the ring with him, and he screams back with much fist shaking. It's all great fun and makes you feel good.

She goes on to describe the actions of Dirty Dick Raines and Kinji Shibuya (boos and hisses) in a tag team event against Roy McClarity and Jack Witzig (beautifully-muscled heroes.) With "dastardly kicks and favorite tricks" by the villains, she was seen to conclude:

Once when the villain was slammed out of the ring a nice old gentleman in the front row arose and shook his finger under the villainous nose scolding him angrily. Fans hung out of the balcony screaming at Dirty Dick and the sinister Jap, and they yaked right back, shaking fists and threatening in most satisfactory manner.

Anyway, the upshot was that the two villains won two out of three falls to the noisy wrath of the crowd. I can't wait to see these same villains rassle the fine heroes again.

I'm sure that virtue will triumph next time

Wrestlers Competing in Winona: A Partial List

Men

Paul Baillargeon—vs. Pete Managoff, 1952. He was tag team partner with Vern Gagne vs. "Hard-Boiled" Haggerty and Joe Pazandek in Rochester.

Tony Baillargeon—Quebec. Competed with brother in 1954, vs. Abe Kashey and Hans Hermann.

Fred Beell—1911, of Marshfield, Wiconsin. The first-listed Winona professional wrestler. He was later killed as a police officer in a theft at The Marshfield Brewery in 1933. Although opposing "The German," in 1911, he, too was German—born in Prussia in 1876.

Don Beitleman—Buffalo, New York, vs. Don Papaleo, vs. Dirty Dick Raines, 1952.

George Bollas—"Zebra Kid." Hawaii Champion 1955, Ohio State Champion, where he played at 360 pounds. He was down to 320 pounds when he crushed and sent Ali Pasha to hospital in 1952. Dr. Tweedy was called in.

Billy Burns—1911.

Carl Busch—"The German," from Brockton, Massachusetts. 1911, lost to Beell in two falls.

Cowboy Carlson—the steer-throwing cowboy, vs. Kayo Hall of St. Louis, 1950.

Les Clayton—1906 and 1911. First Winona wrestler. April 23, 1906.

Joe Corbett—234 pounds, from Boston, vs. Mayslack.

Kasta Davelis—A "Tough-looking Greek," 220 pounds.

Purple Demon—1952.

Jack Dillon—250 pounds, from Chatanooga, Tennessee, vs. Butch Levy, 1951.

Ray Dunkel—Purdue graduate and champion. 1951 vs. Nagurski.

Stan Dusek—228 pounds, from Omaha. His famous wrestling brothers Ernie and Emil traded the Canadian Tag team title with Tiny Mills in 1953. Emil was with Butch Levy in Rochester in 1952. His brother (?) Frank tells the story of how Stan Stasiak became World Champion through pre-arrangement (for eight days). He had eight brothers, and the family name was Hason. Rudy was eldest. In Winona, 1943, after twenty-five years in wrestling (since 1917).

Big Ike Eakins—270 pounds, James D. Harlan, Kentucky coal miner, vs. Butch Levy, 1953. His first time in Winona. Ike died of heart attack (elsewhere) at age fifty-two.

Billy Evans—from Omaha, vs. Bronko, 224 pounds, 1934, at Catholic Rec Center.

Little Fix—from Chicago, 220-pound TV performer, 1952.

Steve Gob—weightlifter of cancelled 1940 Olympic team. 1951.

Stu Hall—vs. Johnny Moochy, 1950.

Hard-Boiled Haggerty—New York, tag team with Eakins, 1953.

Hans Herrman—"Herman the German," 269 pounds.

Vic Holbrook—260 pounds, lost his debut to Leo the Lion, 1950.

Lee Jones—from Mason City, vs. Stan Myslajek, in 1935.

Harvey Kahoe—from St. Paul. 1935 vs. Winona wrestler.

Ivan Kamaroff—"The Riotous Russian" from New Haven, Connecticut.

Abe Kashey—from Los Angeles and Syria (a "weaver's son"). A headline read: "King Kong Kashey Kolorful Karakter." 1954. Previously, 1934, 1936.

"Duke" Kotsonares—"The Greek Apollo" vs. Professor Sason Takahashi of Japan, 1939 ju-jitsu expert, "no holds barred" match, 1939, Armory.

Jack "Sky-Hi" Lee—Toronto, six-foot-eight, 292 pounds. "World's tallest wrestler," vs. Johnny Moochy, 1951.

Butch Levy—"World's top contender," 250 pounds, played University of Minnesota football under Bernie Bierman, coach.

Roy McClarity—Canadian, former hockey star on TV. 236 pounds, was married at mid-ring.

"Handsome Don" McIntyre—1939 Washburn College star, second to Bronko in Minneapolis's popularity.

Bobby Managoff—Hawaii champion three times, Texas champion. Trained by his father. Began in 1942.

Pete Managoff—Known as "Pistol Pete" and "The Mad Russian," 241 pounds, from Newland, North Carolina, vs. Paul Baillargeon, 1952. His father was Russian wrestling champion. He learned "oriental noodle-cracking from Professor Higami, noted Japanese Judo expert," vs. Butch Levy, 1950. "Both wrestlers brought fists into play," read one newspaper. Levy pinned Managoff.

Frank Marconi—from Salem, Ohio, 365 pounds.

Farmer Marlin—from Niles, Michigan, 228 pounds. Tag team with Butch Levy. Marlin's first time in Winona.

Stan Mayslack—from northeast Minneapolis, 241 pounds. Later, he owned Mayslack's Restaurant in northeast Minneapolis.

Tiny Mills—roughest wrestler, from Minneapolis. When Mills retired, he became a sheriff in Minnesota. Tiny vs. Black Panther, 1952.

Francois Miquet—France vs. Ben Hamilton, 1950.

Johnny Moochy—from Balsam Lake, Wisconsin. The "Bad Guy" in first Winona tag team in 1952. Vs. Firpo Zybszko, from Poland, 1952.

Bronko Nagurski

Mike Nazarian—260 pounds, Des Moines native, vs. Farmer Tobin, bearded giant, at the Armory in 1936.

Leo Nomellini—"Leo the Lion," born in Italy, from the University of Minnesota, heir to Nagurski. A professional football player. Tag team champion with Vern Gagne.

Pat O'Connor—from New Zealand. Rated as one of country's best. "A farmer by trade," he fought Von Saxon (of Berlin, Germany) in 1951, in Winona. Was NWA World Champion 1960. Teamed with Tiny Mills. O'Connor was reportedly "a future champ," "fast and shifty" A drop kick specialist.

George O'Hara—A Texan, vs. Caifson Johnson, Minneapolis, 1950.

Don Papaleo—from Boston, vs. Don Beitelman, 1952.

Ali Pasha—from Turkey, 241 pounds. Had "numerous bouts" in Winona. He was described as a balding, slow-moving Turk, 1952. Died (elsewhere) after a match in 1961.

Sergeant Joe Pazandek—former University of Minnesota grappler, weighed 240 pounds. Pinned Stan Dusek, 1950.

Dirty Dick Raines—Waco, Texas. Hawaii champion, 1939. "Country's No. 1 Mat Villain."

Sterling Robinson—vs. Leo Nomellini, 1950.

Von Saxon—from Berlin, Germany, 265 pounds, 1951.

Hans Schnable—vs. O'Connor, 1950. "Wrestling's Drastic Dutchman." Famed for the "blockbuster"—pounding an opponent's head into the canvas.

Ernest Siegfried—German, "a true Nazi follower," vs. Walhek Wodarak, Polish Giant. 248 pounds, 1939.

Ben Sharpe—from Hamilton, Ontario, 245 pounds.

Kinji Shibuya—"Villainous gimmick of a Japanese bad guy." A favorite, he credited Vern Gagne with making him popular as a villain in 1955. Was originally raised in Utah and went to school in California—not Japan!

Lon Sjoberg—from Duluth, Minnesota, 239 pounds, a Scotch Irishman.

Billy Smith—207 pounds, vss Joe Valento, 205 pounds, 1950.

Fred Stoeker—Iowa State champion, vs. Rocky Gallop of Winnipeg, 1953.

Professor Sason Takahashi—from Japan. A ju-jitsu expert—"no holds barred" matches, 1939, Winona Armory.

Charles Taylor—from Des Moines, Iowa. 1935.

Champion Killer Thomas—1952.

Farmer Tobin—1936, vs. Mike Nazarian.

Joe Varga—from Chicago, vs. World champ Zybszko, 1923

Earl Wampher—from Scranton, Iowa, vs. Bronko at sold-out Catholic Recreation Center, 1937.

Jack Wetzik—from Eau Claire, 226 pounds, "good guy." 1952, 1954.

Black Panther—Identified as Bearcat Wright, Jr. A Boxer. Bear Cat Wright vs. Ali Pashsa, 1952.

Walhek Wodarak—"Polish Giant," 248 pounds, vs. Ernest Siegfried, German, 1939.

Abe Zvonkin—from Hamilton, Ontario, 235 pounds, mild-mannered. Often against Ali Pasha.

Firpo Zybszko—from Poland, vs. Johnny Moochy, 1952.

Stanislaus Zybszko—Champion of the World, vs. Joe Varga of Chicago, 1923, Armory.

Women

Bonnie Bartlett—from Hollywood, California.

Mars Bennett—from Detroit, circus performer, 1951.

Lilly Bitter—from Newark, New Jersey. A headline read, "Girls Draw Record Crowd" when 814 packed the stands in 1952.

June Byers—from Houston, Texas, 138 pounds.

Dora Coombs—from Nashville or Kentucky, Hillbilly singer, redhead, 1951.

Dolly Dalton—from Chicago.

Dot Dotson—from Tampa or Orlando. A taxi driver.

Beverly Lehmer—from Council Bluffs, Iowa.

Shirley Smith—from Little Rock, Arkansas.

Therese Theis—from St. Paul, Minnesota, age 21 at the time of her match.

Vi Viann

Elda Waldek—from Custer, Washington, billed as a natural blonde.

A Woman Takes Revenge

Zetta Timms, divorced wife of professional wrestler Howard Osler of South Bend, IN, used rawhide to publicly horsewhip a farmer on Main Street in Niles, MI. He apparently insulted her. Didn't say if she learned technique from Howard.

—*Daily Republican*, April 5, 1902

Other

James McLaughlin–the first named wrestling champion (1870, in Detroit), held the title for seven years.

Vern Gagne–was named "Outstanding wrestler of 1952" by *Police Gazette* magazine. He competed in LaCrosse and Rochester, 1949.

The Crusher–Reginald Lisowski, raised in Milwaukee. His first match was in 1949. By 1954, he was a "barrel-chested tag team success" with his brother Stan. His wrestling cousin was "Dick the Bruiser," for fifteen to twenty years the AWA Champion Tag Team (to 1963).

"Gorgeous George"–drew only 4,197 people at Madison Square Garden in 1949. $14,000 was collected for "the show."

A Gap in My Remembrance

There's a gap in my remembrance.

Practically expected and not unusual for a seventy-year-old, one might suggest. But this remembrance feels a bit like someone suddenly took two teeth from the upper side of my mouth. Suddenly there is a physical gap. Someone created a hole in my memory, causing me to falter a bit.

As a boy I looked forward to days when I could leave school at the end of the day and walk to Grandma's house. She lived in the east end of town. I lived in the west end. Hers was a welcoming space where I could land after another day of figuring out what life was all about.

If I didn't have chores at home, I simply put one foot in front of the other and headed off down Howard Street for a couple of miles. I looked forward to some yard chores, fresh-baked bread, a game of double solitaire and maybe a nickel treat from her leather coin purse if I needed to go to the little grocery store across the alley.

Howard was a street of Rockwellian homes and safe spaces. The Lake Line bus ran up and down Howard (also known as Tenth Street) on its route from Main Street to the western fringe of town. With a wide circle around the blocks of beautiful craftsman homes and abundant churches in the western neighborhood, it reversed itself to head toward downtown and a transfer connection with the Main Line, where one could jump off and give the new driver a paper transfer coupon from the first bus, which allowed the rider to circle the East End.

I seldom rode the bus, except when I was with some "wisenheimer" buddies in the dark of a late winter afternoon. With a fresh snow, we grabbed onto the bus bumper for a free slide down the icy street on our buckled, rubber-booted overshoes. I didn't have a token for the bus.

While I was sliding down the street on my back side, the teachers college expanded. The first Minnesota State Legislature had established the Normal School in 1858, "to prepare teachers for the common schools of the state." This first tax-supported school west of the Mississippi River was created to train teachers for a new frontier.

Citizens of Winona quickly supported the school with donations of more than $7,000 in money and land in 1860. While I attended in the 1960s, it became a 1,000-student State Teachers College. Today's nearly 10,000-student, multi-level university has grown to usurp nearly twenty square blocks of former city lots, taking away portions of Howard Street—and many of my memories.

Today, I attempt to fill in the missing spaces.

What happened to Dorn's IGA store on the corner of Huff and Howard, and the gracious merchant's family who lived upstairs? Always welcoming as I stopped in for a penny candy on a summer day or on the way to Grandma's, a dormitory bulwark is in my way today. Across the street, Betty Lowther's hand-colored photos displayed in the large front window studio of her majestic house are but a fading memory. I remember their beauty as I gazed upon them with awe, having just come from my very elementary school artistic endeavors.

Where did LaVerne Fossum's house go, where I had my first up close and personal look at a 1951 Harley "knucklehead" motorcycle? Where did LaVerne go? There was a sweet shop up the street from McVey's Ice Cream Store on King Street (a block over) that vanished, a family-owned dairy on the other corner of Huff and the homes of Bonnie, Barb, Beatta, Earl Blood and Blanche Lubinski. With hundreds of others, they are all gone—families, residences, memories, fun and life.

The single household neighborhood from Huff to Main, from King to Sarnia Street was banished—in favor of high-rise dormitories, a colossal student center, a statue or two, fountains, cement walkways and a school-wide heating plant. The beautiful brick sidewalks are gone, too.

I tried to walk the path of Howard Street the other day from west to east end. Characters of my youth were absent. Mr. Nelton's booming voice of "watermelon, rutabagas, and potatoes" had echoed across the blocks as he slowly traveled the street offering his farm produce from the back of his truck. Pete, the iceman, drove his truck slowly from block to block bringing blocks of ice to homes with the "Ice" cardboard in the window. I yearned for a "zebra" five-cent ice cream cone from McVey's to eat along the way. I tried to place the missing houses on the open arcade of the college.

After my visits to Grandma's, I loved the late-afternoon walk toward home—always allowing plenty of time, so as not to hurry. Supper was at six and I wasn't about to miss it. Walking down Howard Street, I greeted the folks, smelled the blooms of spring and early summer and wafted in the smell of burning leaves at curbside in fall. A trek in winter snow was equally audacious.

Someone took away my neighborhood.

No wonder I have a feeling of missing teeth.

Chapter Eight

Hold the Torch High:
A Memorial Day Remembrance

I have a red poppy tied to the visor of my car.

The poppy's colored paper is faded and owning a bit of dust, but the meaning is as bright and clear to me as it was on the late May morning when I bought it. It travels the roads year-long with me to symbolize my remembrance and adoration of veterans, as well as treasured memories of my father—now gone for nearly fifty years.

In my childhood home, Pa and I greeted the sunrise of Decoration Day with the hanging of our carefully preserved heavy-cotton, forty-eight-star U.S. flag. There was a singular place of honor on the front porch for the flag to brighten our house, the neighborhood and our thoughts. Pa proudly wore his red paper poppy in a buttonhole of his fresh gray work shirt on that day, and shared his thoughts about the wonderful men he knew who had offered their lives for our country. He bought his poppies at the Labor Temple and explained the reverence and meaning to brothers and me.

Decoration Day was a day off from school, and the day of the big parade in which we marched. I ironed my Boy Scout shirt the night before and set it out with blue kerchief and golden slide. A large "5" on the upper arm of the shirt showed membership in Troop 5 of Madison School. Knowing that the troop would be in the company of some very special men and women who had fought for our country, I was honored to step in stride with veterans of World War II and other service times.

Mr. Peter Loughrey, one of our neighbors down the street, was one of a few remaining Spanish-American war veterans. He would be there to ride in a black, shiny open convertible preceded by an honor guard. We didn't know all the details of his war or his service, but we studied it some in school. Parents and teachers caused us to understand how much he and others had given to all of us.

Mr. Gleason, a neighbor around the corner and down the block, spent his life in a wheelchair due to the loss of his legs in World War I. He was a part of our everyday lives. Even though we were young, we understood the value he had given to each of our lives—and to our future. Seeing neighbors and relatives who had served in the more recent World War II and Korean War increased and deepened our understanding.

We understood the value of country and flag—and the recognition due to military veterans by each of us. Denigration of the flag was unheard of. Memories of service and loss were with us at every turn.

Going about the Saturday morning subscription collection on my paper route (thirty-five cents per week), I walked to the doorways of many individual homes. I came to understand the meaning of a gold star in the window—the loss of a son in World War II. Hanging a banner called a Service Flag, a blue star showed a family member in the service, with gold stars showing those who had died for their country. The banners abounded.

On this big day of late spring, with excitement brimming and early morning sunshine upon me, I was as keyed up as I was each summer with the early morning arrival of the Ringling Bros., Barnum and Bailey train on Circus Day. The assembly point on this Decoration Day Parade was very near those same railroad tracks along the Mississippi River, where we had waited at 4:00 a.m. for the arrival of the cast and animals of the "Greatest Show on Earth." Animals were unloaded and formed into a parade in the early morning hours for a slow walk to the circus site some three miles away. Many of those along the route then would be out today to honor veterans, parade participants and a very special day in America.

With a momentary chill caused by the dewy, damp morning and by the excitement at being a part of such a momentous occasion, I was at the ready with troop members for the boom of the cannon to mark the start of the parade. Each in his place, flags held high, we were ready. A police officer on his freshly-polished, tri-wheeled motorcycle led the way with shining badge, buttons and darkened visor on his official officer's hat all agleam.

The military color corps of the Legion crisply moved out at the head of the parade, with the American flag of forty-eight stars moving gently in the light morning breeze. The high school band struck up "The Star-Spangled Banner" and a chill went down my spine as contingents moved into place. In but a few moments we would be front and center in the downtown area, surrounded by thousands of proud and respectful viewers. Taking a sharp left turn on Main Street, we headed down the elm-canopied, extra-wide street that allowed for good distribution of marchers and straight lines across the formation.

Everywhere could be seen the paper red poppies on marchers and viewers alike, having been provided by VFW members on this special day. Our course was straight ahead to Lake Park, where decorated white crosses were laid out on the field used for picnics and football games on other occasions.

Central to our arrival was the band shell—a 1930s WPA project that stood glorious, gleaming and high for just such occasions. Used weekly for Wednesday evening free concerts of the Municipal Band, we were accustomed to the setting of fixed park benches in a large, semi-circular fashion around the band shell. Hundreds could be seated to enjoy the music and speakers of the day.

As the parade came to a close at the pea-gravel parking lot, we took our place as a troop on the side field to listen to the prayers, speeches, and music glorifying past veterans. Small children with flags, mothers in Sunday best and dads in Sunday suits already occupied the bench seats.

Standing around the perimeter throughout the service were veterans and current military personnel dressed in their best formal military garb. We

Boy Souts continue the tradition of marching and carrying the colors in the annual Memorial Day parade. (Photo courtesy of the author.)

knew that the pins and ribbons on their chests represented acts of courage, distinguished service, and assignments in far-off lands—known to us only through geography books and newspaper accounts in the local *Republican-Herald*.

Decoration Day was officially changed to Memorial Day in 1967. Yet today, members of the Veterans of Foreign Wars (VFW) offer poppies for a small contribution at stations throughout the community in days preceding Memorial Day. The poppies are harder to find in the suburban environments of today, but the paper reminders are there—in original form.

I was fortunate to buy my recent remembrance from a grizzled veteran and his wife at the entrance to a country flea market. I exchanged greetings and thanked them for upholding the tradition of remembrance.

The poppy's significance to Memorial Day is a result of Lieutenant Colonel John McCrae's poem "In Flanders Fields," which is reproduced here.

> In Flanders fields the poppies blow
> Between the crosses, row on row,
> That mark our place; and in the sky
> The larks, still bravely singing, fly
> Scarce heard amid the guns below.
>
> We are the Dead. Short days ago
> We lived, felt dawn, saw sunset glow,
> Loved, and were loved, and now we lie
> In Flanders fields.
>
> Take up our quarrel with the foe:
> To you from failing hands we throw
> The torch; be yours to hold it high.
> If ye break faith with us who die
> We shall not sleep, though poppies grow
>
> In Flanders Fields.
>
> May 15, 1915.

The sound of military marches rang in our ears as the ceremony came to a close.

A solemn and tender moment occurred as ladies of the legion auxiliary, wives and mothers placed flowers on each of the white crosses in the field. As final remembrance of the sons and husbands who would not return again to the beauty of our community, circular bouquets of flowers were placed offshore on the adjacent lake.

With a final twenty-one-gun salute rattling our bones and souls, the memorial was complete. We soon returned to homes, gardens, school, work and daily routine having been challenged to remember, to make a better world for one another, and to hold the torch high. We were now free—in so many ways—to carry on life and growth in our small river town.

Beer, Bowling and Fun

In 1950 in Winona:

We could grab a bottle of **"Zip" Cola**, **Coca-Cola**, **Pepsi-Cola** or **Seven-Up** for five or eight cents per bottle (depending upon size) to enjoy a refreshing break during the day. Pop machines were around every corner. Just outside the door at the **Capitol Bait Shop** and inside the **Owl Motor Company** at a-nickel-a-throw, a one-armed machine spit out a bottle, with the expectation that you would return the empty bottle to the case next to the machine.

In **Ben Wera's Grocery**, at **Vick's Grocery** on East Seventh and many small grocery stores and food shops throughout our small, industrious city, water-cooled bottles awaited us just inside the door—in either a **Coca-Cola** or **Seven-Up** cooler.

If we wanted, we could grab a case or a "picnic" (a half-gallon bottle) of bottled beer (no cans) at the **Hal-Rod Beer Depot** on Huff Street—or at one of the forty bars in Winona. **Ole's Tavern**, **Poot's Tavern**, **The Sportsman's Tap**, **Jack's Place**, **Arnie's Bar**, **Vic's Bar**, **The Main Tavern**, **The Friendly Bar**, **Swede's Bar** of West Fourth and **Ralph's Flame Room** were but a few of the many names emblazoned on the backs of colorful bowling shirts in Winona in the early 1950s.

The bowlers (in men's and women's leagues) were spread across the city for seemingly every-night bowling—although Sunday was usually family night at the alleys. Teams took a well-deserved night off.

These avid keglers were found at the "East End" Winona Athletic Club Lanes, the St. Martin's Lutheran Church Lanes on Broadway, Hal-Rod Lanes

All names listed in bold type are names of Winona bowling teams of the late 1940s and early 1950s—a selected few of the many.

on West Fourth, Red Men's Club Lanes on Franklin Street and Kegler's Club Lanes over the Hurry Back Pool Parlor on West Third.

We gained real sustenance for our days (and bowling nights) from **Potosi Beer**, **Hamm's Beer**, **Bub's Beer**, **Schmidt City Club** (Beer), **Grain Belt Beer**, **Fountain Brew**, **Peerless Beer**, and (Heileman's) **Old Style Lager**. When combined with **Pepin Pickles**, **Mahlke's Bakery** rye bread and **Safranek's Meats** or **Scandian Sausage**, we were fully charged for a night of action.

Boston Bakery's French bread and homemade beans, **Mahlke's Do-Nuts** and the glass-bottled fresh milk from **Springdale Dairy**, **Marigold Dairies** and **Winona Milk Company** helped us care for our bone and growth development—all topped off with **Love It Ice Cream**.

In between bowling nights, we could stop at **Mickey's Diner** or the **Kit Kat Café** for a breakfast or a noon lunch or enjoy an after-work stop at **Sloppy Joe's**. If we wanted to, we could meet with the **Odd Fellows**, the **Dream Girls**, the **Cozy Cornerettes**, **Elks Fawns** or **Elks Does** after lunch, or go to the second floor of the Post Office on Main to get guidance from the **Marine Corps**. We might even be able to find the **Six Merchants** to gain counsel.

Tired of walking, we could venture down to **Red Goose Shoes** for a new pair of shoes, then to **"Nash's Flashes"** at Nash's Clothing Store and get fitted for our new bowling shirt. Or we could go through the alley or around the corner on Third to the equally marvelous **Nevilles's Clothing Store** for a Hart, Schaffner and Marx suit provided by Emil—quality salesman, bowler and star shortstop of the Winona Chiefs baseball team.

We could also find Mr. Enstad at **Enstad's Nash** on Mankato Avenue, ready to provide us with a new or used car. If more to our liking, we could see Mr. Vater at **Studebaker Sales** downtown on Fourth Street for a new Studebaker Commander, or venture off on Fifth Street to see Mr. Seifert at **Seifert-Baldwin** for a new DeSoto. As a "spif" to our new car purchase, Mr. Mosiman on West Fifth would fill our tank on behalf of the **Texaco Fire Chiefs**.

Our jobs were at **Peerless Chain**, the **Winona Plumbing Company**, **East End Coal**, **Swift's Meats**, **Boland Manufacturing**, **Great Heart Coal**, Winona **Cleaning Works**, **Winona Tool Company**, **Neville's**, **Winona Transit** (Bus) and a myriad of non-sponsoring small industries of the sixty-five in our city. If we happened to be in the baking or delivery business for Federal (Sunbeam) Bakery, we could roll for either the **Sunbeam Bread** or **Sunbeam Cakes** team.

Bowlers celebrated the good life of bowling and life in Winona after a 600 series with a burger and fried onions at the **Kewpee Lunch**, or at the kitty-corner **Kewpee Annex**. A big night out for dinner took us upriver to **Wally's** of Fountain City, to the regionally-acclaimed **Hot Fish Shop**, or possibly to **Shorty's**, across from the Milwaukee Railroad Depot.

The "mister" topped it all off with a Winona-made **Manual Cigar**. He might even take "the little lady" on a visit to **Home Furniture** for that special table she wanted for the entryway, or make a stop at **Cichanowskj's Jewelry** on Mankato Avenue for a ruby or a bauble.

Ultimately, we could settle the day by planning for our retirement away from bowling with a visit to **Peterson's Monuments**. At their outdoor show room on West Third Street we could create a personally-designed gravestone—with team name and etched graphic of flying bowling ball and pins—to capture a "strike" for eternity.

Beer, Bowling and Fun Revisited: The First Fifty Years

*I*t is believed that King Henry VIII bowled using cannon balls. Henry VIII also famously banned bowling for all but the upper classes, because so many workingmen and soldiers were neglecting their trades.

—Wikipedia, 2012

In the first half of the twentieth century in Winona, every roll and resultant crash of bowling ball and pins (boom or bust) was reset by human hands. Impossible to imagine! Who would have returned Henry's balls?

Resetting pins on two alternate sixty-foot alleys at the same time, a small teenage boy tucked himself up in the back end of the alleyway—taking quick turns at grabbing and stacking. Pins were flying as the setter ducked back into his niche. As we stood below in the alley near the back door of the Hurry Back Pool Hall, we could hear a constant rumble of thunder above our heads. We knew the setter was earning another dime at **Kegler's Klub**.

Kegler's, one of Winona's many bowling alleys, was loaded with bowlers playing the Kegel game (from the German nine-pin game of *kegeln*) nearly every night. The first lanes—**City**, **Exchange Club Lanes** and **Philharmonic Alleys**—were in use for teams in 1902, with teams including Wacht am

*A few months after my story "Beer, Bowling and Fun," I ran the article "Beer, Bowling and Fun Revisited—The First Fifty Years." It was fun to research and compose a story of Winona fully based upon bowling team names. I loved the richness of team names and the history of places and people in Winona. I felt their action over the years through stories, friendships, and the personal experience of bowling for "beer frames." This was my second stab at Winona's history of the popular game. In this chapter, each name in bold is a bowling team or a bowling alley.

Rhein Club and the Voerwaerts. The Minneapolis Palace bowlers defeated an Arlington Club team one Sunday afternoon at the Philharmonic in 1903.

The first standardized rules for pins had been established in 1895, in New York City. Following those rules, a new, cooperative bowling alley and league was opened in Winona in 1904. With contention from Pythian Hall, **Arlington Alleys** took off into the new century—with "Mayor Brown to Roll the First Ball." It was announced that the "Alleys Are Perfect" as bowlers entered their new home. Paul Lang rolled a new record 258 that year.

Fifty years later, I rolled my first ball—and was hooked. I wasn't alone. A few had preceded me. Primitive forms of bowling date back to Ancient Egypt and the Roman Empire. Indeed, about 2,000 years ago a similar game evolved between Roman legionaries: It entailed tossing stone objects as close as possible to other stone objects (this game became popular with Roman soldiers, and eventually evolved into Italian Bocce ball, or outdoor bowling.)

The Bunch of **West Enders** joined the **Rubes**, **Mallards**, **Haymakers** and **Cadillacs** in the City League of 1912. Playing with them, **Gate City Laundry** cleaned things up at the Arlington. Graves drove his **Cadillacs** with a high score of 535.

The American Bowling Congress held its annual tournament the same year in Cleveland, with "Any Club Able to Bowl." By 1917, the Northern Bowling Tournament was held at Duluth.

Alleys in Winona were soon abundant. **Gate City Bowling Alleys** (later to be **Kegler's Klub**) was showing action upstairs (over the Hurry Back) at 103-105 West Third Street. Ed Steffes and Frank Hamernik led the **Fulton Stars** in the 1910 IBA tourney in St. Paul. Otto Biltgen and Ed Steffes each rolled a 594 in 1914. The trio became recognized leaders of Winona bowling in 1917, with Steffes as president, Hamernik as secretary and Biltgen as treasurer of the Winona Bowling League.

Frank Hamernik started **Gate City** in 1912, selling out to Louis Biltgen, a Sugar Loaf grocer, in 1920. With eight lanes and seventy-six organized bowling teams, it had "the best bowlers in the city" in 1920. Otto spent his life bowling, listed as proprietor of **Gate City** in 1941, soon to be **Kegler's Klub**.

One event that is still remembered today occurred in 1918. One Saturday night at the **Gate City Alleys**, J.M. Frantel showed "an unusual bowling feat" that "was the object of considerable comment "when he challenged and beat Clem Erpelding. He beat Clem bowling left-handed (versus his normal right), scoring a series high 168 to boot."

Ah, for the life and challenges of a Saturday night of 1918!

The Red Men's Club on Fourth and Franklin had a popular set of maples. Team names were creative—and intriguing. In addition to many named after workplaces, local products, gathering places and refreshments, the 1919 league recognized its heritage with the **Pokegames, Mesabas, Wenonahs, Mohawks, Wacoutas, Whiteclouds, Wanetas, Winnebagos, Mineolas, Chippewas, War Eagles,** and **Minnewakans**—all assembled in one league.

One newspaper of the day reported that, "The Improved Order of Red Men's is based upon Revolutionary War concepts of Freedom and Liberty—having tribes in forty-six states by the 1920s." "Patterned after early Native Americans," Wenonah Tribe No. 20 is alive and well today, with meetings held on each third Thursday only a few blocks from their original home.

The 1921 Motorist League of Red Men highlighted some of the autos of the era—**Lincoln, Studebaker, Olds, Nash, Chevrolet, Dodge, Essex,** and **Star.** The **Hudson, Moon, Paige,** and **Jewett** cars were relegated to the Tourist League.

"The Maples Got Rough Treatment" at the Red Men's in the hosted City Bowling Tournament of 1921. Frank Hamernik won with a massive 633! As part of the **Leicht Press** team, Ed Steffes and Hamernik won the 1919 LaCrosse tournament in doubles. The **Hamernik Specials** and **Leicht Press,** "Winona's crack bowling teams," were at the IBA (International Bowling Association) tourney in 1919, as well.

A formidable duo, they led "twenty crack bowlers" to the ABC (American Bowling Congress) Tournament in Milwaukee in 1923, with a special coach provided on the C & NW (Chicago and Northwestern) Railroad for team superstars—leaving at 11:05 a.m. In 1929, three teams (**Leicht Press, Foss Chocolate** and **Whit's Market**) went to the IBA in Minneapolis, led by Hamernik and Steffes. The pair stayed home in 1927, to win the Fountain City tournament as doubles champs.

The Cities League of that year contained Winona bowlers who affiliated themselves with **Long Prairie, Winona, Rochester, Moorhead, Duluth, Eveleth, Lake City, Hibbing, St. Paul** and **Red Wing** teams, obviously recognizing hometowns.

The **Athletic Club** on Mankato Avenue "toppled the maples" in the 1920s and well beyond. Their 1925 tournament featured over 100 teams, of which Al Grabowski led with a 633. Vince Breza of **Nelson Tire** led all bowlers in 1929 with a 192 average.

Alphabetically, a few of the teams who called AC home were: **Bambanek Hardware**, **Winona Boiler Co.**, **Bob's Bar**, **Botsford Lumber**, **Buffalo City Resort**, **Cichanowski Bros.**, **Cities Service**, **Winona Coal**, **East End Drugs**, **Federal Prize Winner Breads**, **Flame Room**, **General Cord Tires**, **Goodyear Tires**, **Griesel Loans**, **Haddad's Cleaners**, **Hirsch Clothiers**, **Leaf's Laundry**, **Leicht Press**, **Miller's Market**, **Winona Milk Co.**, **Morgan's Diamonds**, **Nelson Tire**, **Olson Plumbers**, **Peerless Beer**, **Riteway Carpet** (Bud Berger had a 224), **Safranek Meats**, **Schaffer's Cleaners**, **Standard Lumber**, **Swift's Premiums**, **Toye Plumbers**, **Wieczorek's Market** and **Wingold Flour**.

Also found in the alleys were some of my favorites: **Slim's Specials**, **Red Oak Lunch**, **Manuel Cigars**, **Pussy Willow Inn**, the **Queen Specials**, **Sunshines**, **Unknowns**, **Cherrey's Peanuts** and the **Fox Bushy Tails**. Who *were* these people?

The "pin boys" even got into action with their own two-team league at AC, with the **Giants** and **Yanks** taking on one another. Remodeling the alleys in 1941, AC added fluorescent lights for better "spotting."

Later, **Hal-Rod Lanes** at West Third Street and Wilson was built and named after two Biltgen sons, Harold and Roger. Hal lived upstairs, content to hear the sounds of pins flying night and day. They sponsored the VFW League and Tournament in 1948 and 1950. The World War II veterans' teams included the **Jeeps**, **Doughboys**, **Quartermasters**, **Cookies**, **Bombers**, **Gee Whizzes**, **Gunners**, **Torpedoes**, **Seabees**, **K.P.s**, **Rockets** and **Pom Poms**.

Pom Poms or not, nineteen ladies' teams were featured as early as 1924, with some being the **Knickers**, **Gate City Six**, **Best Ever**, **Let's Go**, **The Fashion**, **H. Choate and Co.**, **Williams Cloak Co.**, **Lucky Strikes**, **Grand Union Tea**, **The Orphans**, and **R.D. Cone Co.** In 1926, the **Best Evers** were in the lead. At the Gate City Lanes in 1928, the "**Bloedow Bakers** Lead Women's Loop," according to one report.

The bakers beat out **Marty's Smart Shop**, **Great Six Overalls**, **Hurry Backs**, **Boston Bakery** and the **Voss Brothers**. Due to increasing popularity of women in bowling in the early 1940s, the Keglerettes formed a second league at **Kegler's Klub**.

Isabelle O'Brien demonstrated her Irish charm at Hal-Rod by rolling a 634 for **Main Tavern** in 1948. **Choate's** was the place for ladies' bowling dresses and bowling team shirts, with Irene Pozanc no doubt well-dressed for her 299 game in 1952.

By 1954, the women of the **Athletic Club** shone across their glimmering alleys, with Gertrude Suchomel of **Main Tavern** rolling a 244 (the singles highest) and Irene Gostomski displaying a **Morgan's Diamond** with her 608 the same night. My aunt, Olga Stever, was a stellar team member to Irene, and a presence in bowling across the years. Gusta Guden sparkled in leading St. **Martin's** women with a 153 average in 1953.

Winona Railway Clerks (Milwaukee Road) traveled to St. Paul in 1915 to beat their fellows, and celebrated afterwards with a banquet. The C & NW League had their **Black Hills Express Team** winning the "loving cup" at the **Gate City Alleys** championship. Sixty men were present for the banquet at the Arcade Restaurant. Ticketing agents had their own railroad league in place at **St. Martin's Bowling Alleys** in 1936, preceded by the Annual Sauerkraut Dinner. Those railroaders sure loved to eat!

The men of Winona had taken to bowling in a serious way with league activity virtually every day of the week—causing them to become more healthy with every frame, according to Logan Clendenning, M.D., noted authority in "Diet and Health" column in the *Republican-Herald*. Clendenning supported their activity in 1940, when he offered, "Bowling is a healthy sport. It is splendid exercise, cultivates coordination, reduces fat people and increases thin."

Sundays were open bowling for families and individuals wanting to "tune-up" for their weeknight leagues from September to May.

A bowling league was organized at the **Eagles Club** in 1933. Six teams, led by Gil Mason's **Newberry Night Club**, scored "in the money" at the Eagles Tournament in LaCrosse in 1942. Oren Turner had a 583.

In 1939, four Red Men teams participated in the Red Men state tournament in Minneapolis, hosted by Chippewa Tribe No. 20. Well-known Red Men bowlers Fred Fakler, Roy Wilgrube, Ray Zywicki, Carl Dielke, Leo Olson and Harry Kowalczyk led the charge. They enjoyed a steak dinner before the roll-off, with a herring lunch afterward.

Led by Howard Clark, insurance owner extraordinaire, a bowlers' German Band of Winona marched extemporaneously and "paraded majestically" through the streets of St. Paul as part of the ABC National Tournament in 1941.

As exciting as the arrival of the annual train bringing Barnum and Bailey's "Greatest Show on Earth" to Winona, a circus of bowling combined with a massive American railway system to move eighty Winona teams—including five hundred bowlers and guests—to the "World Series of Bowling." It was "the first time west of Chicago" for the Holy Grail of bowlers—the place to be and be seen. *Oom-Pa-Pa!*

Some teams of the 1940s included: **All-Sweet, Al's Café, Biltrite Soles and Heels Blue Blazers, Bub's All-American, Coast to Coast, Coca-Cola, Congress Café, Edstrom Studios, Federal Cakes, Hurry Back Billiards, Jack Spratt Foods, Jockey Club, Kalmes Tires, Kewpee Lunch, Left Handers, Main Tavern, Mahlke Bakers, Mankato Bar, Merchants Bank, Millerpax, Neeck's Bar, Neville's, Niggle's Café, The Oaks, Old Style Lager, Peerless Chain, Pepsi-Cola, Poot's Tavern, Rochester Dairy, Schaffer Cleaners, Sinclair Oils, Stevenson Coal, Sugar Loaf Tavern, Sunshine Café, Ted Maier Drugs, Vic's Bar, Western Koal Kids, Winona Flying Service, Winona Motors, Winona Transit** and **Zip Bottling Co.**

"The papa" of bowling came to Winona, in the form of Andy Varipapa, in March of 1940. Brooklyn bowler and world record holder in exhibition bowling, he came to challenge O.F. Koetz (the only 300 bowler in Winona league play), Leo Kemp, who was reportedly an "outstanding bowler," and Mark Kolter, who had beat Andy a couple of years ago. The halls were filled for free bowling lessons by Andy on Thursday and the following evening's exciting exhibition games and trick shots at **Kegler's Klub**.

Wow, What a thrill—the "papa" in Winona.

The 1949 City Tournament brought 188 of the 226 eligible men's teams into action at **Hal-Rod** in an attempt to beat Loren Walski's 697 of the previous year. In 1952, Rich Bell topped male bowlers with a 761 series—and headed off to California.

It wasn't the cost of bowling that drove him away. Bowling cost thirty-nine cents per game in 1951. He probably bought new shoes for travel at the OutDor Store on East Third before leaving. Oxfords for bowling were five dollars and ninety-five cents, a new bowling ball bag only four dollars and ninety-five cents (the same price at Arenz Shoes in 1941)—yet women's shoes were only two dollars and forty-eight cents. Used balls were available at Kegler's for eight dollars.

By 1951, the highest recorded Winona score was 768 by Jess Scott at the Athletic Club Lanes in 1935. Carl Breitlow rolled his 300 game at St. Martin's in 1951. In the 1940s, a 300 game occurred once every 175,000 games. With improved technology of balls and alleys, 300 games are becoming an everyday occurrence today.

Bell probably got the urge for travel after rolling in the ABC Tournament of 1951, when chartered Greyhound buses took seventy-three teams from Winona to world action—again in St. Paul. Some who were there included **EB's**

Corner, Dutchmen's Corner, Jack's Place, Swede's Bar, Blanche's Tavern, Sunshine Café, Fountain Brew, Scandia Sausage, Marigold Dairy, Vater's Shell Oil, Sunbeam Cakes, Winona Heaters, Behrens Manufacturing and **Nash's Flashes.**

In 1953, a sedate league of lady bowlers included **Happy Dan's Skelly Girls, Winona Rug Cleaning, Siebrecht's Roses, Lincoln Insurance, Winona Printing Company** and **Winona Insurance Agency.**

Chuck Trubl, Jr. was a noted bowler of the early 1950s, rolling a 617 in 1948, and a 624 in 1954. (Trubl, Sr. had a 486 in 1918, in a LaCrosse tournament featuring **Schellhas Brewing, Conrad Furs, Park Brewing**—and Otto Biltgen's 631!)

The names sparkle across the alleys and the years. We saw Carl Breitlow's 300 game in the 1930s, applauded John Chapman, AC manager, in his domination of the state tourney in 1938, with an 880 (four-game scratch), thrilled with Irene Pozanc's 299, marveled at techniques of George Vondrashek, Andy Kuklinski, Bud Breza, Rudy Edel and hundreds of others in the 1940s, who boarded the bowling train.

Chuck Kubicek and Chuck Trubl, Jr. of the 1950s, and Gordy Fakler and Jerry Dureske of the 1960s, were but a few who consistently hammered the pins. Hundreds of others created flying pins over the years that shook our senses and thrilled our Thursdays. Jerry had a 709 in 1967, and an average of 196. *Ka-boom!* What fun!

Today, bowling is enjoyed by ninety-five million people in more than ninety countries worldwide and continues to grow through entertainment media such as video games for home consoles and handheld Wii devices. A friend interviewed for this story reported a league of 250 winter Wii bowlers at their abode in Florida.

In our "fun times" of Winona bowling and golf, we continue to shoot for a better average score (one higher, one lower). It's our nature. Setting the standard for bowling, Walter Ray Williams, Jr., male professional Bowler of the Decade (2000-2009), gave us something to shoot for.

With his "cool and confident demeanor," this math and physics major from California found the formula to "over eighty" 300 games, seven PBA Player-of the Year awards and forty-seven career PBA Tour titles. His established PBA average of 226.34 is the second-highest ever. As an aside, Walt's a nine-time world champion in horseshoes.

The alleyways of AC still have a shine on their floor—albeit limited activity. Kegler's closed in the 1960s, with Red Men's going out in flames in

1967. **Hal-Rod** (as **Maple Leaf Lanes**) operated until a major fire burned the pins and everything else in 1990.

Winona's bowling lanes of today are "a formidable duo."

The **Winona Bowl** has sixteen lanes built in 1977 on Cottonwood Drive. It features league bowling "every night of the week," according to owner/manager Brian Fakler, son of Gordy. With over seventy teams competing in evening leagues and plenty of weekend junior league activity, bowling is alive and well.

Westgate Bowl has sixteen lanes at its hillside location. Operating since 1961, bowlers have made many league bowling memories over fifty years. Jerry Dureske helped to bring a shine to Westgate's opening with a 299 in 1961. Original owner Carol Gartner reports today that it took eight years before they had their first 300-game—by Vic Shewe on December 26, 1968. With double evening shifts, a coffee league and Sunday night bowling, the hardwoods rattled—and lasted.

Westgate reports healthy league action five nights per week, with bowlers appearing to challenge the 300-game with regularity. As a "futuristic" offering to open bowlers, Westgate offers Brunswick's "Cosmic Bowling"—a surround sound light show offering a "glow-in-the-dark bowling lanes" experience.

In my Lakeville neighborhood today, I find a **Brunswick Zone** that offers thirty-eight lanes of bowling, billiards, a "gamezone" arcade, bar, grill and rental shoes (for three dollars and sixty-nine cents, versus the thin dime of my teenage years.) Bowling is two dollars and ninety-nine cents before 5:00p.m., three dollars and ninety-nine cents thereafter. It's fun to visit.

Absent are the remembered cat-calls, camaraderie and alley-wide cheers of bowlers across an eight-lane **Kegler's Klub** or **Hal-Rod Lanes**. I can still hear the voices, see the colorful bowling shirts and resonate with bowling "*ka-booms*" of all the Franks, Buds, Carls and Gertrudes. They set the pins to flying—and made for the lively history of Winona bowling. King Henry's cannon balls may have started it all, but today's lighter and faster bowling balls still shake the pins.

They cause the "thunder from above" at today's re-incarnated **Kegler's Klubs**—to thrill another generation of bowlers.

Kent Stever bowled on the St. Clair's Bowling Team of the early 1960s. In the search of over 1,000 newspaper stories for this report, his scores didn't make the news.

A Conversation with Pa

Following a lifetime pattern, I shared some few quiet words with him—thanking him for guidance, care, comprehension, and concern.

It's hard to imagine that I spent all the years growing up with my father and yet today have little remembrance of conversation with him. There must have been moments. But they all seem to revolve around snippets and snatches of a few words here and there.

A large, red-faced man, he resembled the meanest outlaw ever seen in the Saturday afternoon movies, with nothing delicate about him save for his sparkling blue eyes and the friendly smile that occasionally broke through. His face was coarse as sandpaper. Large, bushy eyebrows dominated his forehead. At six-foot-two and 210 pounds of muscle, he usually dressed in gray, workingman shirt and pants.

On his oversized, overworked hands were most often a pair of leather gloves that were white-crusted from a day's work of sweat and cement. His extra-large brass-buckled Big Mac bib overalls had seen days of use. Boots with leather laces were large and similarly encrusted with cement dust, giving evidence of his days of construction labor. He seldom wore short sleeves, but could be seen on Saturday nights in suit, white shirt and tie as he set off to the Labor Temple for a night of cards and friendship.

He was our Pa. We understood what that meant. He set the rules (once) and didn't need to clarify them. With our mother's passing at an early age, my brothers, sister and I (six total, ages two to thirteen at the time) internalized those expectations and performed accordingly. It was simple—trust, respect, decent behavior, and hard work, with no excuses. Conversation was limited.

He wasn't there to be our "friend." He didn't take us to ball games or events or entertain us. He was there every night with supper at six.

We understood. We even understood when he didn't go to our graduations, or to school for any issues, awards or problems. We simply solved those issues ourselves and understood who we were to become.

Each day we would rise in the morning and head off to school on our own. In summer days of vacation from school, we found our way out of bed, dressed and headed out the door for adventure in the shed or with buddies in the neighborhood. If Pa was working, then we were alone in the house to get ourselves up and dressed and out the door. If he was laid off in the cold days of winter, he roused us for school with a holler up the stairs.

"Hey! It's time to get moving."

There might even be a word or two to engage us more quickly when he added, "There's snow out there." The possibility of earning fifty cents before school for shoveling a neighbor's walk got the heart pumping. With a splash of cold water on my face, I was "up and at 'em"—another term he frequently used. I headed for my snow shovel and the early morning dark.

When I headed out on the bread route at age ten as a rider/assistant or later on as a milk route rider/assistant and then driver (at age fifteen), he used his "Hey!" at the foot of the stairs as my alarm clock by 4:30 a.m. Dressed for the day's chores, I offered a quick greeting to him as he sat at the kitchen table with his coffee. If I were headed off to the woods or trails for a day's adventure or to a weekend Boy Scout campout, I told him where I was going and when I would be back. Our conversations would go something like this:

"We're going up to Witoka and Wilson on a bike ride. Isn't there an old road that goes up Pleasant Valley toward the top of the hill?"

"If you go out past the cemetery at the bottom of the hill and then head off to the east about a half mile, you can see the cement of the old road. You can cut around the fence posts that are there. The road may be overgrown with weeds and branches, but I think you can find your way up to the first ridge. From there, it connects back to the main road up the hill to Witoka. Witoka's about seven miles, Wilson three miles more, and then you can cut down from the ridge through Gilmore Valley and come out behind St. Mary's College. Be careful coming down the hill. It's long and steep."

"Thanks, Pa."

My part in conversation was as limited as his—just get the direction and then head off into the day. Working all day in the shed or cleaning up the backyard, I was always pleased to show him my accomplishments when he drove his 1936 Chevrolet into the yard at the end of his long day of labor at the construction site. As the first to greet him, I gained the leavings in his metal lunchbox—always a half-sandwich or a single snowball or a bite of pie that he somehow wasn't able to eat.

"Thanks, Pa."

Then off to the shed or yard for his inspection and a "Good job!"

As he headed toward the back door, he said, "I moved up to 'mud mixer' for the bricklayers at the teachers' college today. I get ten cents more each hour for being the mixer. Now I'm at two dollars and twelve cents per hour. Better get supper started."

As centerpiece of our well-worn and clean kitchen, the porcelain-faced, cast iron wood/gas combination range invited attention. It was a beacon of warmth in the center of the worn linoleum-covered floor. To the left, on the backdoor side of the room, were hung his bib overalls, jacket, workman's hat adorned with chauffeur's badges and AFL-CIO union pins—all next to his World War II air-raid warden billy club hanging on its leather strop.

To his right, as he fried pork chops or turned buckwheat pancakes, stood the wooden Hoosier cabinet containing all the essentials of cooking. It faced a large kitchen sink with a single cold-water spigot. A wooden icebox and large wood table with seven chairs completed the furnishings in the neat, usable room.

My conversation at age sixteen was most often at the kitchen table. When I returned from one of my football or basketball trips to another city, I was dropped off at the high school by the bus, "Big Bertha," at 11:30 p.m. I headed for home in my first car, a 1950 Nash "bathtub." Home games were held at Jefferson Field or away in our Big Nine Conference.

When we traveled, I was always late getting home, but Pa would always be up—seated at the kitchen table with his coffee cup and Raleigh cigarettes. Even though he never attended a game, I found out in later years that he and some of his mates at "The Hub," a neighborhood bar, listened in to the play-by-play on local radio station KWNO.

"Did you have a good game?"

"I was okay. We lost thirteen to seven. We almost tied it in the last few minutes. Roy had a heck of a run that brought us down to about the fifteen, but we fumbled on third down and Faribault recovered. I had my hand on it for a second, but couldn't hang on."

"I'm sure you did a good job and tried hard. That's all that matters."

"I handled my guy pretty well. He was pretty heavy—but soft. Harders and I teamed up a couple of times on him and made a good hole for Roy. We had some pretty good gains. I even got in on a couple of tackles tonight. Usually I play offense only, but Liver got whacked on one play and I played defense for a while."

Pa knew all the guys, since they often came by the house and played nickel-dime poker in the kitchen. They knew him as Otto and called him the same. He was well-accepted by the guys and occasionally sat in for a few hands. They were comfortable with him and kidded him. Parents were an accepted part of our routine as we visited back and forth.

Some of the parents were a part of our lives and were more welcoming than others. Others were aloof or not included, by their choice or ours. At Otto's table there was a comfort and friendliness that made me proud.

He was always there. In the raucous 1930s and throughout life, he was involved as union leader for drivers and tradesmen. His World War II air raid warden block duties were recognized in the city, as was his union leadership. Work as a truck driver and construction laborer kept him busy and fully employed through the warm months. In his truck driving days, his usual work outfit was gray work shirt and pants, with chauffeur's hat. Later, in construction work, he added the layer of bib overalls as he went off to work with his black metal lunch box containing coffee, lunch and the ever-present salt pills for extremely hot days.

He was worn out by age fifty-nine, with a stroke immobilizing him. For several days, he lay without word or conversation in his hospital bed. Following a lifetime pattern, I shared some few quiet words with him—thanking him for guidance, care, comprehension, and concern.

Excepting the use of a few more words of conversation with my own kids, I am proud to follow his lead.

At Day's End
A Dedication to Otto

Dressed in workingman gray, he shed the encrusted coveralls.
Brass buckles showed bright contrast to ground-in cement
Made hard by the sweat of day.
Kitchen hook held them at the ready for another dawn.
Concrete dust covered gnarled hands.
Day was ended.

Lunch bucket unopened, a treasure to find,
Pocket watch on leather twist took its place
Near choppers in the water glass.
A quick rinse by the single kitchen spigot gave a semblance
    of indoors to a rugged face.

Deft hands transformed potatoes into chunks for boiling.
With a "whoosh" heard throughout; gas stove ignited.
Another's evening meal set to frying, chops for seven,
    beets in tin bowl,
Potatoes and gravy, enough for all.

A cold beer now. Supper at six—always.
Greet the kids, directed homework.
The twilight of eve was his.
Folded newspaper on request.
No question this.

October, 1982

Chapter Nine

Early Morning

Glowing cigarette in hand, the driver of the very large truck negotiated the roadways through the hills of Southern Minnesota on his pre-dawn journey. Before sunrise, Harold and I had covered miles of deep valleys, hardwood forest and curving farm fields cut away from the river's edge.

Small trout-filled streams gave way to hills and ridges in our steady, slow uphill climb. Farms were spread across the ridge for miles, with fresh-cut hay, alfalfa or just-picked corn—all in their season.

As we had done a hundred times, we were on our way toward distant farm customers at 4:30 a.m. with a truckload of empty, gleaming and galvanized six-gallon milk cans. As a lean and strapping twelve-year-old assistant, I had loaded them, steam-cleaned and hot, at the creamery the previous day. With the load enclosed in a double-decked, oversized truck box with doors on sides and rear, we began our day's work.

We passed through Hart for a first stop at "Leapin' Lena's" farm just off Highway 43 for milk pickup and some raucous, early morning banter on her family's 100-year-old farm. After a hoot with Lena, we continued on to Wilson and Money Creek and Houston and Hokah to soon make our way to Spring Grove, a small town of Swedish-Lutherans some fifty miles distant.

By 6:00 a.m., as the first customers of the day at the local, just-opened bakery, we shared a quick stop and a friendly greeting with the proprietor to hustle out the door to our farm stops. In the cozy cab of the truck, Harold shared his Thermos jug of coffee and the still-warm donuts—our breakfast and sensory delight.

Traversing the hills and valleys daily from spring through winter, Harold would gather his full load of farm-fresh milk and deliver it by noon to the creamery at Altura—the end of his circuitous route. I was fortunate to be his summer assistant and semi-occasional weekend rider during the year, building my muscles with every toss of the eighty-pound cans.

We listened to the AM radio station out of LaCrosse ("Katy at 580") to be updated on news and weather, commodity prices and jolly offerings of real country music—ranging from old-time polkas to the nasal twang and melodious sounds of Hank Snow.

Even though we had traveled the route many times, we were always filled with excitement and anticipation of another great day with one another—and with the special welcome of each farmer to his milk-house or barn. We were warmed in their barns by the body heat of cows in stanchions waiting their turn to contribute to the supply of milk becoming whole milk and cream and cheese and ice cream that sustained the population of our area.

Passing Yucatan, a country crossroads, we delighted in sighting a deer in the headlights of our new 1950s Dodge truck. It was a truck in which we both took pride and comfort. The well-tuned heater gently pushed away the early morning chill—soon to be replaced by the warmth of sunlight. As the rising sun shone over the well-polished hood, the chrome Ram hood ornament was highlighted—a proud emblem of our "Job-Rated" truck, known for its strength and durability.

Each day we started fresh with our clean, freshly gassed truck—a shine retained inside and out by a quick hose-down and interior cleansing at the completion of our route and day. As a final task I so enjoyed, I was allowed to back the huge truck up to the gas pump in Harold's yard, top it off and then park it in the yard—headed out for another day's adventure.

Harold had a good business. His second truck was driven by "hired man" Bud. Bud, a neat, fit and dedicated driver, proudly wore his chauffeur's cap and button. He traveled a second route leading to the same destination. His truck was the well-maintained earlier version of the truck we drove.

Grant, a large, burly and rugged outdoorsman, drove the large firewood truck for Harold. From the farms of western Wisconsin, he gathered the winter supply of wood for Harold's secondary business of wood supply to city customers. Grant occasionally filled in as driver on the milk routes, but I seldom chose to join him.

Harold always had us in a new or nearly new truck with a leather seat that made us feel comfortable and proud as we waved to farmers in their fields and to drivers we met on the highway. All received the "v" greeting from Harold, who casually lifted his two strong, callused fingers away from the top of the large steering wheel to offer a friendly sign of greeting.

I have traversed the hills and valleys of my youth continuously in my mind. Driving off to my place of work in intervening years, I have not forgotten lessons learned from the hard work and quiet conversations with Harold.

My days started with our gleaming work tools. A computer, briefcase and fresh business suit today take the place of blue jeans, a ram-charged truck and shiny milk cans. It is my turn to have the thermos of coffee—albeit replaced by the modern coffeemaker in the corner of my office.

The radio, the scenes, the senses, the anticipation and dedication to start a day fresh with shiny tools, a donut and commitment to quality work continue. Rather than gassing up the truck at the end of the day, it seems that I was the one needing to be re-fueled for the next day.

Over fifty years have passed since I took my first ride in that milk truck and over the route through God's country. Although travels have taken me across many miles and many stops at donut shops, I seem to have come full circle to arrive back where I started. I begin each day in a remarkably similar way. I enjoy the early morning news and music, the anticipation of another sunrise and the opportunity to work hard and do well for those I serve.

The resilience of the human mind and body amaze me. How we are able to work so diligently at our tasks, sometimes for as many as sixteen hours in a day, and yet awake refreshed and ready to give even more is stunning. I am refreshed by the thoughts of the hills and valleys that God made. I travel to them when the need is there to re-fuel my mind and body.

My quiet thoughts in traveling those same hills and valleys and rivers and streams are as God would have them. I am led into His valley where I will fear no evil. At creek side on a day of trout fishing, He sustains me; He refreshes me. My mind is calm. As I travel to my workplace these days, I see the stars of morning, the beautiful moon, the buds of trees and the beauty of a snowfall. These are God's gifts, the treasures of life that guide me through the reality of my days.

By age fifteen, with my own truck and milk route, I negotiated the hills, valleys and eighty-pound milk cans on my own, to deliver my own load to the creamery. Over the years I moved similarly from beginning driver to experienced executive—often describing myself to others as "just a good truck driver."

As Harold taught me to drive that large, lumbering truck with its two-speed, multi-geared, "double-clutched" gearbox at age thirteen, I have been able to take charge of the vehicles and the roadways before me—to negotiate the most challenging situations. The strength, pride and confidence I gained through the trust Harold placed in me as helpmate and fellow truck driver was essential.

Today as I clean my garage or shine my tools of work on the computer, I come to appreciate the gleam of morning sunlight off my hood ornaments of quality work and teaching I carry to the workplace.

Harold would be pleased.

The Cab Driver

Eight! Where the hell are you?"

With a cigarette in yellow-stained fingers of his left hand and a coffee mug in the right, Shorty hollered through the mic at Driver Eight. With his two-way radio before him, he reached up and down the streets of our small town enclosed by the bluffs of the Mississippi River Valley to control movement of the several drivers on shift for Vets Cab Company.

Eugene's crackled response said, "I'm at 567 Carimona."

"I told you 467—not 567—get your ass down there," Shorty spat out with another lungful of smoke. As he spoke, the little man in charge rose up off of his pillowed wooden chair and nearly put his face through the microphone. As was his fashion, Shorty was red-faced and hollering at one or the other of his drivers.

We knew Eight to be Eugene, the semi-philosophical Korean War veteran who was working his way through the local teachers college as an English major—and currently taking Shorty with a grain of salt.

As I checked into the small office of the Vets Cab Company to start my shift at 5:30 p.m. to end thirteen hours later, I was put at ease to see Shorty at the desk, in spite of his bluster.

Like Eight, we all took Shorty's outbursts with a smile. With him at the helm, it would be a night of fun. A warm and comfortable human being about five feet in size, he enjoyed the theatrics of domination when in charge for his twelve-hour shift. His ever-present cigarette and flattened leather-brimmed cap worn year-round were his signature and stature.

The tin-and-metallic chauffeur's pins tacked to the front represented his many years of service to the people of the community. There was no need for the embroidered "Shorty" over the shirt pocket. Everyone knew who he was. Besides, as always, too many notes and paper tags stuck out of his left front shirt pocket and covered his name.

His right pocket contained the extra-long Pall Mall cigarette pack, to be emptied and exchanged for a new one every eight hours or so.

Shorty ran the shop and the drivers with his younger brother, Dave, a big old galoot who seemed to live on huge hot pork sandwiches that came through the door of Ruth's Restaurant. With a mound of catsup and a side of fries, Dave enjoyed sandwiches that we often drooled over—but the dollar-eighty-five he spent was always beyond our means.

With thirty-eight percent of fare payment and a few meager tips, we knew that a good night on our twelve-hour shift would probably produce a total of twenty dollars—already earmarked for purposes of tuition and clothes and gas money. A full meal at the new McDonald's with burger and fries and malt garnered for forty-five cents would suffice as our mid-shift treat.

Shorty and Dave shared the same chair—and kept it occupied nearly twenty-four hours a day, with short relief shifts from Eugene. When Dave was there, the pillow was off and the mood was somber. He was definitely in charge of the operation, with Shorty deferring to him in matters of business. Together they lived as bachelors in a big old house on the West End of town that they shared with their black labs Henry and George.

Dave and Shorty were competitors in championship dog trials for hunting dogs. Dog and handlers' abilities were tested in retrieving the muffs tossed into the cold, murky backwaters of the Mississippi. At Prairie Island, a slough on the west edge of town, state and regional competitions were held on Sunday afternoons throughout the fall.

In this sport for the gentry, Dave and Shorty were an anomaly. They were a couple of local guys who never hunted a day in their lives, didn't own a shotgun between them and yet continued to sweep up the medals and ribbons of this gentleman's sport—all to festoon the walls of their immaculate kennel.

"Hey, Seven! How's your noodle tonight?" Shorty greeted as I closed the door behind me. The room was only big enough to swing the door from the outside past the edge of Shorty's desk—with a similar door swinging in from the adjoining Ruth's—where Shorty garnered his endless supply of coffee (and Dave his sandwiches).

I had known Shorty and Dave a bit as a kid growing up down the block—occasionally stopping by their house on King Street to greet the dogs and throw a muff or two. Six months ago, I approached this same office to make my application as a driver. With my chauffeur's license and several years behind the wheel of large trucks and my 1953 Nash, I was a driver skilled beyond my years.

From paper routes and bike rides around town, I knew most of the street names and numbers—and the orientation of the folks we would chance to meet in the varying neighborhoods of our small town of 25,000. Shorty and Dave were well acquainted with my pa, since Pa was a neighbor and a local union official. Vets Cab was the choice of union members in the town.

Without hesitation, they took me on and gave me the basics of how to be a driver, how to approach potential customers as they arrived at the local train stations and how to demonstrate customer service and etiquette (not exactly their words).

Shorty basically modeled how we were to function, since he was both driver and dispatcher. Dave restricted himself to dispatching and handling the operations end of their successful business. Shorty was gracious, respectful and ambitious in caring for the needs of customers—from the "drunken sailors" we hauled from bar to bar to the little old ladies who had the standing 6:40 a.m. Sunday morning pickup to take them to their little Polish Catholic church for seven o'clock service.

Their appointments were usually the last run for one or the other of us coming off a thirteen-hour Saturday night shift. Although Shorty and Dave used a few harsh words across the airwaves when drivers were alone, they were extremely professional and polished when customers were present in the cabs.

They knew the difference between when the taxi was occupied by driver and customer or driver alone. It was customary to check in with our call number and destination when we picked up the rider, and also acknowledged completion and availability when the run was finished.

Shorty was a fierce competitor for riders off the trains at the three stations in town, during this heyday of railroad transportation. His pleasant smile and manner drew customers to him. Competition was not only with Shorty, but also between those of us who drove for Vets and the rival Royal Cab—an excellent company housed at the Steak Shop on Main Street. All regular calls incoming to the Vets number at 3354 were dispersed in a fair rotation to drivers, so Shorty had no advantage in that rotation—thank the Lord.

Our trips varied from moment to moment. A pickup at her home on Bierce Street of the cigar-smoking stub of a woman accompanied by her wisp of a husband who never uttered a word was a "regular." So, too, were the female telephone company operators who truly appreciated a safe ride home at midnight.

We had calls from home to bar, from train station to hotel, from bar to home. We had short runs for fifty cents and longer runs that reached several dollars.

The rides from the stations were usually better paying, since those riders were often visitors to our lovely, industrious community.

These riders seemed more attuned to the world of tips when delivered to hotels and sites within the usual fifteen-mile radius of home base. Town regulars were more inclined to use the taxis as an after-hours alternative to the city bus line that ran all day long for a ten-cent token fare—with transfer included.

We especially liked it when we snagged a visitor from the train with a destination away from the city—even an occasional run down the river to LaCrosse. A call to Shorty or Dave on the radio established the rate—we operated a standard in-town fare, but our leaders calculated longer fares, considering distance and time.

Calls would come in through the night to Shorty or Dave, with a major surge for all drivers at the "bar rush." When empty from any call, we returned to the taxi stand at the office facing Third Street—the "main drag" of our bustling downtown—where we hung out in the cabs.

The action settled down from 2:00 to 5:00 a.m.—a chance for a quiet snooze or some early-morning chats with fellow drivers. In these quiet, dark moments, Eugene was a favorite of mine, since he had great stories of his war experience to share. He also shared his continuous interest in writing of stories and poems he composed in pencil on his yellow pad on the front seat of his cab.

He satisfied both college requirements and personal interest through his writings—and encouraged me, as a neophyte, to find my way into that larger world. Like a columnist for a newspaper, Eugene kept quotes and notes of interesting people whom he met while driving his cab. Being a math major and a non-literate personality, I was less inclined to see or note those "fantastic snippets" of personality or conversation.

Rosie, the cigar smoker, was a favorite of ours. She worked hard all week in the factory on Fourth Street, converting rags and waste materials by machine into stuffing that was ultimately oil-soaked to become the "Felpak", a standard fill in connecting boxes of railroad cars.

Well-paid as a line worker, along with a hundred or so others who worked the three-shift day at the "Waste Mills," Rosie headed out with her Friday paycheck. First stop was the Eagles Club on Center Street for a few beers and probably a shot or two. After two hours or so, Rosie's call brought one of us back to the Eagles—with the grocery store as the next stop.

"Son-of-a-bitch," the well-lit Rosie exclaimed. "We get the college boy again. We want you to stay with us at the Piggly-Wiggly when we shop, help us pack our groceries and then drop the bags off at home—then we'll have some fun!"

From past experience, I knew what this meant. Rosie and Otis were off on another toot—and I was to be the paid chaperone. My job was to hold their hands as we went from store to home—and from bar to bar. I explained the standard waiting rate of four dollars per hour to Rosie. She agreed. With a call to Shorty to let him know I was on the clock and unavailable for calls, I set out with groceries, burly cigar-smoker and her mate for destinations yet to be determined.

There was the Midway Bar just across the river that was a favorite of Rosie's, "Sloppy Joe's" on East Third and the Black Horse on Homer Road. With more than 100 bars in the city and nearby small towns in the beautiful hills and valleys of southern Minnesota and nearby Wisconsin, a cashed paycheck and a designated driver, my riders were out to have "fun." I was invited into the bars, had Coke to drink in excess and hung around the parking lots—with occasional updates to Shorty on my progress or availability.

By ten o'clock, the partygoers were fortified and ready for a quiet trip home. In usual flourish, Rosie offered too big a tip—which I refused. I accepted the total fare, as well as a fair, negotiated tip from a "regular," a friend—and one who needed to be cared for by the best that Vets Cab had to offer.

"Seven! Time to wake up. Get your butt to the police station." Shorty hollered across the airwaves. He took pleasure in shocking us out of a restful slumber—knowing full well that we would be relaxing in the front seat. My rest was in the new 1959 Studebaker V-8 Champion—one of the powerful cars that were replacing the older Plymouths in our ten-car inventory.

It was a special night when I was assigned to a new car. With a bucket of soapy water, sponge, towel and quick rinse-off at curbside, I had that new car gleaming before I started my shift. If the evening were slow, I would even polish the car in bits and snatches by the street light at Third and Market, our home base.

The police station was at City Hall, a block off Center Street. Interestingly, it had a neon sign of blue indicating "Police" that hung over the alleyway entrance to the station that was used a bit throughout the day, but exclusively at night when the City Hall was locked down. The six-block jaunt from cabstand to station took but a moment.

Pulling up to the side door, I headed into the station and up the several stairs to enter the office on the right. Ever-fascinating was the padlocked wood-framed glass cabinet on the wall with the collection of firearms, hand-cuffs and robber's paraphernalia from the 1930s—when our town was "wide open" to illegal liquor, gambling, prostitution and associated illegal behaviors during Prohibition. It was alleged that the now-retired chief of police had been "on the take" during these years.

Not so fascinating or glorious was the presence of red-faced Sergeant "Bull" Tiegarden, who manned the counter. He was known to all in town as one not to mess with. He was reputed to be a specialist with his billy club—a nicely formed hardwood hand club with a leather strop that he wielded with impunity at the slightest hint of trouble.

He was feared by all, having gained a reputation of busting heads in the Labor riots of the late 1930s and 1940s, as well as in quelling Saturday night bar fights that emerged in some of the shadier bars of the East End.

"Hey, kid. What do you need?" Bull asked in typical, blunt fashion as I entered the swinging glass door. Bull and I had a nodding acquaintance, since his brother was a dump truck driver I knew from my summer day job of hauling blacktop and crushed rock to county road projects. Unlike Bull, he was a pleasant chap with a ready smile who always had a funny story or two to offer as we waited in line to unload our trucks.

"Someone called a cab." I said.

"Oh, yeah. It's pizza time. We need you to head over to Sammy's and pick out seven pizzas—five for the cells, one for the desk and one for the two guys out on patrol. Here's fifty bucks from one of our inmate's brothers who wanted to pop for the pizza, your two trips and an hour of cab waiting time.

"You figure out with Nick your best deal, pick up a couple of six-packs of Coke and whatever's left over is your tip—and you get a piece of our pizza when you get them all here."

"Sounds like a deal. Shouldn't be much more that an hour." I offered as I headed out the door.

Nick, the owner of Sammy's Pizza, and I had worked together many times in getting his greasy, delicious pizzas delivered to the dorms of the local colleges. I knew his menu, prices and his efficiency—and he knew that I hustled across town quickly to deliver his product warm and tasty.

It was a combination of a warm cab and the special twist that Nick gave to the large paper bag in which he enclosed the pizza and cardboard.

The bag was always "puffed up" about six inches on the topside before closing to keep in the heat and keep the paper off the pizza. Nick knew his stuff. And I knew that Nick would work with me to provide his best price to me.

Figuring his premier pizzas at four dollars and ninety-nine cents each, my need to pay the office for two runs and an hour of waiting time, plus the two six-packs of Coke I would get at the little grocery down the street, I figured I was on a tight budget. I explained to Nick and he shot me his best price of four dollars and twenty-five cents each. With my math major enhanced by strong skill in seventh grade math, I was easily able to calculate, meet my payments and plan for a tip of ten dollars or so—a new record for me!

Nick complied, Bull cooperated and pizzas were delivered to everyone's satisfaction. With my pizza slice oozing down my fingers, I heard Shorty holler "Seven!" on the car speaker as I returned to the cab. Pleasantly enough, he informed me that I was needed again at the Midway in Wisconsin to pick up "Bruce." Unbeknownst to me, Bruce was to become my next baby-sitting mission.

A suave dresser in his mid fifties with a tan too deep for Minnesota habitués, Bruce brought charm and style to the places he visited. He was the skilled leader of the well-regarded local company—strengthened by an eastern private-school background. As I entered the Midway, his fellow barflies listened intently as he told of his recent trip to Puerto Rico—a long way from their farms in southwestern Wisconsin.

After another "bourbon neat" for Bruce and a Coke for me, I was getting nervous and decided to check with Shorty.

"It's okay. Just hang in there and give him the rate as a reminder. He's good for it."

With his final "bump" for the road complete, we set off to his next stop, the semi-exclusive Exchange Club in the heart of downtown—an enclave for the well-to-do of the community. Bruce seemed to fit right in with the beautiful wood surroundings and the equally successful patrons, moving from table to table with the ease of Humphrey Bogart in *Casablanca*.

I was comfortable on a high leather stool at the end of the bar. With another Coke in hand—compliments of Bruce, of course—I had a ring-side seat to observe the relaxed social workings of a class of which I had no part. His smile and charm had only grown after settling in with his peers. Not to be ignored, Bruce stopped by to check on me and pleasantly rewarded me with a friendly pat on the back as he returned to the tables.

After an hour or so, he was ready to go.

We set off in the Studebaker and meandered the streets of town, with a leisurely swing down Lake Drive to enjoy the beauty of the late evening. Making small talk, Bruce told me of his ventures in Puerto Rico, his love for New York City and the grand comfort he had in being settled in our small town. Now divorced, he lived alone in a fine apartment across from the Central Park.

He loved his job. Making conversation, he invited me to see his apartment. With a small bottle of rum promised as part of my tip, I was anxious to get such an unknown and illegal gift—as well as conclude my evening of travels with Winona's finest.

It was time to "get off the clock" and get back to the business of seventy-five-cent runs of bar patrons and telephone operators. Promising quick pay and a quick glance at his apartment, Bruce patted me on the back as we headed up the double-wide staircase. Only then did I discover my discomfort. I was entering a new experience, a new phase of my life. At age eighteen, six-foot-four and 210 pounds, I was facing my first homosexual encounter in the adult world.

With the guys, we sometimes talked about the "queers" we had known or encountered—but nothing "real" was known. My only real experience was with a toothless, old scrawny guy named "Roy" who frequented my friend's father's second-hand shop. At age fourteen or so, Roy, my friend, was asked by his dad, Edson, to take the other Roy home in the 1949 Kaiser called "the Geezer" when old Roy needed to leave.

Even though young Roy was illegal as driver due to his age and absence of license, we made the venture more than a few times with Roy driving, old Roy in the center front and me in the "shotgun" seat. It soon became obvious that the ninety-pound Roy wanted me along for the two-mile journey.

He kind of "cooed" and moved too close to me, but I didn't know what that was about, only that it was uncomfortable. When it became obvious that old Roy had a passion for me, I was teased relentlessly by my friend Roy about my "new boyfriend." I did get the understanding that old Roy was different. Thereafter, the two Roys made the journey without me.

With one final touch on my back from Bruce, I entered the huge and expensive apartment, got the quick tour and abruptly headed for the door with my payment and tip in hand, before Bruce could take one more step.

I told him that Shorty expected me back within minutes and that he had a call standing for me. I made a quick exit to my Studebaker and headed off into the safety of the dark night on the streets of Winona—with one more experience under my belt!

Looking up from his desk with eyebrows raised as I entered, Shorty greeted me subtly with, "You've had quite a night, Seven!" It was only approaching the midnight bar rush—halfway through my shift—and I had already turned in personal record earnings.

It wasn't every night that one had the likes of Rosie, Bull and Bruce and been occupied virtually every moment of the shift. More than that, I think Shorty knew that these were unique experiences I gained from my contacts with these assigned public personas. He probably had a good sense of what Bruce was all about and the potentialities for his young drivers. No wonder Eugene was able to write a book.

There were others like Rosie and Bruce, who needed babysitting in their travels. There was Pete, the Studebaker man, and Curt, the local furniture dealer—both known to go on their "toots" around town. They mainly went about their business of "getting loaded" and quietly stumbled at night's end into their well-maintained homes in the adjoining village of Goodview. Essentially they were harmless—maybe just personally festive or lonely or some extrapolation thereof. Fortunately for me, I wasn't required to babysit any more adults on this particular evening.

Having been too busy for a stop at McDonald's and with a break in the action, Eugene and I stopped our cabs at Shorty's Bar (not the same Shorty)—across from the Milwaukee Road train station—before they drew their shades at 1:00 a.m.

With one of their well-known greasy burgers covered with fried onions dripping down the fender of our Studebakers, we recapped the evening and fortified our spirits with the delicious and delectable treat. Eugene always had the Studebaker, since he was a senior and trusted member of the cab corps. I recapped the evening's events with him and he made notes on his yellow legal pad—more fodder in his writings.

With calls from Shorty over the next few hours, the four cabs on duty all stayed busy. A favorite run for the barflies was to finish up at 1:00 a.m. at Shorty's or Sloppy Joe's or the Main Tavern (on Main Street) in town and then grab a cab to the Midway across the river for a final bump or two before their closing at 2:00 or 2:15 a.m.

As we traveled back and forth on the ten-minute journey, we frequently met other cabs (Vets and Royal Cab alike) with top lights lit to indicate "on duty" status. We repeated the trip in reverse an hour later and sometimes grabbed two or three returnees headed in the same direction—

which increased our fare, income and potential for tips. We dropped many of these patrons at their spartan homes on the East End of town.

They were often workers at Peerless Chain Company, Bay State Milling or the Swift's meatpacking plant—many of them second-generation Germans and Poles whose fathers had worked in the booming lumber business of the late 1800s, until it was exhausted.

As we finished our late Saturday night/early Sunday morning shift several hours later, we might stop again at the same residence to take "the woman of the house" to the local Polish-Catholic church for Mass.

Somehow (and no wonder) the "mister" was still sleeping in.

By 4:00 a.m. the action was over. I bantered with Shorty, philosophized with Eugene and even played a little nickel-dime poker on the hood of the car with other drivers. When taking a snooze in the front seat of the Studebaker at cabstand, one was certain to be awakened by Shorty's shout over the two-way.

If we turned the volume down too low to avoid any early morning chatter and to rest quietly—and thus missed a call—Shorty would be out his door fifty feet away, pounding on the car window and telling one or the other of us to "Get your ass in gear!"

With bleary eyes and a final cup of coffee from Ruth's at 5:00 a.m., I looked forward to the end of my shift and the exchange of the cab with a day shift driver who came on duty at 6:30 a.m. By 6:00 a.m., my eyes reopened and the action picked up with church calls, getting folks to work and the return of denizens of the night to their homes.

It was a successful (and profitable) night, not unlike many I spent winter and summer on the streets of Winona during my beginning days of college.

The occasional day shifts were days filled with a different type of excitement—the many trains to meet at the three stations, action all over town with traffic and folks in a hurry, all requiring a little more hustle of the foot pedal and Studebaker.

Downtown was a-bustle with traffic and shoppers. Skill was needed to avoid jam-ups around town. With an eye out for Bull Tiegarden and his buddies, we cut around corners and hustled through alleys to serve the customers of Vets Cab with the quickest possible service.

Robert E., "Shorty," appreciated our hustle.

"Attaboy, Seven!" he would offer when pleased with my effort.

What a Way to Ride:
A 100-Year History of Taxicabs
in Winona

*I*n 1949, a New York woman called to request a taxicab come to pick her up. With a new-fangled radio system from office to cab, the dispatcher gave details to the driver who was near the address. Barely hung up, the driver arrived.

"I won't ride with you," she said sternly.

"You drive too fast, young man."

She proceeded to call another cab company.

—April, 1949

In Winona of the 1950s, there were lots of pleased passengers who took radio-dispatched, quickly arriving cabs from home to downtown—or from work to bar. With three full-time train depots serving the many daily arrivals of passengers to town, taxi drivers were kept busy morning through night with train arrivals and serving local customers. I was pleased to be one of Vets Cab's part-time drivers in the late 1950s.

Arthur S. Cunningham proposed his cab company idea in the early 1930s. From observations while attending Winona Normal School (Winona State), he felt he could do better. Working part-time at the Oaks Supper Club, he noticed that some of the cab drivers were drinking on the job. Art suggested to his brother Frank that they join the competition (without the drinking drivers), with the older brother becoming co-owner. They would operate out of the small annex to Frank's Duncan Hines-endorsed Steak Shop Restaurant on Main Street.

To get a start, according to his daughter Sheila, Art visited the nuns in charge of St. Teresa's College—since several of his family members were already nuns—seeking student business. Given their endorsement, Royal Cab (named after a soap that their mother used) became the exclusive cab of choice for nuns and St. Teresa students—who most definitely followed regulations.

Throughout the years, "Tel. 3331" was posted in Lourdes Residence Hall and across Winona. The number today remains a part of Yellow Cab Company of Winona at 260 West Third Street with the same, albeit extended, phone number (507-4523331).

After a sorting out of companies over the years, the Royal Cab Company at 125 Main emerged in 1946 as Winona's only cab company.

Soon to follow in 1947, the Vets (Winona) Cab Company joined in, located in a small office behind Ruth's Restaurant at 126 East Third Street, telephone number 3354. Five cabs were licensed in 1948. As had been done in neighboring Rochester, Vets Cab was created to become the favored company of city laborers and veterans. Following original proprietor Willard Mayotte, Shorty and Dave Krause were soon at the helm—and on the radiophone. By 1953, Royal had twenty-four full-time drivers, with Vets showing sixteen to eighteen full- and part-time drivers.

In 1948, Cecil Baldwin joined with Mr. Seifert (as Seifert-Baldwin Dodge/Plymouth) and the owners of Nelson Tire Company to purchase the Beyerstedt Building on Fourth and Johnson. Cecil remembered working from that building as one of the first taxicab drivers in Winona. The oversized building originally housed the largest horse and buggy livery in the city, yet allowed space for two taxicabs in 1915.

From 1903 to 1909, the city created a listing of owners of autos (with a two dollar state license fee). It included J.R. Watkins, Max Conrad and other distinguished Winonans, but no taxi owners. In the "Years in History" section of the newspaper, it was reported that the first taxicab actually arrived in town in 1912—"not heretofore offered here."

In October of that year, Nevius added a seven-seat taxicab (possibly a Haynes "of medium size"), "with continuous service day and night." The Haynes vehicle, with a leaky radiator, may have been involved in an accident with Mr. Smart several years later, "breaking both legs," to result in a $25,000 lawsuit against Nevius.

Taxicab company owners Bert Beyerstedt and Mr. Mallery, of Mallery's Livery, were at a city council meeting in 1916 to address concerns of safety—possibly due in part to Mr. Mallery's running his taxicab into the side of a streetcar. Mr. Mallery's taxi was "of the new Ford model and presents an attractive appearance"—at least previously to the accident.

Nevius Livery and Transfer continued as competition in 1915, with their "latest type of taxicab"—the Dodge "winter car." A "short circuit in electrical wires in the car" caused a Nevius taxicab fire in 1918. A Safety Cab Company vehicle collided with a streetcar in 1930, at Fifth and Center streets. (Those darn streetcars!)

Cecil reported that the horses were gone by the early 1920s.

Nevius Livery and J.P. Cooley of the Ross Livery were reportedly bilked by an "alleged tax sharper" in 1919, who claimed to be representing the state in collecting a per vehicle tax on taxis. He collected forty dollars from Nevius, with Ross losing a few dollars. Although suspicious to each, neither reported the incident to police—yet it made the news on April 26, 1919.

There was apparent concern for the safety of drivers, as well. In 1918, Mr. F.R. Stevenson, night clerk at the Park Hotel, shot and killed Elmer Mead, a taxicab driver, at the Home Hotel. In 1923, a Nevius cab was commandeered by Officer John Malosh to "overtake a drunken driver at Broadway and Liberty."

A.H. (Harry) Beyerstedt and his brother Albert (Bert) had "the oldest established taxicab company" (among five) in 1933, with Harry having been the early manager of Nevius. Bert appealed to the city council that there "needed to be city regulation of the cab companies to give a living wage to drivers." An ordinance was passed, with licensing and insurance required. The ordinance included a stipulation that "no driver can wait at any place for employment without approval of the Police Chief"—subject to arrest.

The Beyerstedts offered a Christmas special for shoppers—"a round trip downtown for a one-way price"—in 1933. Before their special, they took some time away from the cab business, with the sale of their company to Harry and Al Voss in December, 1926, creating the Voss Bros. Cab Co. (Phone 80J.)

Harry and Al did well. They advertised prominently in December of 1929, that their twenty-seven vehicles were used for all manner of transport—people, funerals, trucks and buses. The advertised taxi rate was "50 cents anywhere within the City of Winona." Their apparent success led to the resale of the company to the Beyerstedts in 1930.

One of the competitors of the time advertised itself as the Sayboy Drivurself and Taxicab Company at Third and Johnson Street. You could get a ride or rent a car from this early Hertz affiliate. The Winona Taxi and Baggage Company (phone 2618) advertised a rate during this depression-era time of "25 cents—for one passenger or five." Cabs were heated, insured and "drivers are all a 'hand-picked' lot of men with courtesy for all passengers."

During the very challenging and competitive era of 1933, the rate for all companies was down to twenty-five cents, with Royal Cab and a newly formed Safety Cab and Transfer having joined the fray. From the home farm at Janesville, Minnesota, Frank came to Normal, with Art following. Soon came their company's success and Art's meeting of his future wife, Marion, in his taxi.

Marion recently explained the circumstances in the story "How I Met the One I Love" in the *Winona Post*. He "got her to sit in the front seat of the taxi—and I stayed there for 69 years," she recalled from the family home on West Broadway, where she today resides at age ninety-seven. It's the same home to which Art occasionally brought taxi "fares" home for dinner, said Marion.

With twenty-five-cent fares, cash was limited for all the companies, but the Cunningham boys had a steady income. The Beyerstedt boys needed to chase after theirs—at least on one occasion.

In June of 1933, a swarthy smoothie of a horse trader from Cavalier, South Dakota, rolled into town, took a Beyerstedt cab to Minneapolis to buy a new Cadillac with a dealer-accepted $4,000 check—and proceeded to return to Winona with two girls gathered for the occasion. One was in the cab and one in the Cadillac. The taxi driver lost the Cadillac and ended up alone in Winona with a girl he hadn't intended.

The swarthy dude had crashed the "Caddie" in Red Wing, and needed further rescue. A second trip was made by cab and driver to return the girls and the dude to Minneapolis—where the authorities took over.

By 1934, the boys had recovered and bought a new fleet of Ford V-8s from the newly refurbished Owl Motor Company on Fourth and Main, with the addition of a new ambulance to their fleet. Harry Beyerstedt died in 1937, Albert in 1939. Descendants are still looking for that fare for the two unpaid round trips to Minneapolis.

There was a bit of a rush on taxis by car thieves, and thieves in general, over the years, with Royal Cab losing cars in 1933, 1935, 1936 and 1938. All were recovered. Kelly Cab and Ambulance lost one in 1938, a 1936 Chevrolet. In 1935, a Royal Cab driver was robbed and his car stolen by three Minneapolis youths who then received "up to 20 years in state prison."

Visiting soldiers in 1944 (probably from Camp McCoy) skipped out on a fare and broke a window of a Royal cab—not to be found.

In September of 1938, Eitel Guthman, late of the Green Bay Reformatory, "was sentenced to a term of up to ten years in prison" for three separate abductions of cabs and drivers in July and August. The Kelly Cab driver was forced to drive to Wisconsin under duress of Guthman's "two revolvers." Drivers two and three were directed to Houston, Minnesota, and the Michigan border, respectively, by "the blonde taxi bandit." "On all three occasions, Guthman had been smoking marijuana cigarettes," the police chief commented. He added, "the location of marijuana beds in Winona is being checked."

Accidents were prevalent throughout the years, with icy roads generally to blame. A little sand on icy streets didn't make for ease of stopping in winters of Winona. Listed Royal incidents are shown in 1942 (overturned), 1943 (five), 1944 (speeding), 1947 (three), 1948 (two) and 1953. Of particular interest was the collision on November 7, 1947, at the Airport Road between a Royal cab and a 1936 Chevrolet, whose driver was smacked in the side as he turned into the passing cab. He said that he had "opened the left door to signal the turn." Apparently the cab driver missed the unique signal.

The term "taxicab" was defined in a 1932 *Republican-Herald* ad for the new Webster's Dictionary (Merriam) with a drawing of a goat as the header—suggesting the two to be similar. Taxicab is an abbreviation of "taximeter-cabriolet"—a vehicle carrying an instrument to measure fare. The French word *cabriolet* has meaning of a leap—thus likened to a goat, since the carriage has a light, bouncing motion.

The cabs continued to bounce along, but World War II was a challenge for all drivers, due to a shortage of rubber for tires. Federal guidelines were imposed to reduce their overall mileage—thus using less of the tire where "the rubber hits the road." Cab companies were particularly challenged to reduce miles in New York, Minneapolis—and Winona, too.

An initial May lockout, in 1946, led to a ten-day strike in June against Royal, "Winona's only cab company." The strike resulted in a signed contract with Royal and the new competitor borne of the strike—Winona Cab Company, led by Willard Mayotte. In 1951-1952, Winona Cab was awarded the annual contract to carry special students to school each day, with Royal just a few cents behind. In 1953, both companies increased rates for the "first time since 1947"—as high as seventy-five cents to the 1800 block west.

Today's Yellow Cab of Winona retains the quality of service and the "Royal" treatment started eighty years ago. Continuing on in a tradition of family ownership, the Walter and Vernetta Nustad family purchased the business from the Cunninghams in 1967, becoming Yellow Cab of Winona. The initial leadership came from Bruce, an experienced "cabbie" in his own right at Yellow Cab of LaCrosse. Interestingly, Willard Mayotte, founder of Winona cab (Vets) moved on to a Yellow Cab franchise in Austin, according to his daughter.

With Bruce's passing, current owner Janet Nustad "fell in love with the business" and took over as president in 1997. Now operating four taxis with dispatcher Mike Szewell at her side, these service leaders have many shared years and exciting moments of responding to the needs of Winonans. Both have a great sense of history in cabs, with Mike remembering his "free rides with Shorty and Dave" (of Vets Cab) in the 1950s.

Economy Cab Company today operates six Winona cabs and provides handicapped van services to Winona, LaCrosse and Rochester from the space formerly dedicated to Rocky's Tackle Box at 200 East Third. Bob Christopherson, owner, purchased the business in 1992, after driving for the White Cab Company. Sheri Meyer, his "right-hand person" has been driver and dispatcher over the twenty-year history. She suggests the company "has grown far beyond their early imaginings."

Economy and Yellow Cab drivers continue to share their service to Winona, meeting the two lone trains each day at the Chicago, Milwaukee and St. Paul Railway Company (Milwaukee Road) Depot. Rochester Express joins them to meet the trains and provide shuttle service to Rochester. The depot, across from the former Shorty's Bar, was built in the late 1800s, and placed on the National Register of Historic Places in 1984.

Radio calls continue to take today's drivers to their many patrons with maximum speed, efficiency and concern. Drivers of both companies continue early-morning runs to church services, offer special service to downtown on snowy days and shuttle regular late-evening regulars to the "hot spots" across the river.

It has been "A Century of Personal Service"—of which all can be proud.

Kent Stever has "been around the block" in a taxi. He loved time spent on the evening streets of Winona—and the activity generated from Winona's downtown in a "boom time" era.

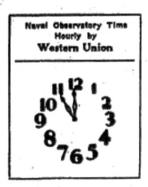

New Train and Bus Schedules

(Published June 3, 1930)

--- TRAINS ---

C. M. St. P. & P.

East Bound	West Bound
1:35 A. M.	4:02 A. M.
11:30 A. M.	5:53 A. M.
3:12 P. M.	11:35 A. M.
10:10 P. M.	4:30 P. M.
11:30 P. M.	7:25 P. M.

C. B. & Q.

East Bound	West Bound
10:35 A. M.	3:35 A. M.
10:05 P. M.	8:15 A. M.
	7:00 P. M.

C. & N. W.

East Bound A. M.		West Bound A. M.	
Arrive	Lv.	Arrive	Lv.
10:10	10:15	5:15	5:30
		7:35	7:40
P. M.		P. M.	
Arrive	Lv.	Arrive	Lv.
5:00			
9:30	9:40		2:00
10:35	10:45	7:00	7:10

G. B. & W.

Arrive	Leave
3:00 P. M.	9:05 A. M.

Naval Observatory Time
Hourly by
Western Union

Phone TAXIS TO ALL TRAINS AND **Phone**
80-J BUSES **80-J**
Bus Station, 121 West Third St.

For
Correct Time
Night or Day
Phone 80-J

To La Crosse, Madison, Chicago and intermediate points.
12:30 P. M.
6:15 P. M.
9:05 P. M.
11:50 P. M.

To Eau Claire

Arrive	Leave
7:55 P. M.	8:30 A. M.
11:30 A. M.	4:00 P. M.

To Merrillan
Except Sunday

Arrive	Leave
11:50 A. M.	4:00 P. M.

To Wabasha, Red Wing, Minneapolis and intermediate points,
7:50 A. M.
1:30 P. M.
3:50 P. M.
8:35 P. M.

To Rochester, Mankato, and intermediate points.

Arrive	Leave
4:00 P. M.	1:30 P. M.

To Rochester

Arrive	Leave
12:00 Noon	5:00 P. M.

Before entering any taxicab, in Winona or elsewhere, always demand proof of the driver that the cab is insured. Our drivers have credentials.

Clip this out and save it.

A train and bus schedule which appeared in a Winona paper, June 3, 1936. (Courtesy of the Winona Newspaper Project, Winona State University.)

The Truck Driver

I t had taken awhile for the heater to kick in.

But once it did, I was sailing, and adjusting doors of the heater to deflect the continuous blast. Although the temperature outside was four below zero, my travel through the west end of town out to the highway was warm as toast. I had been out of bed by 4:30 a.m., at my truck by five o'clock and on the road within minutes.

I really liked the early morning travel. Getting onto the highway, I cruised at sixty miles per hour, slowing only for the curves around the limestone walls of the hillside bluff. I had traveled the road hundreds of times. In the summer after my fifteenth birthday, I was given full command of my trusty Ford pickup truck.

With driver's license secure in hand, I was finally legal to be driving on the highways. I passed the driving test on the second try with a lowly seventy-two, just two points past the lowest possible passing score. It wasn't due to my operation of the clutch, floor shift and steering. I was well-coordinated and skilled from three years of driving large milk trucks on country roads, backing and shifting and guiding the vehicles through the hills and valleys of this beloved countryside.

The problem was in the rules to be observed. It was obvious that I needed to dedicate more time to the driver's manual of the state and to the official rules of the road in order to be the best driver possible.

On the country road some fifteen miles from home, I was at peace with my truck, the warmth of the vehicle and the task before me. I coached the truck up the hill, over the fresh snow, with ease. Traveling over the frozen road, I downshifted as I came to the tight curve before the uphill climb. The truck growled as I put it into creeper gear for the pull.

This left turn into the woods and country of Lewiston Hill was one of my favorite spots in my county travels. The singular beauty of the winter day, the early morning, the quiet of the fields I passed and the strength I gained by handling the truck and accomplishing work on my own all led to inner warmth, security and confidence.

As I turned into the crushed rock road leading into the Miller farm, it was like arriving home. The Millers were always so pleased to see me. Early morning winter or mid-morning summer, I was greeted with a warm smile as I entered the barn. Inevitably, the ever-present litter of kittens scattered every which way upon entry. They were constantly hanging around the barn for a fresh squirt of milk directed at them by one of the Millers—John or young Jack or brother Peter—who together milked the cows twice per day.

An open metal bowl of milk, occasionally refreshed by spills from the Surge milkers being carried from barn to milk house, was there to be to be lapped up. Kittens tumbled and tossed around the bowl, well-fed and satisfied. The yield of carried pails from cows to milk house would be six or eight filled eighty-pound metal cans that rested in the cold water cooler.

Slightly below ground level, the cement-encased cooler received a steady stream of fresh water from a pump attached to the small windmill. The cement-block-and-stone milk house was the headquarters for milking equipment and cleanup. My job was to pick the cans out of the cooler and haul the abundance to the Pleasant Valley Creamery on winter weekends and summer days.

Milking was a chore, a routine and way of life around the Miller farm, as it was with neighbors who ran their own 160-acre dairy farms. On most of the farms milking thirty to forty-five cows, the routine was similar. Each day began around 4:30 a.m. and finished up with the second milking by 8:00 p.m. In between, depending upon the season, the lives of the farmers were filled with activity and with necessary meals to sustain the effort.

Breakfast came after the first round of milking in the morning. Then the barn and stalls were cleaned, with new bedding laid down for the personally named cows. Grain was mixed, calves fed, chickens watered and fed, and a plethora of chores were accomplished to maintain equipment and a healthy environment for the animals.

In planting and harvesting seasons, tractors were running nearly all day long with one or the other of family members at the wheel. They were most often not even shut down, save for re-fueling and lunch breaks that were taken in the field. My favorite was the John Deere B, with its distinctive *thump-thump-thump*.

After the stop at the Miller farm, I proceeded west to the Wirts. A three-generation family operated the farm, noted for having the best Guernsey herd in the entire county. Every year, the Wirts won blue ribbons at the county fair for record milk production of herd members. Their herd was bigger, as was their barn.

To step inside the barn in the early morning was to step into a model of efficiency and cleanliness of a milk production facility. All family members went about their designated jobs with cool efficiency—feeding, milking and carrying. Early morning country music offered by the AM radio was punctuated with reports of cattle prices from the previous day's sales at market, with news updates on happenings in the area.

Grandpa Wirt, in bib overalls and oversized work coat, quietly moved through the barn with a gentle nature shared with cows and kittens and family members. As patriarch, he had turned over the major physical chores to his son Russell, a burly farmer with arms as thick as fence posts. He and his sons carried gleaming stainless steel buckets of milk from their new Surge milkers to the milk house, to be poured through cheesecloth covering the tops of the six-gallon cans. Cans were soon filled and awaiting my transport to the creamery.

With their larger herd and quality production, I always had a real chore in loading the usual twenty cans or so. I was always thrilled to have them stop for a moment from their chores to share a word as I loaded the cans onto the truck. There was a fresh apple or even a piece of apple pie on occasion that made for a great start to my day.

In the best fashion, they made me feel welcome and special. They held great pride in their product and their work. They also made me feel like an important member of the team—the one who transported their precious commodity to market.

My third and final stop was at the Nahrgang Farm. On the corner before the straight stretch into Lewiston, the home farm was majestic. A windbreak of spruce trees graced the crushed rock entry road and front yard—with milk house, silo, windmill and barn at center stage beyond the trees. It was like arriving home when I pulled into the circle drive next to the milk house. Off to the left was the immaculate white farm home that had stood the test of time. Being there nearly 100 years, these were truly early settlers of the county.

It was a special place, a quality dairy farm operation rivaling the Wirts for quality and production. In addition to annual prizes for milk production, the Nahrgangs also garnered ribbons at the county and state fairs for their pigs, beef cattle and assorted small animals.

Five kids, including three girls with spark and beauty, were constantly primping and cleaning their animals and the cherished setting. The girls were always there to giggle and greet me. They were much younger, but it was already evident that they were ones to watch and remember. The qualities of their mother were already showing through.

Mom was the real social director and event organizer. Unlike the farm wives of many other farms I visited, she lived beyond the kitchen. She could be seen on the tractor, in the barn or in her sensational garden with an ever-effusive and gracious nature. Offering a soft hand callused from work, she greeted all with warm welcome.

On this day, she greeted me in the barn with her usual smile and a warm, fresh-baked breakfast roll. An additional special gift for me—double wrapped in waxed paper and newspaper—was a fresh loaf of home-baked bread to take home. She offered strict instructions not to unwrap it until it hit the kitchen table at home.

The dad was a gentle soul who quietly led the enterprise. He was definitely in charge of all aspects of the farm. His boys were skilled tractor drivers who maneuvered large wagons and the requisite manure spreader with ease. By the time most young boys were getting a handle on how to hold a bat, they were already tossing bales, cleaning barns and doing twelve-hour days on the tractors. Like their dad, their muscles were taut, their expectations clearly understood. They enjoyed every minute of life on the farm.

By the time the load was ready from the Nahrgangs, I had over 3,000 pounds of milk on board for the trip to the creamery. With a wave of thanks and my fresh loaf of bread at my side, I set off for home. Making a brief stop at the bakery in Lewiston to enjoy the world's finest glazed donuts, I turned right onto the main highway and headed down Lewiston Hill. At the bottom of the hill some four or five miles ahead was a beautiful trout stream and entry to a county park called the Arches. Even in the midst of winter it continued to flow openly between the mounds of snow at creek side.

From spring through late autumn, families, churches and organizations from throughout the area made great use of the park. Between 400-foot bluffs were playfields, a center pavilion and a remarkable open-air auditorium with a roofed, natural limestone presentation platform set into the bluff—all within throwing distance of the clear rippling stream.

It was as if one had entered the land of the twenty-third psalm. This was home for true family enjoyment, outdoor church services, school patrol picnics (with all the ice cream and hot dogs that one could eat), pickup kitten-ball (softball) games and "tag" football in the glorious days of autumn. To wander along the stream and up into the bluffs would take you from thoughts of city life to nature's simplicity in a matter of minutes.

My route from Lewiston through the Arches took me east toward Stockton Hill. With the sun coming up on a frozen day in the country, I gave the usual two-fingered wave of truckers and farmers to early morning travelers whom I met. Today, as every time I made the journey, my thoughts were of the farm and the job and the special pleasure of being in charge of my own truck.

I looked forward to the pull up Stockton Hill a few miles ahead. It was fun to match the power of my truck against the pull of the 600-foot hill. With clear roads today, the hill was no match for my trusted steed. Winter snows and drifts had often turned my forty-mile trip from home to farm to creamery into a several hour adventure—especially in the early morning before the plows had made their pass.

The trip out to the farms with the shiny, empty milk cans was more treacherous than the return trip on those days. Once I was loaded with over 3,000 pounds of milk, it felt that I could buck the drifts and challenge the hills without worry.

I rounded the gentle curves through the valley and hit the straight stretch approaching the village of Stockton. Cruising at fifty around the curves, I looked forward to this three-mile stretch of straight road to add a little more power and speed. Empty, one summer day I had taken the old Ford up to seventy on a downhill stretch.

Today, fully loaded and winter-cautious, I boosted it to fifty-five as I hit the straight stretch. Ahead, one of the local farmers in typical, accustomed form drove his old sedan at forty or so. I turned out easily to pass and head by, ready for the familiar wave. Before I got to that friendly waving place, the driver made an abrupt left turn—directly into my path and firmly into my right front fender.

With the unexpected sideways shove, I firmly grabbed the steering wheel in my callused hands to hold it steady and straight—with the grinding and collision forces screeching in my ears. Momentarily locked together, I was forced off onto the opposite shoulder of the road. Strong as my fifteen-year-old arms were from the lifting of milk cans, they were not strong enough to hold off the simultaneous forces of his car and the cement drain built into the shoulder.

The world turned over—and so did the milk cans. My stout red truck flipped onto the driver's side and skidded down the roadway for an eternity. Sparks flew, milk sloshed—and I hung on for dear life. After interminable moments of sheer fear, my sideways ride finally stopped, dead center in the highway. The highway patrol officer later measured 130 feet from the point of the original impact with the drain to the final resting spot.

Finding myself upside-down in the truck, I assessed damages and proceeded to cautiously stand upright on the bottom door to gain leverage, a sense of awareness and to set myself up to pull out of the wreck. I was unable to lift the top door. By cranking the window sideways, I was able to gain access to the frigid air and freedom.

Standing on the steering column and dashboard, I forced myself through the window opening to an upright-seated position on the doorframe. Hitting the cold air, I felt the need for my gloves. As was my practice, I had shoved them into the crevice in the middle of the seat. I reached down for them, found my fresh bread on the floor/door and scrambled out of the truck, down the fender and onto solid ground. It felt so good to be standing upright once again.

I walked the frozen edge of the road to avoid slipping on the spilled milk, covers and cans that flash-froze on the roadway. Carrying my bread in one hand and my milk route logbook in the other, I avoided the topsy-turvy can collection and headed back toward the farmer's car that had come to a stop on the right shoulder.

Feeling shaken but okay, I approached the farmer, who was alone in his car. He appeared frozen to the steering wheel as I saw him through the cracked windshield. I rapped on the driver's side window to get his attention. It was as if I had awakened him from a sleep. He recognized my presence, but didn't respond. By then, other drivers had stopped, due to the accident, access being denied by the overturned truck, and cans shining in the early morning sunlight.

Soon thereafter, local police from Lewiston and the county sheriff's deputy were on hand to direct the flow of traffic. One of them invited me into his car for warmth, where I remained until Officer Hittner of the Minnesota Highway Patrol arrived. He checked to find me basically uninjured. He proceeded to the farmer's car, where the driver remained immobile.

Officer Hittner was able to open the right side door of the farmer's car and took his place in the passenger's seat. He spent a long time with the farmer—who apparently needed some time to unravel after the shock of being slammed by my sturdy rig. The officer placed the farmer in the highway patrol cruiser and took him up the entry road to the farm where he had earlier attempted to turn—apparently his home farm. The officer returned some minutes later to coordinate the wreckage and cleanup. He called in a wrecker and a separate truck to pick up the cans.

I was able to watch all the action over the next hour or so as the roadway was cleared of cans, the car was pushed safely off onto the shoulder and my rig was righted. The driver of the big Mer-Kohn Wrecker out of Winona wrapped his steel cables over the F2 as it lay sideways across the highway. With a steady pull of the cables from the back of the wrecker, the smaller truck was upright in minutes.

He unlatched and pulled in the cables and reset his truck on the shoulder to best lever the front end of the pickup into the air for transport. My truck was headed for the Ford garage in Winona, where it frequently saw service—this time to receive a full treatment package. Although the sturdy fenders of the truck had taken a beating, I was assured by the officer that the truck would soon be back on the familiar route.

Leaving the accident scene, the officer took me to his home in Winona, where we filled out the necessary report forms. He called Harold, the truck owner, and my pa to explain what had happened. We enjoyed together the sandwiches prepared by Mrs. Hittner. Apparently, I happened to hit the noon hour routine of his house. It may also have been an hour or two of calming what I thought were my steady nerves.

The adventure of the day was completed by mid-afternoon when Officer Hittner dropped me off at home. Harold stopped by to check on me and pick up the logbook for insurance purposes. He assured me that all would be well and that I would have a substitute truck for the next day's duties.

He did tell me that if I built up my arm muscles a bit more—by lifting even more cans—that I could overcome any bounce from a drainage lip on the highway shoulder in the future. I was pleased to have survived my frozen spill, and looked forward to my run the next morning in my replacement truck.

As a part of supper in the warmth and comfort of home, the fresh bread was delicious.

Chapter Ten

Moments to Remember

In early summer vacation days, a bike ride to the Witoka Store took us up the brick paved road past Sugar Loaf Hill. Taking the better part of the morning, we wound through valley and limestone bluff ever-upward to arrive on the ridge and the village of Witoka—about nine miles out. After a short rest on the weathered and slanted front porch of the ancient store, we hustled a few miles across the ridge to Wilson. From there we sailed down through Gilmore Valley toward home at what seemed like sixty miles per hour.

Trusting limited mechanical skills gained from turning a pliers and a crescent wrench in the backyard, we were dependent upon our New Departure brakes and a set of new Goodyear "Double Eagle" tires purchased from paper route money.

The downhill trip was completed in minutes. It was a hope and a prayer as we sped down the hill and through the of woods and farm fields. The smells—the beauty of it all! We were the harbingers of the "zen of motorcycle maintenance" and didn't know it.

The trails of East Burns Valley, West Burns Valley, Stockton Hill, Wiscoy Valley, or Knopp Valley limited our travel plans during elementary, junior high and early high school days. Whether hiking up the bluffsides or bike riding around and through them, each journey was a visit to a land of enchantment.

These were visits to the roots of our county; visits of biking and hiking simplicity and joy. In high school years, the loud rap of a friend's 1957 Ford V-8, the squeal of tires of a 1932 Ford hot rod or the roar of a Norton, Zundapp, Indian or Jawa (motorcycles all) or Whizzer (just a purr) took us over the same routes at a higher rate of speed.

Did we really have our driver's license at age fifteen, and then own and drive the 1936 Chevrolet, the 1950 Nash "washtub," the Kaiser, the Hudson or the 1955 Plymouth four-door? How did we survive trading our car for a friend's BSA motorcycle for the evening and not get it wrapped around a tree? How did we survive the "boys' night" trips across the river?

Were we rebels without a cause like James Dean?

A Sunday afternoon ride with our best girl in a 1952 Plymouth convertible to visit an uncle's farm nestled in the woods and hills above the Arches Park near Lewiston took a slower pace. The presence of a special friend, a hillside trout stream overlook and the crispness of autumn brought apple freshness to our cheeks. In our leisurely outing, we walked the beautiful woods and deer trails and rested amidst natural piles of leaves under oaks and hickories and sugar maples—a panoply to behold and perfect setting for young love.

Like Archie and Veronica, comic book characters of the time, we would drive Mom's car (or an older brother's 1948 Mercury Coupe) to our country ventures, to a night out at the Sky-Vu Drive-In Theatre or to a post-football game dance.

Boys' night out was often a bit more risky and dangerous—and probably not suited for the pages of comic books. Driving Pa's 1936 Chevrolet Coupe across the river took us to Galesville taverns at age sixteen to "belly up" to the bar for ten-cent glasses of beer.

On weekend evenings we ventured to the Wine House on the Wisconsin bluffside or Czechsville to purchase fifty-cent quarts of beer to be brought back to town and drunk in the secluded areas visited years ago on childhood bike hikes.

We sometimes returned from away football games and found our earlier stash of cold beer bottles cooling in a stream on the fringe of town. With a head of steam gathered from our quart of beer, we then sauntered around town and acted "cool," before the word was invented.

Wisconsin's Merrick State Park's lack of rules and supervision somehow allowed us the weekend nighttime pleasure of beers and "hanging out" at the pea-gravel covered outdoor vestibule and covered jukebox where we played into the night without interruption of parents or constabulary.

Entertainment in the woods adjacent to the jukebox and snack bar/beer store often featured some inebriated tough guys duking it out for bragging rights on who was the toughest or drunkest.

We were the generation that mimicked the ways of Roy Rogers, Red Ryder, Joe Palooka, the Three Stooges and the Everly Brothers. Fabian was hot. Elvis made his beginnings on the Ed Sullivan show—and Teresa Brewer was seen on the Saturday night *Hit Parade*. Patti Page asked in her number one hit, "How much is that doggie in the window?" Could there have been a deeper lock on philosophy than this?

We heard all our favorites on the jukebox at the "Vars"—our teenage hangout for Cokes and hamburgers. When not at the Vars, we shared forty-five-rpm records with friends on Saturday afternoon home visits. Joining friends to ride the carnival "Octopus" or the Ferris Wheel on Main Street during Steamboat Days was the zenith.

How much more could we hope for? If only we could win our way into the state basketball tournament and go to "The Cities"—then life would be complete.

Our skills were tested at hula hoop and limbo contests (how low can you go?). We learned ropeclimbing in phy. ed., protozoa from Bugsy Moore, and *Reader's Digest* words from Charlie Stevens. The girls' GAA was a sham of recognition of the inherent competitiveness and skill of the female members of our class.

We were not exactly gender-fair, were we? In a reverse way, the Inner Circle was indeed that, an inner circle of girls that we could never see into. We did, however, meet them at the public library—a groovy place to be at night. It was handy to the Vars and served as a good excuse for us when we left parents at home.

High school was a state of mind. Surrounded by good friends and good activities, with school providing us a place to be and a reason for being— we were on our way to becoming. These were times for lessons of safety, sensibility, security and sex—and recognition of the importance of friends.

We seemed to enjoy every moment. Not content to leave our schoolmates at the classroom door, we made arrangements for Sunday afternoon touch football games at Lake Park, dances, campfires and dates—always the dates. They took us off to places where we had never been. So many choices. So much fun.

These were truly "moments to remember."

Characters to Remember

There was always adventure on Grand Street.

With a rainstorm on a summer afternoon we got in our bathing suits to play in flooded streets. On fall Saturdays we listened to Gopher football games on WCCO radio as we raked leaves or played touch football in the street. Fresh snow was shoveled and snow forts built during Christmas vacation. There was something to do every day of every season.

We were often productive—with a morning hoe of the garden weeds, a cleanup of the wood ash pile in the back yard or the gathering of trash from the shed set out for a trip to the dump in Pa's borrowed truck. After school on a winter's day we used a buck saw to cut wood for the fire, then hauled sleds full to the back porch for stacking.

We kept the walks shoveled and dusted with non-slip ashes. Every Saturday all year long was wash day. As two young boys (ages eight and ten), we even painted the house one summer. Tomatoes from the garden were eaten on the front porch and occasionally tossed at cars in evening forays.

Each day seemed to bring new options. We never thought to be bored. There was just too much to do—and too many people to see. At every turn, we met and enjoyed the daily characters of our small town nestled in the Mississippi River bluffs and valleys.

On a sunny, summer day we could hear across the block the early-morning sounds of the Schneider brothers as they cut their winter wood supply with a large buzz saw screaming across the neighborhood. Driven by an old Ford Model A motor, we were invited to participate by the startup of the engine before 8:00 a.m.

The transplanted farm bachelors allowed us to stack wood in the shed on their small city lot for a couple of hours—and earn a few nickels. They seemed not to fit so well on the sixty-foot lot in town with their burly structures and heavy-duty machinery. Neat and orderly in their bib-overalls, they were efficient and welcoming in an austere, German-heritage kind of way.

Like the woodcutters, we lived only a couple of blocks away from the busy train tracks that bisected the city. Railroad conductors feared traveling through Winona due to the abundance of crossings and the frequency of fatal accidents. With only a few traffic regulators and even fewer skilled drivers, we saw and heard the constant passing of trains—and the all-too-frequent auto-train wrecks. Sometimes we were there first, having heard the grinding collision of locomotive and auto. Other times, our attention was drawn to the scene by police sirens.

Our arrival on bikes often coincided with the ambulance and newspaper photographer Merritt "One-Shot" Kelley—a legend in his own right. Every picture in the local *Republican-Herald* newspaper had Merritt's byline. He was with us from grade school through high school as the official photographer, with large camera and flash, broad-brimmed hat, trench coat (in season) and a constant Missouri Meerschaum tobacco-smoking pipe in his mouth. His bright eyes and mustachioed face focused clearly on his subject, whether football star, accident victim or homecoming queen.

Annually, on the second weekend of July during Steamboat Days, we awoke to the steady early-morning whine of multiple outboard-engined hydroplane boats preparing for afternoon race competition on the Mississippi River. We took off running to the river, less than a mile away. The exciting days of community celebration brought us new, and sometimes unusual, visitors to Main Street and to Levee Park. There were the roaring sounds of race boats, megaphone messages of carnival and midway barkers, marching bands from everywhere for the Grand Parade and the soft music of a queen pageant to stimulate us in pre-teen ways.

It was hard to avoid the lure of the exotic inside the huge, hot carnival tents. The bright-colored artistic displays painted on tent fronts and the quick flashes of skin from covered talents standing on the runway promised greater exposure within. Each was hyped with "a deal" by the barker to entice the "rubes" inside. We needed to be careful to avoid the shady operators of carnival sideshows and others with their games of chance (like knocking down the bottom-weighted milk bottles with a thrown baseball) that promised furry prizes, but more often took our money. We learned that first nickels lost could soon be multiplied into dollars unless we kept our single dollar bills tightly clasped in a clammy hand in a front pocket.

As years progressed, we learned of dwarfs and fat ladies, tattooed Indonesians and snake handlers, sword-swallowers and even (and maybe especially) "Margie the Wham-Wham." She really brought a "wham" to Winona—the first exposure of teenage boys to real, live, exotic female performance.

Her act was shut down by the police the next night.

Not so forceful as the whirring engines, twirling baubles or exotic creatures of Steamboat Days, but equally mesmerizing, was the slow and melodic shout of the vegetable farmer from the valley outside town who traveled slowly down the bus route street shouting, "strawberries, tomatoes, potatoes, rutabagas, watermelons," all in their own season, of course.

We made a beeline for his call to see the fresh treasures of nature brought to us on that given day—always in anticipation of a sample or a special deal to be struck with the nickel or dime in our pocket. Mr. Nelton, the local truck farmer, entertained us over many summer and early autumn days.

A most genial man, he drove his well-kept farm truck slowly down the street and boomed out a message of simplicity, delight and anticipation bringing housewives and small children at a scurry. He had a way about him that was always welcoming, whether purchaser or not. If we garnered a free slice of watermelon or a cucumber half, we were delighted. We enjoyed his company and the beauty of his produce. Mr. Nelton seemed to believe that God's treasures were meant for sharing.

Pete, the iceman, quietly brought huge chunks of ice from the storehouse of the Western Coal and Ice Company in the east end to homes on our street. His presence on hot summer days was felt, not heard. With a slow-moving truck, he made frequent stops as he circled his route of city blocks.

We knew he would be around our block at mid-morning. Pete always had a kind word and a small sliver of chipped ice for each of us to take away from the back of the truck as he scored and broke the 100-pound blocks into appropriate sizes for the various iceboxes with his ice pick.

With huge ice tongs and leathery arms, he hoisted the block across his leather apron and onto a leather shoulder patch, to be carried around to the back of the house. He comfortably entered the kitchen to place the large chunk in the icebox. Like the milkman before him, he was an acknowledged part of the extended family, occasionally stopping for a cup of fresh coffee and a moment's rest.

It was a given that we would be allowed a sample of ice, but only if Pete said so. There was not to be any taking without permission. As we respected and appreciated him for his thoughtfulness, he respected us for recognizing his small gifts and consideration. Pete was a friend of the family for all of the years. He still visited our kitchen on occasion after we achieved full electrification—and a real refrigerator.

Mr. Schumacher, the old German butcher, was a favorite of ours as we visited his shop on the corner of Seventh and Olmstead Streets, across from Madison School. The gleaming offset varnished wood-and-glass door with tinkling brass bell overhead signaled our entry. His extremely neat shop, immaculate glass-fronted cooler and fresh, sawdust-laden wood floor welcomed all.

He would emerge from the cutting room to take his place behind the counter with a gracious and booming "Welcome!" He always asked how the "bald-headed kids in the first row" were doing today. With a large smile on his reddish face, his white apron and burly frame, one could imagine him as an opera singer on the Munich stage in his earlier days of his home country. His smile was infectious, and he genuinely cared about kids. Whether we bought or not, he liked to have us stop by.

Out back, the smokehouse scent of Shumacher's was an olfactory pleasure to behold when we approached his shop from the back side. His old wood-framed building stood twenty feet tall on a small space right behind his store. It was always padlocked, as it should have been. For inside, a treasure of sausages and wieners hung from horizontal pegs at alternating heights above the smoking wood fire at the base.

When showing us his garlic-laced treasures, he reached, placed and sorted various sausages using a long, varnished stick with a hook on the end. Placing one's head inside the building gave us a lifetime sensual experience—all of Mr. Schumacher's making.

Tom, a retired railroad shops mechanic, often rode by our house or schoolyard on his bicycle. Leisurely smoking his pipe, he usually hung an assortment of metal pieces around and about his person. It was amazing to see the largesse that this elderly gentleman could gather and carry on his bicycle. He made his way home from regular scavenging operations to sort his treasures and prepare them for resale.

One day he could be found riding with an old metal pipe three times as long as his bicycle, or with a broken shovel and parts of an old bike somehow tied to the basket and frame of the bicycle ridden with obvious care. Another day would see him with large onion or burlap bags filled with tin cans for crushing and resale. Ever-purposeful, Tom was one we knew only by sight and reputation. He never stopped to talk.

There were the neighborhood grocers from whom we gained sustenance through their supply. Mr. Julius Deilke, in the store started by his father, with a carved "JLF Deilke 1900" marker stone at the roof peak, was a favorite. We spent much of our time in and around his corner store with the polished wood floors across from school.

We often fished for pennies through the grate next to the sidewalk in front of the store with a stick, string and wadded, used piece of bubble gum. He was always officious, yet cordial and affable, seeming to know when we needed a free piece of penny candy. Mostly we hung out there as kids, but didn't buy a big supply of groceries. He did buy our used comic books for two cents each, to be added to the pile for resale at five cents per. I wonder if he occasionally tossed a few pennies through the grate to entertain us.

Pa's designated store for us was at Kindt's Grocery, a block away, where Eddie Kindt and wife Trudy, Aunt Elinor and Billy the deliveryman (Elinor's brother) took care of our needs and wrote down purchases on a small tablet with a carbon between pages. We had occasional credit and "charge" rights from them when income was lean—or absent.

We occasionally brought produce from our summer garden to Eddie's store to apply as credit to our outstanding bill. On occasion, Grandpa Kindt could be seen in the store. A slight man in his eighties who lived next door, he apparently founded the store. He needed "salt-free" butter (an unusual remembrance for us) that we occasionally ran next door for Eddie, a gentle soul and good friend who seemed to often defer to Trudy's more aggressive style.

Tucked between the Kindt Store and Grandpa's house was a small barbershop run by Dick Fredrickson, with his quiet, impeccable nature and appearance. Dick kept up on each of us as we sat in his old leather-and-porcelain barber chair over the years. After getting our "ears lifted," we were treated to a splash of "Cat's Paw" around the ears that left us smelling beautiful. Dick was like an extended uncle in the family as he watched over us.

Mrs. Thorn, in her small store above the beauty shop on West Howard Street, and the McVey Ice-Cream family members all were fixtures in our lives. They taught us about who they were and what was expected. Like members of an extended family, they watched us grow—and let us know what they saw.

Anytime during the week we could expect to see Johnny LaBale cruising his very nice bike (a new Schwinn cruiser, I think). Johnny was a fixture around town. He was a gawky man with limited intellectual and social skills who somehow was allowed by his well-to-do parents to traverse the streets of the community from morning to night.

With plastic ribbons hanging off handlegrips of his shiny bike, Johnny would show up at the playground or city park, or pass by on the street throughout the days and years. He had one characteristic trademark sign that was shared with everyone he met. Without a word, Johnny would draw his finger across his throat one way and then the other as if cutting it with a knife. With a smile, he continued wordlessly on his travels. He never seemed to stop anywhere. He just traveled by and entertained all of the kids of the community.

To a person, virtually everyone in the small city of 25,000 people knew Johnny and looked out for him. It was unknown for us to taunt or make fun of Johnny. We would just extend our greeting in return and expect to see him somewhere else tomorrow. To this day, I don't know whether Johnny was able to talk. Needless to say, he communicated with all of us.

Two people who communicated to us in a negative way were Stanley "Chinky" Beerman and Charley Falk. They were two local ne'er-do-wells with a few years in age on us. Even though we weren't the king's pride in cleanliness and the ways of slovenly behavior, Chinky and Charley out-classed (or under-classed) us. They seemed to live somewhere in a world of grime not unlike the boys of the streets in *Oliver Twist*.

Chinky, the stubby one with a constant need for a shave, was outfitted winter and summer in his black leather jacket and "chain-drive" billfold. Charley was a lean, tousle-haired creature who may have cleaned up to look like James Dean, except for his rather large, protruding front teeth.

But to those of us who were yet to test our strength and prowess against tough guys, they were just plain scary. We kept our distance.

They were always ahead of us in getting the good snow-shoveling jobs in the neighborhood, though. They must have maintained themselves with these and other small jobs throughout the year, for they could be seen doing cleanup at the sites of fallen trees after a summer tornado or in shoveling hardily when the best snow falls occurred. Whether they targeted only our neighborhood or spread themselves across the city we didn't know, but they were known as two to avoid.

With regularity, they could be seen at the Hurry Back Pool Hall in the company of other equally scary gentlemen. By the time we reached high school and the maturity of regular attendance at the Hurry Back, we learned that Chinky and Charley were harmless, but still scary. As a group of strong high-schoolers, we always felt secure in their near company—but only with our own group present. On a dark night walking home alone from the alleys of the downtown area, one steered clear.

Our summer hangout at the school playground brought us acquaintance with Bob. He, like Johnny, seemed somewhat limited in his abilities. He walked with a crossover step, wore a trench coat a lot and incessantly smoked his pipe. Bob was probably in his late thirties when we knew him. He was unable to speak, but always engaging.

He stopped to see us, raised his eyebrows with assumed understanding when we talked with him and shared a genuine heartfelt smile. Every time we met Bob, we felt good. He could only grunt out some sounds as he chewed on his pipe and listened expectantly to our explanations. Bob smiled, chuckled (or chortled) at the words of nine-year-olds playing marbles or sitting on the swing. He seemed to enjoy the conversations. Bob didn't mean to give us lessons, but some of us learned from him the genuine art of human communication.

Gil Keelin, a neighbor down Grand Street, brought the sound of motorcycles to the neighborhood. He lived next door to the sedate Mr. Newman, who quietly tended his goldfish in his backyard pond. The rap and rumble of the old Harley motorcycle being driven down the street by Gil, a Marine veteran of the Korean War, often followed the quiet putter of Mr. Newman's immaculate 1930s Ford one-ton stake truck. Gil's rumbling return from work passed a mother's gentle call to supper of "Bergie Allen"—as she reclaimed her child.

Gil kept the Marine haircut throughout his time with us. In early evening hours after supper, we often traded stories with him on the family's back porch—and shared the bounty of a Concord grape vine encapsulating it. We were sorry to see Gil aim his Harley toward California, and the grapes of Napa Valley.

"Skinny" Maxworth was an older guy with glasses (not too skinny, either) who was regularly seen in front of the Hurry Back Pool Parlor on Third Street. He did not challenge us or communicate with us in any way except for slathering back and forth across his face an overly large tongue in constant motion. He seemed to be chewing it, when not wiping.

We didn't know whether he could talk. He was a fixture in front of the pool hall and was never removed, to our knowledge. You could be assured that you would get a tongue wipe greeting when you passed by his space on your bike. Maybe he was the owner of the Hurry Back—or a retired English teacher.

A favorite place for comic book trading and camp items at a cut-rate price was the Swap Shop on East Third Street. Edson greeted us with his usual "hey-ya." A little, bantamweight guy, he was usually seated at his desk in the midst of the second-hand store's ordered clutter. From there, he had full-range coverage of customers and his extensive inventory. He seldom left the desk, since he could respond to customer inquiries and make "deals" without leaving his station.

He was always pleased to see us and greeted us as real customers— not just "kids." He kept his money drawer next to him, alongside the latest of his projects. Edson was known far and wide as the guy who could fix anything, particularly old and new-fangled radios for home and car. He would interrupt the smoky soldering on his project to ask one or the other of us what we had been doing, and was sincerely interested in the response.

He was a good guy who knew his stuff and his customers. He seemed to like to have folks and kids around. As a consequence, everyone treated him fairly and didn't attempt to shoplift any item—as was known to occur with frequency at the five-and-dime just down the street. It may have been that Edson was known as a former competitive boxer while serving in the Navy in World War II. He was no one to trifle with.

Hustling down Third Street, we often stopped by the Woolworth's Store to get a dime's worth of candy from the glass cases supervised by Viola, Bill's mom. Bill was a part of our "tribe." He lived with his mom and a couple of sisters in a small house about a block from the river.

We had fun with Bill and used to have fun with his dad, Ray. Most exciting was when Ray took us to the professional "rassling" matches in the small auditorium of the Red Men's Wigwam—a club for locals that had little to do with Native American heritage, other than the name of the place. We cruised there in his sleek Hudson car, with the famous "step-down" entry. You stepped down into the car—a cool modification—or at least we thought so.

Body slams of the humungous visitors from the Twin Cities almost landed one or the other of these behemoths in our laps in the small auditorium of the Wigwam. Ray kept us safe and entertained us with popcorn and his comic commentary. Unfortunately, Ray passed away, leaving Vi alone to raise the kids and exude her special spirit throughout the household. She was just fun—always smarting off and joining in with her wisecracks. At Woolworth's, Vi gave us an extra ounce of ju-jus, root beer barrels or "blackies" for our dime purchase.

Emil, the shortstop of our famous hometown Chiefs baseball team, was ever a favorite. Like a grandfather, he always had time for us. Even though we buzzed with questions and excitement about his past career and his recent ballpark exploits, he nodded, cajoled and took in the scene. He looked us in the eye and made us feel like the most important people in his world.

We engaged Emil as he walked to or from his work. He passed by the playground to give us words of encouragement or personal tips on baseball technique. Short stories from his famous past gave us visions beyond the tetherball activity our playground. We could almost hear the crowd of Wrigley Field in Chicago when he described an afternoon game between the Cubs and the Cleveland Indians.

He had seen the great Bob Feller, the anxious Early Wynn and even had a chance to see Casey Stengel at Yankee Stadium. His excitement (and ours) rose when he spoke of the Washington Senators, the Boston Red Sox and his night as a youth in Fenway Park.

A distinguished gentleman in black known to us only as "Blackie"—due to the clothing he wore—would often cut diagonally across the playground, probably on his way home. We didn't know where he lived or what he did, but he always took time to greet us and watch our progress at softball or tetherball. He was always friendly, complimentary and interested. We found out later that Blackie was a veteran of World War II who had served with Colonel Mason, a gentleman we met through Edson.

One day, we made a few trades with Edson at the Swap Shop to enhance our stock. We were about to head out the door when he asked if we would each like to earn a quarter. He had just completed repair on a small table radio for a customer who lived in the West End near our homes. The customer doesn't have ready transportation to pick up the radio. Would we deliver?

Of course we were willing. We would do it for no charge for Edson—but he insisted on payment for services provided. With Edson's call made to the customer, a scribbled note and invoice and a quarter each in our possession, we headed out the door, hearing the overhead bell chime as the door closed.

Our destination for delivery was off West Seventh Street. We knew by the number that it was just a couple of blocks west of Davey's house. We couldn't place the house—even though we knew the neighborhood like the backs of our hands. Cutting out of downtown, we passed the YMCA, a favorite hangout for pool, swimming and basketball, slid through the diagonal walkway of the park and headed west on Seventh Street with big "rich folks" homes where we shoveled snow off their drives in winter.

We arrived at the Schumacher Meat Market corner across from our home school. In another block or two, we recognized our principal's house, then the three-story where Patsy lived, to soon come upon the house number that called for mission completion.

We were shocked to see that it was the little old house that always appeared to be boarded up. Only a block from the General Hospital, we had passed the house a thousand times—but didn't know that anyone actually lived there.

The dark corner lot had a stack of lumber in the front yard, with weeds overgrowing the whole of the property. There didn't seem to be any sign of life as we stepped onto the small front porch entry. Surprisingly, there was a shiny brass plate on the weathered front door. It had been there for years, judging by the wear around it—but it gleamed in the late afternoon sunlight. Inscribed in majestic script was "Col. Robert L. Mason, USMC (Retired)."

We were stunned by the contrast of the beauty of the plate with its natural surroundings and the fact that a real, live soldier lived here. From our vast reading about wars and heroes, dating from the Union and the Confederate armies of the Civil War through the more recent World War II, we were aware of the significance of a colonel's rank. To find a colonel of the U.S. Marines in our small town was beyond our comprehension.

With trepidation, we rapped the metal clapper on the right of the door. Before time for a second rap, a booming voice from inside announced, "Come on in!" Turning the shiny metal knob, we found ourselves face-to-face with a man of considerable girth in a wooden wheelchair. He was dressed in a starched white shirt and sharply-creased khaki trousers.

His ruddy complexion and considerable size were not unlike the features of Santa Claus. The main difference was that his hair was closely cut and his face cleanly shaven, as if he were expecting a visit from the commanding general to his home. Presenting the radio and invoice, the colonel thanked us and offered that Edson was "a remarkable fellow."

The colonel introduced himself to us as Bob Mason. Asking each of us our names, he inquired as to where we lived and who our families were.

When learning that we all attended Madison School, just a block or two away, he was excited to tell us that he had spent his early years at the same school and playground.

He knew all of the local characters—from Schumacher, the butcher, to Old Man Deilke, the grocer, to our friend "Blackie"—the man who often walked across the playground and told us funny stories. He knew Blackie from his elementary school days and through mutual service in the Marines. He assured us that he was "an upright fellow."

Once he began to tell us of his Marine experiences, sharing pictures of his comrades at Iwo Jima along with various awards and polished plaques, he absolutely lit up in his pleasant and ultra-neat surroundings. He had begun his career as a private in the Marine Corps during World War I and steadily rose to full command of a battalion over the next twenty years.

He was excited to know about our comic book heroes and the commitment we all had to becoming future soldiers and protectors of our nation. We told him about our night encampments in the woods across the lake and our travels in the hills. He verified the need for us to continue to build our strength. Colonel Mason invited us to stop by for future visits.

With our teacher's permission, we invited him to school to meet our class and share his ventures. It was a special day when several of us assisted him in his wheelchair across the two blocks of brick sidewalk on the way to school. Bill Groves, the school custodian, assisted us with a temporary ramp up the back steps. The colonel was thrilled to return to his old school. We were greatly honored by his visit.

These visions and mental pictures of the wonderful people of our small town are in no particular order. Some are a mixed, yet juxtaposed, part of memory. They are characters who impressed my youth and imagination. They brought the "stuff" of life to us at every turn of the corners around Grand Street in Winona.

Our lives were enhanced and enriched by their presence.

Speed, Sunday Rides and Flaming Tunnels: A History of Motorcycles in Winona

The Harley-Davidson advertised by Winona dealer Nic Steffes in 1914,

... has every feature to be found in the motorcycle field ... and in addition it is the only motorcycle with the Step-Starter—Double Clutch Control—Ful-Floating Seat and Free Wheel Control. The brake, clutch and the step-starter can all be operated by the feet, leaving only the spark and throttle for hand operation, making the control the same as that of the highest priced automobile.

In Winona, by the time of the Harley ad, there was already quite a following of motorcyclists. Motorcycle day trips by Robert Henry from Independence, Wisconsin, to Winona and those of R.E. Haesley from Winona to Utica made the news. Additionally, there were "Good Races Here Sunday," according to newspapers of the time. Indian Motorcycles stomped the competition at the fairgrounds, winning nearly every place in the races. Races were reported as "spectacular."

The races at the fairgrounds were "good races." In August, 1912, an event held "Rain or Shine" pitted auto against auto and motorcycle against motorcycle in separate three-mile events. The winner of each race faced off against the other for a two-mile race of motorcycle against auto. It wasn't stated whether the winner was from the three-man Indian or Davidson team, but the motorcycle won.

The Winona Motorcycle Club (later called the Wenonah Cycle Club) was already in operation by 1912. Club members had decided that "speeding among club members will not be tolerated—at least in the city." The Winona Club traveled together as a club outing to Altura in May of that year "as far as the roads would take them." Soon thereafter, club visitors from LaCrosse scooted upriver to join the gang to enjoy a shared ride to Witoka. The next meeting was "to be held at Nic Steffes Shop."

Along with Mr. Steffes as Harley representative, other shops in 1912 included Kiral and Deeren's on Lafayette Street and R.E. Haesly (Indian) of West Third Street. He offered the Indian Powerplus for $320. William Sonnenberg carried the Excelsior and Henderson models in his shop at 118-120 Walnut Street, with the Henderson four-cylinder later becoming the $500 model of choice for the Winona Police Department (capable of 110 miles per hour!)

Nic Steffes was the early leader of "wheels" in Winona. At Winona Cycle Livery in 1902, he offered "A Fine Line of Ladies' and Gents' Wheels." He first was located at 118 W. Third Street, with a move to the Motordome at 205207 Main Street in 1907. Pierce, Crescent, Cleveland and Gendron were but a few of the "Serviceable Bicycles" available for approximately twenty-one dollars each.

A committed rider, Nic crashed his bike into a curb in March, 1906, "smashing the front wheel"—with no mention of personal injury. He continued with bicycles, yet added Mitchell, Maxwell and Jeffrey autos by 1912. The Mitchell was advertised as "Quietly, easily, smoothly dependable, powerful and accessible, with 4 1/4 by 5 inch cylinders." Some were available for hire, along with Nic's general repair and Miller tires.

Nic gained the Pierce motorcycle dealership in 1912 with a five-horsepower, four-cylinder model intended to "push other motorcycles off the market." His Harley dealership came soon thereafter. Dedicating his time to motorcycles for several years, he raced from Fountain City to Winona with six others in 1921, and led a charge of stunt riders from the Winona Motorcycle Club in local venues over the years. One of the motorcycles under Nic's charge in 1919 was in flames at 9:30 p.m. at the Motordome, causing a fire alarm in the city.

Mr. Haesley held an Indian Day in February, 1915, featuring the "Little Twin" and all the new Indian models for that year. By 1921, he had become the Harley and Indian dealer outright. Winona Fire Power on West Fifth Street offered the English James Motorcycle in 1948, with C. Paul Venables's Pontiac dealership on Main Street offering Cushman models for more sedate riders during World War II and beyond. The Whizzer ($150) and Doodle Bug (thirty dollars) were available at Western Motor Sales. Something for everyone!

Allyn Morgan, well-known master jeweler of Winona, set up his shop in 1946, at age sixty-two, in the basement of his large home overlooking Lake Winona—to become the "appointed distributor for INDIAN Motorcycles for this territory." With his full-time business as master jeweler, owner of the Garden Gate and Candy Box restaurants and the Morgan Block on Third Street, as "first Winona businessman/aviator" *and* motorcycle enthusiast, he was busy. He offered in 1951 (at age sixty-seven), "It's the plow that isn't used that gets rusty."

After the demise of Indian in 1953, and in moving into the 1960s, Morgan became dealer for NSU Quick and NSU Fox three-horsepower, Jawa, BSA, Triumph, C.Z. 125, and James. As competition, the Yeske Brothers of East Belleview Street carried the Harley badge into the 1950s.

The "Motor Cops of the Winona Police Corps" must have seen the advertisement in the *Winona Republican* in 1914. They took matters into their own hands in 1916, when just too many speeders were racing up and down the streets of Winona. With a full City Council discussion and action, it was decided that two "motorcycle cops" would be assigned—instead of purchasing an automobile for the chief of police.

Officer Thomas Mrachek was the first "cop" to "easily chase speeders and answer various calls in cases of boy fights, ball playing in the streets, dis-

Allyn Morgan Kept "A Shiny Plow"

One of Winona's pioneers, Stephen (S.W.) Morgan, came to Winona by steamer in 1861, from Oquaqua, Illinois. He established the Morgan line of quality jewelry products and a personal theme of continuous community service. He laid down the first stone sidewalk in the business district, and continued to be a rock in the center of Third Street shops in an era of real "downtown" life.

Allyn, the youngest son, continued the traditions of his father, finding his way through glass in the eye, typhoid fever, a broken collar bone, a lost night in the slough, challenges of bicycle racing and near asphyxiation at an early age. He brought the first motorcycle to Winona in 1905, and tinkered through his nights on jewelry making and carburetor tuning for more than fifty years. His "plow never rusted."

He studied watchmaking, manufactured original jewelry and hosted a variety of business interests. Along the way, he played handball at the YMCA, ran for school board, flew a plane with international aviator Max Conrad and "hit a horse on Stockton Hill." He moved into an exquisite home on Lake Boulevard, leaving behind a new home he had built across the lake in the 1920s, on Johnson Street.

At age eleven in 1895, he was the original door opener and greeter for customers entering the Morgan store. From there, he went on to lead the jewelry enterprise with quality service, continuous and innovative advertisements and exquisite products for more than fifty years. Along the

way, he donated newspaper space and generously advertised for Liberty Bonds to "bring the boys 'Over the Top'" in 1917.

At one time he offered "a free silver spoon for the newborn." He created Duncan Hines-recommended restaurants Candy Box and Garden Gate, also known as "The Morgan Tea Room." A Music Corner of the oft-remodeled Morgan's store followed Allyn's early interests in the violin, featuring the Aeolian Vocalion—a machine to play all records in 1919. The Indian shop in his lakeside home's lower level probably reverberated simultaneously with sounds of harmonic mufflers and highbrow music.

He led Winona motorcyclists through the Indian era and continued to bring quality cycles into the 1960s, from England and Czechoslovakia. In 1948, he hosted 100 motorcyclists to a Sunday Picnic and "1,000 wieners" at the Arches Community Park. Alone on a motorcycle side trip to St. Charles that same year, he was reported to having "Beat the Heat" of August by traveling at seventy miles per hour through the valleys from Winona to St. Charles. He offered that there was "a vagrant cold breeze through the valleys."

On the quiet side, he introduced Winonans to "High-wheeled bicycles of the Gay Nineties Era." His son Steve joined him in the jewelry business and in riding high bikes selected from Allyn's collection—for Winona parades of the 1940s and 1950s. Grandson Kent today recalls his grandfather teaching him how to ride one of the high wheelers in the 1950s.

A crowning achievement for Allyn occurred in 1924, when he led the all-male production of "Dream of a Clown"—as the clown. With nearly 100 male community leaders in the cast, the clown was to "Dream the show . . . And keep the audience in a constant uproar."

Allyn was a man for all seasons, a one-of-a-kind model, a legend who operated on four cylinders all of the time.

turbances and calls from across the lake." He also drove the "paddy wagon" during his twelve-hour, seven days per week evening shift.

A year later it was decided that the automobile was "Better than the MC" and that an auto needed to be purchased. It was seen as "risky business for the officer on the motorcycle to chase a speeding automobile." In addition, sighting of a motorcycle automatically caused speeders to slow down. Thus, an auto purchased by city fathers caused a "marked decrease in speeding here." No more was said of capturing those errant boys in their fights—or those otherwise upsetting the world by playing ball in the streets.

The race was on in 1922, when Officer Sievers, on motorcycle, chased after a speeding car to ultimately decide that "Now I've got them!" Indeed he did—after a roundabout race when the car sped on. No arrests were made when the officer "captured" the offending speeders—Officers Winkels and Bronk—who were themselves chasing a speeder.

Motorcycles had come to Winona to stay—and stayed all the way into the 1960s at the police department. In the 1940s and 1950s (preceding parking meters), the three-wheeled Harley-Davidson used by Officer Irv Przytarski aided him in marking the tires of downtown visitors with a chalk line, to be ticketed for overtime parking if the vehicle remained too long in the space—according to his timetable. He also led all of the parades over many years, having most probably been preceded by August Bingold, motorcycle officer and future chief, who regularly collared speeders and violators in the 1920s.

In 1953, Chief Bingold proposed adding a second three-wheeled motorcycle to help with parking issues and the "traffic snarls at the churches on Sunday!" A replacement Harley-Davidson Servi-Car from Yeske Brothers in 1948 cost city fathers $804, less the $400 trade-in of a 1941 model.

In 1923, Bingold hauled in Mr. Kingsley for a too-loud motorcycle—as decided by neighbors and a judge who visited the noisy motorcycle to conclude that a three dollar fine was appropriate because "the law requires that cut-outs must be closed." The future chief may have also been the one, in 1922, who nailed Harry Johnson of Duluth for speeding on his motorcycle on East Broadway at "30 miles per hour."

The same judge offered a flexible sentence. Either Harry could spend fifteen days in jail—or his motorcycle could spend thirty days. Wisely, Harry allowed the police chief to supervise his motorcycle's incarceration for the full sentence. In 1928, Officer Bingold skidded on some mud at roadside near Minnesota City on one of the last days of November to hit a tree and "not badly damage" the motorcycle.

In 1930, Officer Bingold was ably assisted in motorcycle patrol by George Fort, future sheriff of Winona County. Each was assigned a brand-new Henderson four-cylinder machine. Fort didn't apparently tangle with Mrs. Ziegenfuss on West Broadway, who "endangered the life of August Bingold" by "wanton disregard" of him in her automobile attack on him. Bingold escaped—and she was fined twenty dollars.

On his own, in the chase of a speeding car in October, 1925, Bingold swerved around a parade float on East Fourth Street to crash broadside into a passing vehicle, sustaining a wrenched back and a bruised knee. August was off duty from noon patrol on Broadway for a while.

Concern continued about "reckless motorcycling" over the years. The City Council reported in 1948 that, "Third Street had become a racetrack, that three separate riders had been seen on Broadway standing on their bikes as they rode past and that people are just speed crazy."

Accidents and tragedies occurred from 1912 into the 1950s, with few deaths, but many collisions—including motorcycle and cow, boy bike rider and motorcyclist, train and motorcycle, streetcar and motorcycle and a few injured racers. With a crushed leg or broken wrist, scalp wound or twisted back, the riders seemed to get right back on and head down the road.

Many watched (10,000 in attendance!), but apparently few were endangered as the Izaak Walton League held its 1st District Picnic in June, 1948. Crystal Springs, in the Whitewater territory, served as the host site for motorcyclist scrambles and Walton picnic events for thousands over many years since the 1930s. On this day, there were trout ponds to visit, a horseshoe tournament, diamondball game, fox and hound trials, coon chase and a hill competition that drew cyclist climbers from the four-state region.

Hill climbers furnished thrills of the day as they traversed the bluff and climbed to a record 318 vertical feet. The event was safely hosted by the Rochester Motorcycle Club. In 1952, the hill climb at Crystal Springs was sanctioned as an American Motorcycle Association pre-trial event for national riders.

Many Winonans developed their motorcycle fantasies at an early age. As they aged, some risked a ride to Altura or Independence. Another took off for a ride about Winona and ended up in Key West, Florida. With a springed-seat and a hard-working four-horsepower engine, others climbed hills and tipped their machines over to get up and try again. With multiple gears and levers to operate, it was amazing that one could maintain a two-wheeled machine on flat ground, let alone climb it up a 600-foot bluff.

"Jimmy" Naas, son of Springdale Dairy owner Oscar Naas, in his second year of motorcycling in 1935, took a trip to visit a couple of folks in California. He made a 5,000-mile round trip in about three weeks, covering the West and Southwestern United States. His longest day was 610 miles, with an average speed of fifty to fifty-five miles per hour. The total cost of gas and oil was twenty-seven dollars. Save for the skinned face he received in a "spill" in Salt Lake City, he declared himself "a motorcycle enthusiast" upon return.

Thousands turned out to watch these daredevils at the Galesville Fair, Crystal Springs Izaak Walton gatherings and the LaCrosse Races. There were more thrilling moments at the fairgrounds in Winona and "across the river from Bay State" at Walton Park. Galesville motorcycle acts in 1940 included members of the Winona Motorcycle Club, with featured players Cecil Whetstone and Ernest Yeske. Rider activities included a balloon burst, surfboard race, broad jump through a flaming hoop, flaming board wall and a fifteen-foot "Tunnel of Flame."

In 1938, Irving Schildknecht came on the scene. Known as the "Flying Milkman" and "Suicide Schildknecht," he performed with Ernie Yeske and other members of the Winona Motorcycle Club. In one incident, they staged a hare-and-hound race through town and up Garvin Hill, with "hare" Irving being given a two-minute start.

Chasing across town, Ernie and others roared after Irving and caught him "on the old birch trail" up Garvin Heights. Irving and Ernie were the "two daredevils who crashed their motorcycles through inch-thick plank walls at speeds of 6070 mph at the grounds near the airport on a quiet Sunday afternoon"—and lived to tell about it.

The motorcycles, the "Famous James" English model, the reliable Cushman and the smaller NSU Fox and even-smaller Doodlebug gave some a reasonably safe (and slower) ride as the era progressed. The Excelsior, Henderson, Jawa, Norton, Zundapp, Harley, BSA, Triumph and Indian gave extreme choices of power and speed.

More than once, someone took their machine to 110 miles per hour on Highway 61 toward Lacrosse. On a Morgan-sponsored picnic in 1948, for over 100 motorcyclists at Farmers Community Park ("over 1,000 wieners consumed"), the newspaper reporter of the day was given a ride at 120 miles per hour.

The "reliable" Cushman motorcycle of 1949, sold by C. Paul Venables. (Photo courtesy of the author.)

One who had an early start in motorcycles was Allyn Morgan. Born into a family with a silver (or possibly golden) spoon, this son of master jeweler S.W. Morgan took over the jewelry business, bought an Italianette villa on the bluff across from Lake Winona and served motorcyclists of Winona from his garage for over twenty years. As a boy, he had won the half-mile race on his bicycle in a Fairground race in one minute and twenty-four seconds. He reportedly wore out fourteen bicycles in his races, some as far away as Detroit. He was off and running, reported as having "brought the first motorcycle to the city in 1905—a Glenn Curtis experimental machine."

Before age twenty, Allyn was attempting to create lighting for his motorcycle for night rides. He tried acetylene and petroleum lights and was reportedly "trying a storage battery electric light" in 1907. On a daytime trip that year, he made a "motorcycle trip in two hours, twenty minutes to LaCrosse."

Over the years, his hobby became his passion as he evolved the business into the Hiawatha Valley Motor and Cycle Company. He offered all Indian models—from $225 to $1,800 by 1949. Working with Maynard Whetstone, he sold the Indian Papoose (English) in 1950 for $199 and Indian models including Arrow, Brave, Scout, Warrior and Chief. An Indian Scooter sold at $160, with a six-horsepower Briggs and Stratton motor. All on Lake Boulevard!

Business was conducted out of the drive-in lower-level area—a fully designed underground shop/garage in his exquisite home. It was not reported how many late-night baffle-rattling startups of new and repaired Indians shook the upper floor sleeping quarters of Mrs. Morgan.

The Yeske Brothers were very active in the Winona Motorcycle Club. Meetings were held at their shop. Herb was president of the club in 1937, with Ernest as the vice president.

Herb attended the Harley-Davidson conference in Milwaukee in 1947, as the Harley-Davidson dealer in Winona from the 1930s to 1950s. Brothers Ernest, Herb, Hugo and Fred all stayed near their mother at 527 East Belleview and participated in some measure of the business. They later located their shop to East Sarnia and Hamilton—nearly in their backyard, where they sold the three-wheel Servi-Car (Harley-Davidson) to the Winona Police Department in 1948.

By the 1950s, Ernest had moved on to machinist at Winona Tool Manufacturing, residing at 464 Grand Street—only a block away from Nic Steffes's home. Ah, the tales they could tell!

Kawasaki, Suzuki, Honda, and Yamaha all came to Winona from Japan in the 1960s, some in teak-framed boxes—to provide quality motorcycles of size and speed sufficient for any buyer. Motor scooters were added along the way, with the tiny ninety-eight cc, two-stroke Italian Vespa early on the scene in 1948. Vespa was started in Italy after World War II—taking the place of their former fighter-bomber factory.

The improved Harley and Japanese/American models are here to stay, providing exceptional engineering, efficiency and speed. Rides on Gold Wings or Fat Boys to Altura are today but a brief after-work outing. A night return after a hill ride is led by strong three-lamp headlights that would have blown away the young Allyn Morgan as he struggled to light his bike in 1907.

Only two Winona dealers remain to serve motorcyclists' needs. Harley-Davidson models can be found at the Harley-Davidson Shop of Winona on Mobile Drive, where it's been located since April, 2000. Run by the Fosaaen family, they also own outlets in LaCrosse and Waukon, Iowa. Daniels Hardware on Second Street is the only other dealer in the city—with Yamaha featured.

A century has passed since motorcycles gained a foothold in the bluffs and valleys of southeastern Minnesota. Pioneers kick-started their motorcycles, realigned their chains, took off the baffles, modified every component and blasted through tunnels of fire to give us memories of rapping mufflers and hell-bent youth. Hardy fellows like Nic, Herb, Ernest, Jimmy, August, Irv, Allyn and unnamed hill climbers created the traditions—and took their lumps. In a more sedate fashion, the tradition continues with Winona cyclists.

The author takes short rides on his motorcycle, as he has done for over forty years, when not researching. He reviewed nearly 2,000 stories of the Winona Newspaper Project and other sites to gain support for this story.

Early Motorcycles of Winona: Company Histories

There were 150 brands of motorcycles made in 1911. Only a handful survived the 1910s.

Henderson—Known as "The Rolls-Royce of Motorcycles," it was created by William and Tom Henderson in Detroit. With a four-cylinder, fifty-seven cubic inch, seven-horsepower motor, it was the largest and fastest of the time, favored by police of New York and Winona, and sold for $325. Started in 1912, the company was sold to Ignaz Schwinn (of Schwinn Bicycles) in 1917, with production moving to Chicago. In July, 1931, due to the national depression, he announced: "Gentlemen, Today we stop."

Excelsior—Originated in 1905 in Chicago, they produced bicycles, then a 344 cc four-stroke single speed with a top speed of thirty-five to forty miles per hour. They introduced their famous engine configuration—the "v-twin, sixty-one cubic inch, 1000 cc" in 1910. By 1911, Schwinn purchased the company. By 1914, it was the most successful company, offering the first 100 mile per hour motorcycle. Henderson moved to Excelsior in 1917, to become Excelsior-Henderson. Will Henderson died in 1922 in a motorcycle accident, testing a new model. The company closed in 1931.

The company was re-started in Burnsville, Minnesota, in 1993, with manufacturing in Belle Plaine. All rights had been purchased from Schwinn. Although the company was bankrupt by 1999, models made during the short era are "highly coveted."

Indian—Founded in 1901, the Indian won the Gold Medal for Mechanical Engineering in 1904. A trouble-free run on an Indian was made from San Francisco to New York City in 1906. The New York City Police Department bought the motorcycles in 1907, to "chase down runaway horses." Manufacturing was conducted on a seven-mile assembly line in Springfield, Massachusetts.

The company had 3,000 employees by 1914, with Indian holding every American speed and distance record from 1910 to 1919. They worked steadily for the War Department in World War II, including the production of 5,000 machines for the French government. Following World War II they struggled; by 1953, they faltered.

The company was re-started in 2008 in Spirit Lake, Iowa, today being owned by Polaris. They produced three models for 2012—the Chief Classic for $26,500; Chief Dark Horse, for $28,000; and Chief Vintage, at $36,000.

Harley-Davidson—Founded by childhood friends William Harley (age twenty-two) and Arthur Davidson in a ten-by-fifteen-foot shed in Milwaukee, they received great assistance from Ole Evinrude, creator of Evinrude outboard motors. Harley graduated in 1907 from the University of Wisconsin-Madison with a degree in mechanical engineering.

Incorporated in 1907, they proceeded to introduce the v-twin in 1911, and went with a majority of v-twin models thereafter. It was one of few motorcycle companies to make it through the Depression and enjoy a century of service to riders.

Famous James Featherweight—An English motorcycle company, founded in 1897 and lasting until 1966. Henry James, after a background in bicycles, introduced small, Whizzer-like bikes in 1902—the ninety-eight cc Autocycle, the 125 Comet and the Commando 200. One man, Kent Morgan, sold his in 1950—taking a summer off. His ad of June, 1950, said: "Leaving city for summer. Sell Famous James MC very cheap. See him at 1750 Gilmore for 'demonstration.'"

Triumph and Norton—The real rumblers of the 1950s from Great Britain to appear in Winona were the Triumph and Norton—two "hot" 750 cc machines. Triumph (BSA-Triumph) was the biggest model maker, merging with Norton, which was founded in 1898. They sold 100,000 for wartime service in World War II. Norton's Dominator Twins 500 cc and 750 Commando were stunning; followed by the Norton Big Four of 1952. The most famous model was the Triton—with a Triumph twin and a Norton Featherbed frame.

NSU Fox and Quick—along with other models, these were made by NSU Motorwerke of Germany. Founded in 1873, their early machines were built in a sewing machine factory. The company was later acquired by Volkswagen.

Cushman—Started by Everett and Clinton Cushman in 1903 in Lincoln, Nebraska, the business was incorporated in 1913. From 1936 to 1965, they produced the Motor Scooter, with the well-known enclosed engine shroud and step-through design. Cushman became a big military manufacturer in World War II. Eagle was their most successful motorcycle post-war for sixteen years, through 1966. They moved on to golf carts, Cushman Truckster and small business applications, and were sold eventually to Textron.

Doodlebug—The 1946 Hiawatha Doodlebug was manufactured in Webster City, Iowa, by Beam Manufacturing. Very simplistic, it had a Clinton motor, a gas tank on the rear of the seat, lights and clutch. It was offered for sale for thirty dollars at Western Auto of Winona in the 1940s—and is still available today in various versions and manufacturers.

Jawa—Made in Czechoslovakia, it was merged with CZ. Janacek purchased the rights of Wanderer motorcycle in 1929. Thus the name JaWa.

They produced a 500 cc in 1929—four-cycle, eighteen horsepower. The JaWa 175, in 1932, was very successful—with economy. In 1946, *Popular Mechanics* announced the "light and fast" one-cylinder—topping out at sixty-two miles per hour. They also had a 250 cc two-stroke and 350 cc. Machines were marketed as JaWa and CZ brands. By 1962, they had a 600 cc model. The company is still producing today, with a large market in India. They have had marginal success.

On Memory

In the baked-in warmth of the Federal Bakery of my hometown youth was an ever-twirling, electric and elliptical machine that continuously spun off unbaked bakery globules. They had been deposited on a stainless steel surface of the machine by another machine set up above, in similar Rube Goldberg fashion, to spit out sliced chunks of dough.

Dependent upon placement of the globule on the spinning elliptical disks—and the distance from the eccentric center—the ride of the bakery item in raw form varied in speed and formation. On the inside it started a quick ride around the inner loop to gradually move out to fall into place on a second metallic spheroid. As centrifugal force increased, the dough ball whirled, changed form and flattened.

With a slide across an ever-greater diameter and a fall to a lower level that slowed the speed, the item ultimately slipped off onto a downslide chute. From there, transfer was to a conveyor belt to whisk straightaway the soon-to-be-baked items for uniform deposit onto a greased metal pan headed for the oven.

In the midst of the lightly flour-dusted machinery stood an operator in a white paper hat, white t-shirt and matching pants. Feeling satisfaction with his machine and his second-shift progress, Ed hit the red "stop" button on the wall and stepped out the screened side door of the bakery onto the warm cement walkway. On this summer evening in the river valley, he gave the machine a break, enjoyed a smoke and a bit of the natural breeze.

I often think of the machine and the operator. In the small side room behind the sales counter of a large bakery on Third Street, the complexity of the machines, the ingenuity and cooperation of the operator and forces of nature and invention cooperated to allow a simple product—a roll or a donut—to evolve. For me, it was fascination with complexity that yielded a simple result.

Over time, I sense that my answers to life's questions have gone through a similar process. From somewhere above, questions have been dumped onto a Lazy Susan and spun for a while—gatherng ingredients together and falling out the chute. In the process, I have listened, pondered and talked as ingredients cogitated. Sometimes I continued to talk knowing that the result was cogitating in there and would soon fall out.

Responses twirled and formed. Sometimes my mental machine spun unknowingly for a full shift or shift-and-a-half until there came clear a nugget to share. Sometimes my mind and words wandered in conversation as I waited for the machine to do its work. I off-loaded the question to the Lazy Susan and went on with conversation. It would catch up with me.

Today we have machines to do our thinking for us. As we work and write, we can reach across the screen to a thesaurus or Google or Wikipedia to update a topic before we move on the next paragraph. Responses to questions have become instantaneous. We need only "Dial A Friend" or call our mother to get an instant response. It's even possible that if we don't know the answer to a question on a quiz that we can text-message our friend across the classroom and receive the answer.

We can sit in a classroom, listen to the instructor speak and reach across the world with our iPhone or Blackberry to find out whether the instructor is right on, or whether we need to make a challenge.

We can get a recipe for Mom, look up a sine value on a calculator or otherwise spin answers instantaneously that previously caused our mind to ponder (at least for a moment). I have seen beginning (and some advanced) math students use their calculators to add three two-digit figures.

Cognitive decline has begun—in the third grade. It's no longer the sole domain of old folks. Frequently I see cashiers of the new generation confused when I give one an extra quarter over the designated breakfast bill amount to account for the cents owed. They get confused and ask the machine to figure it out for them. We have diminished our minds by not using forced remembrance and structured patterns to accomplish tasks. The Lazy Susan has been retired. We don't look to solutions. We look to answers. Every answer must be on the web or in a text message.

Levers, fulcrums, inclined planes and the negotiation of human problems require us to use skills learned through investigation and application. With trial and error, use of hands and brain, we stimulate invention and creativity. As we work with one piece, we may see a divergent path that may take us to a different problem, to a new solution. The answer lies in the integration of our skills and knowledge to create power—the rate of doing work.

It is done in a Lazy Susan kind of way. We blend our experience with our knowledge and create a solution. How exciting!

Yesterday I caused the minds of 100 exceptionally skilled high school seniors to go quiet and read a passage for nearly an hour in class. Once settled, they became truly engaged with their own wonderment and response. It is fascinating to perceive the possibilities of their wondrous minds, as they let them wander and twist their way through the reading to solution or to sensate memory.

The quiet of their minds caused them to ponder new possibilities. I suggested quietly that I could "hear their minds whirring." When they invest their time in a million text messages a month (as some teens do), they miss the chance to engage the brain in meaningful action.

Discovering the beauty of the mind as it pops and fizzles to drop globules on its way to mechanical solution is remarkable. Yet in our soft side of memory, nuances prevail. Little is sharp and clear—yet the vision, the sense is crystal.

The flower in bloom, the fresh-baked bread, the warmth of sunlight on a spring day in the garden all drift, then tarry and lead us to wonder. We remember, but sometimes wonder—is it real or not? Memory is fragile, most certainly delicate. It wisps and turns and then abides like a lookout stone at creek side—unyielding, rock-solid.

We feel the sensate and remember—a brush against Pa's coarse stubble, the touch of a friend in the moonlight of a winter night, the sound of geese in formation on their southern trace in cool nights of autumn.

Chapter Eleven

Chipmunk Crossing: A Garden Remembrance

Flowers stretched up the soft pea gravel and crushed rock entrance to the small home. A former driveway, it headed toward a double garage in back. The cement was gone. Flower beds to the left and right and center stage blended instead, as on the palette of a master.

It was a scene reminiscent of a Monet painting—with roses and daffodils, sweet peas and ivy, hollyhocks and lavendar, irises and pansies, asters and coleus, zinnias and petunias, peonies and morning glories, all bringing profusion and harmony to the English cottage environment.

Forever seen in the garden, she was a wisp of a woman, yet master of her domain. She talked as she walked—especially when pulling more than her own weight in the two-wheeled Montgomery Ward garden cart. She was there from sunup to sundown on a steady pace of planting and pulling—interspersed with lemonade breaks on a small, shady side porch.

Although located on West Ninth Street in the Village of Goodview, the bucolic setting was seen by gardener Ernestine to be in the village of "God's View." With a supreme personal effort in her gardens and in the surround of blue skies and valley-wide limestone bluffs, she was in her own Garden of Eden—a heavenly place.

Married for years to Anton of the local college staff, Ernestine spent her early years with Anton and their precocious daughter, Eldora. They attended college events and shared a good life with Eldora and neighbors. The post-World War II village invited young community professionals to seek the open air, yet keep proximity to the benefits of the neighboring established college river town.

They came to Ninth Street in the 1940s, shortly after sand burrs were cleared from medium-sized sandy lots. It was a good life of church and school and home and family. Together they enjoyed Sunday afternoon automobile rides to the hills and valleys surrounding their small river town. Ernestine tinkered with garden and wheelbarrow and thoroughly enjoyed her role as a mother and wife. She was thrilled with quiet evening moments of radio broadcasts and music. An accomplished pianist, she gave lessons to a few children of the village on Saturday morning.

After Anton's passing and her daughter's permanent move to California, she created "Barth's Space," a cornucopia of flowers that entertained all through the frost-free days in Minnesota. She was enthralled with colorful catalogs and the spending of quiet winter moments selecting and ordering seeds—to begin again with spring plantings in her south-side, glass-enclosed day room.

A 200-year-old seed company in Connecticut provided her with packets of her favorite organic varieties of sweet peas—including Blanche Ferry, King Edward, Lord Nelson and Black Knight—"so dark maroon it is nearly black." Music, planting and tea often made up her days in March and April.

Known to neighbors in later, singular years simply as "Barth," she toiled with planting, weed removal and composting—and loved every moment. In facing a weed, she felt as Ralph Waldo Emerson, who offered, "What is a weed but a plant whose virtues have not yet been discovered?"

She was perpetually in motion, seeming to pull her cart everywhere throughout the village. From tulips and hyacinths peeking through the waning snow of her picket-fenced yard to colorful mums of autumn nestling against the back fence, she planted, cut back, and trimmed—with finite design, precision and continuous soft watering provided by an underground pump.

I was recently reminded of Barth as I re-formed one of the garden beds in our small lakeside home, where my wife and I drag around our own garden carts and buckets. I discovered again the small, metal "Chipmunk Crossing" sign that has kicked around our various gardens for over thirty years. It's a small remembrance gained from Barth as she gave up gardening.

She offered some items of her small collection of hoses, figures and garden tools at a garage sale conducted next door by her good friend and neighbor, Evie. We happened to be in town and next door for the seemingly small event and sale. More than a simple sale, it was the closing of a garden, the loss of a guide and friend who showed the way—and the ending of an era. Barth had been unique—an everlasting garden treasure.

Each year I buff and shine the Chipmunk Crossing sign, and place it conspicuously near our front entry for guests and chipmunks to observe.

If only we had purchased the Montgomery Ward garden cart!

Epilogue I:
Up North

Following the path from his cabin through snow-covered evergreen boughs, Davey can see snow accumulating on the deck of his fishing boat. Anchored as it is inside the craggy shoreline that deflects the north wind's gusto, the wind spread waves beyond into riblets—a scene with a sense of the macabre.

Alaska's early morning dawn in mid-December is forbidding. To those who dare enter, there are obvious signs of warning. Gray sleet, clods of rock and wind-driven snow mixing with sands at the bayside foretell danger to those who dare enter.

It is an easy five-minute walk from cabin to dockage for Davey. He has traveled the solitary route so many times these past thirty years that he can count the rock steps as old friends who ease him toward his next step. The flurries of the morning are a sign of welcome to a new day, another adventure.

The wind, the snow, the sunrise and the old wool mackinaw on his back feel like old friends. Each day brings its own glory, its own special grace to share with routines of life and survival in the land of Alyeska, the chosen land of settlement for Kodiak bears, "grizzlies" and a young man from the bluff country of Minnesota.

Life is simple for those who understand the fragile balance between existence and natural cooperation. Fragility and strength hang in the balance. Davey understands it. He has been tested. He is a survivor. His every day, virtually every movement hides the depth of his understanding from those who observe.

They see a man committed to the elements, committed to his own frailties, committed to his work and achievement. They do not discern the nuances, however. In every one of his measured steps, in his every action, he operates on a plane just slightly apart from that of the work-a-day world of his remote neighbors, who operate the "fly-in" fishing and hunting resorts dotting the landscape near Bear Island.

For them, the weekly visitors who arrive by float plane are their source of income, their hope for sustenance, the ticket to color televisions attached to satellite dishes and cash for trips to the lower forty-eight. For Davey, it is the everyday quest of living with nature. The necessities take care of themselves. He is not in it for the money.

Davey's task for this day is to do end-of-the-season maintenance to the hoses and fittings of his well-maintained trawler, the *Lucky*. He purchased her on payments over the past ten years.

Davey's background in mechanical power transmission had been gained first as a service representative in the Upper Midwest Office of General Motors and then as a teacher in the vocational school of Hanley, Montana. Through these experiences, he gained essential background and technique needed to keep his trawler's diesel engines functioning in all kinds of weather.

With no service station to pull into, each boat captain needs to be a jack-of-all-trades when it comes to service, repair and preventative maintenance of his or her craft. Wiring, diesel engines, radar, electronics, hydraulics and water systems are but a few of the necessary mechanical and engineering skills essential to keep his lifeblood and passion afloat.

The challenge of engine maintenance is not as difficult as maintaining the freedom that he needs. For years, he has had to acquiesce to the more mundane needs of banks, interest rates and bureaucracies. In just three more payments, he will be "home free". The boat would finally be his—lock, stock and barrel. Davey anticipates the impending freedom. His sense of personal freedom hinges upon his ability to not answer to too many masters. The bank is a master whom he would just as soon not have.

It was a blustery day in mid-December many years ago when Davey decided to move on from his teaching job. Just the night before, he had seen a report on the department leader's desk that said that enrollment for the upcoming semester was limited and tentative.

Having been aware that enrollment had been hard to come by these past few years, Davey was not surprised. He truly liked the work with his salt-of-the-earth students who came from the nearby ranches, hastily built mining towns and from the families of hardy western stock. There just weren't enough of them.

When the oil economy of nearby counties and the coal-gasification plant in Beulah finally giving up the ghost a year or so earlier, the handwriting was on the wall. How could one even begin to consider a future of stimulating young minds toward the excitement of power mechanics when the future was so bleak for the region and for each of the graduates? Davey cared for them all, but it was time to move on toward his dream of Alaska.

First Bank of Soldatna was terrific. When he dropped in to see Tom ten short years ago, Davey had established a reputation as a most qualified hand on the trawlers, rentals and salmon fishing boats that moved away from the Homer Spit each morning. After working with the whole range of captains along the coast, Davey gained a set of experiences that would stand him very well when it came time for him to put out on his own trawler.

He had worked with the best and seen the worst. He knew the weather, the dispositions and idiosyncrasies of the captains, as well as the habits of the waters and the fishes. He felt himself to be uniquely prepared to be off on his own, to create a space in the fishing community that would rival the best of the catches, provide him with necessary adventure, financial return and the freedom he craved.

Tom was equally aware and immediately supportive. Over the years, through payments and conversation, they had become good and lasting friends. When Tom could get away from his commercial responsibilities, he often enjoyed a late evening or two in the everlasting sunlight helping Davey with the nets and a heavy summer catch.

Early on, Davey had settled on the small island of Unalaska. He was able to purchase forty acres of woods and rocky coastline upon which he built a log cabin, that today suited the needs of his wife, Tumuara, and their son, Peter. They had the conveniences of a wood stove, a small generator for back-up electricity and plenty of woods from which to harvest berries and wild game.

From his daily quest, fish was a staple of their diet. They had a small garden for vegetables. As needed, they made the trip to Soldotna for staples. Davey kept an old pickup truck at Homer that he reached by boat for medical necessities, showers and appointments. Peter attended a one-room schoolhouse on the island that was reached most often in the winter by snowmobile.

Peter was well-adapted to the life and style of Alaska and loved his home. Just a few days ago, at age thirteen, he had shot his first moose. Davey skinned it out and proceeded to quarter the carcass for further use. From the thousand-pound beast, roasts, chops, and ground burger would be made.

His homemade sausage would be smoked and dried in his smoke-house, just outside the cabin door, in the fashion that he had seen neighbor Schumacher, the butcher, smoke his meats and sausages. As a young boy in his hometown of southern Minnesota, he ventured down the block and often assisted "Old Man" Schumacher in loading and extracting the wieners and sausages from his tall wooden smokehouse.

Davey spent a long season and long days on the water from spring to fall. He had a contract with a major fish company for salmon, halibut, and any tuna that he could garner. Davey was successful and appreciated for his consistent catches. He loved his work and generally operated alone until the heavy catches of the summer, when he hired a college student to assist him.

He was out by 4:30 a.m. and sometimes went until 10:00 p.m. with the long summer days. In fall and winter, his schedule was more relaxed to give him time for maintenance, hunting, and setting up the stores necessary for the long winter.

Tumuara maintained the household and garden and cared for Peter while Davey was at work. She was a wonderful native of the island who loved her most natural life. They made a terrific team, often sought out by their few island neighbors for advice and counsel.

Davey had found his home with nature so many miles away from his early ventures in the woods and bluffs of southern Minnesota. As he sat by the fire in his log home on the craggy shores of Alaska, he often thought of his early friends and the beginnings of his natural living and wonderment.

Next to him in his "parlor" was a hand-made shelf not unlike the one his mother had in her small front room in Winona. Now at rest in his old wooden chair with a bearhide cover, he enjoyed his collection of hand-carved Eskimo figures, his pictures of Tumuara and Peter and a few of his old polished knives.

All gave way to the central item of display—a tattered and worn black-and-white photo encased in a beautiful silver frame. He had contracted with a native silver artisan outside Anchorage to create the frame—a montage of leaves and knives and vines intertwined with four youthful hands—all containing the picture of two young adventurers standing next to a small showcase, which held a skull.

It was his most prized possession.

Sugar Loaf of Winona:
An Historic Landmark

*N*estled in the heart of the Upper Mississippi River Valley between the southern border of Minnesota and Lake Pepin is a land, by "consensus of those
who traveled the old World and the New," to be "not surpassed in beauty and mag-
nificence anywhere on the globe."
>   —Art Work of St. Croix and Mississippi Valley from Stillwater, Mn
>   to Lacrosse, WI. Art Photogravure Co., 1899

From Trempealeau Mountain of the south to Red Wing's Barn Bluff of the
north are panoramic bluffs up and down the Mississippi River. Interspersed
over these miles of sparkling water are Queen Bluff at Dakota, Le May Bluff
at LaMoille and the Maiden's Rock, a "domed-shaped cliff" on the Wisconsin
shore of Lake Pepin. Central to the approximately eighty-mile stretch of winding river and magnificent views of southern Minnesota is the historic Sugar
Loaf of Winona.

It is a place of beauty and a landmark associated with the city, initially known as Wapasha's Prairie when inhabited by Sioux Indians. It is also
a place of wonderment for those who have passed by. Growing up within daily
sight of the bluff on walks to school and skating rink and Grandma's house
was the Sugar Loaf.

In late afternoon, it shadowed the historic home of Bub's Beer, with
its underground limestone caverns used for storage of kegs of German beer.
It also cast a shadow on the nationally-acclaimed Hot Fish Shop—home of the
world's best walleye lunch.

"In ancient days, the famous Cap of Wapasha, afterwards known as
the 'Sugar Loaf,' was of massive proportions, and in great favor as a resort to

Sugar Loaf of the late 1800s. (Photo courtesy of Wikipedia.)

kill war-eagles, but it has succumbed to the demands of commerce, if not of civilization," reports one source. Jutting out some two miles off Lake Pepin yet today is a nearly identical outcropping matching the original size of Wapasha's Cap.

I lived in the city and enjoyed the view. In recent years, I ran the wonderful full loop around Lake Winona on many occasions. As a boy, I thrilled at the exploits of youthful climbers of Sugar Loaf. They were obviously forbidden from climbing—and thus enticed to climb its precipices. In school, I heard Sugar Loaf mentioned in school, but teachers never fully explained its history. Thus is my quest.

Samuel Champlain first explored the area known as Miche-See-Bee (Mississippi) in 1609, but didn't visit Wapasha's Prairie. French explorers first found the area. Father James Marquette, in 1675, journeyed from Mackinac to pass through Dog's Prairie at La Prairie du Chien while traveling south.

The Sierur DuLuth, or Daniel Greysolon, Sieur du Lhut (1639-1710), was a French soldier and explorer who is the first European known to have visited the area of Duluth and the headwaters of the Mississippi River. He visited Isanti (Izatys) in 1679, where Father Louis Hennepin preceded him. This was fortunate for Hennepin, since DuLuth rescued him from a Sioux village near Mille Lacs.

Hennepin had previously traveled the area and was responsible for naming Trempealeau Mountain. It was, however, Nicholas Perrot ("the ablest of

French explorers") who first raised the French flag at Lake Pepin in 1689. He stayed downriver at the "wintering ground" of Trempealeau—only ten miles as the eagle flies from Wapasha's Cap. The French originally gave the name "Wing's Prairie" to Winona, settling on "Wapasha's Prairie," after the great Sioux chief.

Lieutenant Zebulon Pike arrived in 1805, and was "presented by Wapasha with a pipe of peace." He visited Minneowah Bluff, three miles south of Winona and Wapasha's Cap, to get "a bird's-eye view of the village itself." He wrote in his diary "a beautiful description of the views from the Winona bluffs." At Red Wing's Barn Bluff, he was "the first American to gaze upon the magnificent scenery of the lake (Pepin) and the winding river and bluffs above from such a central coign of vantage."

It is believed that "Red Wing, named for a chief, was an old Dakota village at the foot of a remarkable bluff known as Rem-ne-chee, though the village was called Ous-shoots-cah. Sometimes the name Rem-ne-chee was applied to the chief of the village, as was the name of Wa-Pa-sha to the modern Sugar Loaf in reverse order."

The "fire canoe" arrived in the form of the *Virginia* in 1823—the "first steamboat to reach the mouth of the Mississippi." Chief Wa-Pa-Sha remembered the steamboat to later visitors, with whom he shared his "great admiration of the power of the steamer."

Upon arrival in the Winona area in 1852, with not a place to stay, Reverand Hiram Hamilton headed toward a haystack in the distance. Approaching, he soon found the haystack to be Sugar Loaf Bluff. He settled his shanty across the slough, stayed for a bit and soon moved to the "bank of the river"—an area that became the foot of Main Street.

He retained 160 acres near his shanty in what became known as Hamilton's Addition, including the road leading to Sugar Loaf. Known as the Stone Road, Mankato Dike and Mankato Avenue, this "macadamized road" was "raised to five feet above the slough" in 1873, thanks in part to Henry Lamberton of the "flouring mill."

Although Mr. Hamilton was probably driven off by the mosquitoes, Mr. John Wonder from Holstein, Germany, found the southern slope of Sugar Loaf to be a cornucopia of growth for his "market garden" in 1857. He established greenhouses and hotbeds, with a flower shop to follow on Kansas Street. Richard Jackman must have succeeded him, for in 1866, Jackman listed himself as "the most skillful and successful gardener in Winona." He offered to "deliver punctually every morning to home or hotel."

It wasn't clear who the deliveryman was in August of 1872, but Van Gorder's fine dray team, Spotted Tail and Red Rye, were getting a load in downtown when the driver loading baskets aboard the dray at the depot happened to toss one "clean over the horses' backs." They misunderstood it for "go," and they went. So did the baskets.

Anxious to have a good audience, the horses ambled gracefully down Third and Second streets. Office Miller darted out from the Big Red Coffee Pot and bared his blazing star to the dilated eyes of the wild animals. They heeded not, but dashed forward on their "mad career."

Miller, never having had any experience to speak of in riding a dray bareback, didn't get on. The lines were down, and there was no use. Just after he had given them up, some fellow demonstrated his sagacity by rushing out with a club, which he excitedly hurled at the runaways. The team passed on and sought the familiar door of their stable, where they were captured.

Oh, for the excitement of a sunny August morning in downtown Winona!

Jacob Weisbrod came along to establish the Sugar Loaf Brewery on seven acres below the "Cap" in 1862, with Peter Bub of Bavaria and Milwaukee joining him as foreman soon thereafter. Mr. Bub married the widowed Mrs. Weisbrod in 1870. The brewery burned in 1871—requiring buildup of a major facility with capacity of 20,000 barrels by 1882.

In 1883, the city granted R.D. Cone and others a fifty-year right to create and maintain a street railway "from Winona Wagon Works (West Fifth Street) to macadamized road leading to Sugar Loaf Bluff (Mankato Avenue.)" The five-cent fare took one "over line."

A great amount of excitement centered in the Sugar Loaf area in early years, with quarries, saloons, gardens, picnics, fires, "German Sharpshooters Schuetzenfests," maple syrup ("the pure article"), Big Sugar Loaf Patent Flour by the barrel, breweries and a proposed new school all vying for attention. Bub's, Schellhas, Winona Brewing, and Becker and Neuffler all created homemade beer in the shadow of Sugar Loaf.

The breweries alternated sponsoring picnics on summer Sundays in the 1880s at Benson's Park, Bub's Grove, and Becker's Grove. Entertainment included the likes of "turning exercisers" (turners or tumblers) and the Germania Band. An added feature of the picnics was a taste of well water drawn from Artesian wells tapped 450 feet below the rock. Bub's was the first to sink a sand point for the water to create their fine, German beer—with the City of Winona following for citywide consumption.

On other days of the week, August Ruhnke offered "cigars, wine, whiskies, Bub's Beer in kegs or 'on draught' at 113 West Third Street—and free lunch every morning from 9:00-11:00 a.m." The Artesian, Phil Feiten's place, opened on the first day of 1897 at Sugar Loaf to offer a saloon and bowling alleys—with a free bus provided on Sunday afternoons.

By the Prohibition years of the 1920s, Bub's was the only remaining brewery, serving up root beer and near beer, with storage in five sandstone caves.

For unknown reasons, Bub, Schellhas and other notables opposed the new school in 1892, with Schellhas stating the idea was "truly a folly." Built soon thereafter, the school closed in 1923, to be sold in 1935. Passing by the school today, the nearby property "in the shadow of Sugar Loaf" has been developed into three subdivisions of housing: Glen Mary, Glen Echo and Glen-View, commencing in 1948.

A "Sugar Loaf" was first made in Jordan in the twelfth century. Later, in the heyday of sugar trade in Brazil in the sixteenth century, "blocks of sugar were placed in conical molds to be transported on ships." This named form became the designated title of the 1,299-foot Sugar Loaf Mountain at the harbor of Rio de Janiero, Brazil—thus preceding Winona's named 500-foot bluff by several hundred years.

Winona's Sugar Loaf Bluff is 500 feet, with an extended eighty-five feet created by quarrying. The view of Sugar Loaf of the early 1800s was substantially changed by the mining of limestone, probably used to create the base for roads in and around the city.

A "thesis read at Winona Normal School" in 1867 suggested the hill to be composed of "silicious sandstone, bluish limestone, argillaceous sandstone and magnesium limestone."

The Sugar Loaf Stone and Lime Quarry owned by E.S. Smith, Jason Jacoby and Warren Powers advertised in 1857 "the best and purest selected stone sold in any quantity—at kilns or delivered." Suggested were stones for stone houses, cottages and public buildings, "to protect ourselves and our families against the extremes of all seasons." Terms listed for purchase stated: "Stone and lime will be sold for cash so low as to defy competition." Mr. Bauder assumed exclusive ownership of Sugar Loaf Stone Quarry in 1867.

Purchasing the property in 1878, quarrying operations were increased by John O'Dea, who ceased operation in 1887. With a call by the citizenry in 1897 to preserve "the Sugar Loaf rocky pinnacle" as a city landmark, interest was present—but the challenge to city ownership was slow in coming, taking an additional half-century. Mr. O'Dea reported that strong interest remained in 1919 to cut Sugar Loaf down further, since "2,500 cords of quality limestone remained." He assured the public that he would not move forward.

The cap was further reduced in size by the "cascade of tons of limestone down the northwest slope" in 2004, caused by the cycle of freezing and thawing in Minnesota winters.

For all of the years, there has been concern for safety of individuals who risked the challenge of climbing or otherwise playing on the hill. In 1912, the police chief reported that "coasters" of winter were taking advantage of the "fine sleighing" and running their sleds onto the highway at the base of the hill. It was "dangerous to children and drivers." He said the "bluecoats have instructions to arrest the offenders."

Some have climbed it—and others have tried.

Locke Lester, age fourteen, was marooned at the fifty-foot level for three hours in 1922. With a strong climb by his older brother Charles, a small rope was tossed to him. He pulled the rope, which was attached to a larger rope provided by the fire department, and affixed it to a long iron peg—to safely slide down the rope.

An early family member of this writer was instrumental in rescuing Ruth Keller, age fourteen, who had fallen 200 feet off the bluff in 1924. Rudy Naas and friends Frank and Paul Zenk were there to help her down the hill and to medical attention on a fine June day. In 1952, a twelve-year old girl died from a similar fall, with her sister sustaining injuries to arm and leg.

In 1945, a brother of mine left a fistfight and his education behind in the halls of Winona High to venture off with a couple of ninth grade buddies. "I guess that's what encouraged me and a couple of the other freshmen to skip school one day," he said. "We'd had enough. So we took off at noon. Our thoughts were to get the hell out of town so the truant officer wouldn't pick us up. We headed west towards Sugar Loaf Bluff. We got there in decent time and proceeded to climb the bluff to the top, where the large rock was located called Sugar Loaf.

"Years ago they quarried rock off this bluff to make crushed rock, I presume. In the process of quarrying, they left this gigantic rock monument now called Sugar Loaf. I have no idea what the size of it is, but it's big to say the least—and damned high to the top of it. Us dummies stood there and looked at it a while and we noticed that somebody at some time in the past had pounded pitons into the face of the cliff. So just for the hell of it, we started climbing up the face of this monolith. Every now and then we would have to grab hold of one of those pitons to help ourselves up. (Scares the hell out of me to even write about it now—sixty-five years later.)

"We eventually made it to the top, no easy chore, I might add. Now as we stood there observing the town of Winona from this vantage point we marveled at the view. All of a sudden it dawned on us that we now had to climb back down that damn thing! That was the scariest part of all.

"I will guess that monolith is at least as high as a four-story building. Maybe even more. One slip of the foot and down you would come—most likely to a very painful conclusion. Neither of the other guys would go first, so I took the lead. I made damn sure they waited until I got to the bottom so if one of them started out above me and lost his grip he wouldn't knock me off the face on his way down.

"I'd heard several times since that kids have climbed that thing and had to be rescued by the Winona Fire Dept. I guess we showed them. By God, we didn't need help getting down off that damn thing.

"*Whoa!* Wait a second, maybe we did have help after all!"

My brother didn't return for any more education, but he had a lasting memory of the day.

Eventually, the Sugar Loaf land moved to the Bohn family, where it remained for many years. Adolph Bohn reported in 1942 to have grown "strawberries as big as walnuts," with a follow-up ad suggesting them to be "as big as eggs"—with twenty-nine packed to the standard box, versus the usual 100.

Following the instructions of Mrs. Adelia Bohn Hogan, family representative, the land was put up for sale in 1948—marketing the edifice and adjoining twenty-two acres "to any suitable buyer." A Grand Street neighbor of mine, Adolph Engel, was named agent of record. "$8,000.00 Will Buy Landmark" read the headline.

Fortunately, a strong cadre of seven strong Winona women in the Wenonah D.A.R., led by Mrs. Carl Baumann and Mrs. George Kissling, came forward to initiate a community-wide fundraiser. They worked diligently for two years to achieve their goal, culminating in the presentation of the deed to the City Council in May of 1950. Winonans and visitors are forever thankful for their grand effort. They preserved a landmark for all to enjoy.

The natural bluff site and adjacent Peter Bub Brewery are separately placed on the National Register of Historic Places in Minnesota.

Original Sugar Loaf Bluff, before mining reduced its size. (Photo courtesy of the Winona Newspaper Project, Winona State University.)

Sources:

Winona Newspaper Project, Winona State University.

History of Winona County, 1883. (Republication by Winona Historical Society, 1977.)

Art Work of St. Croix and Mississippi Valley from Stillwater, Mn to Lacrosse, WI. Art Photogravure Co., 1899.

Wikipedia—Information and photographs. Photos, 1898 and early 1800's (west side)

Robert Voigt Story

Naas Family information

As a young boy, the author enjoyed day hikes and adventures to caves and bluffs facing Lake Winona. His single-speed bicycle strained to get up Garvin Heights and the brick roads of Sugar Loaf Hill and beyond.

He also enjoyed a cool tap beer in the cave of Bub's Brewery when he was a bit below legal age.

Epilogue II:
Yet at Home

The dance was about to begin. As always, first arrivals were one or two singles—anxious ninth graders coming to their first dance—or a few of the quiet, studious types from the upper classes. The first of two spit-and-polished boys arriving in front of Everett were truly dressed for the dance—as their parents had decided.

One reminded Everett of Woody, a high school classmate. With wire-rim glasses, a docile style and a mother-directed shine on his shoes, the young man's appearance was just too much to believe. It was déjà-vu all over again. Woody had been reincarnated.

When Everett was in high school, Woody and Myron were the co-managers of the basketball team. They did all things right, from theme papers in history class to saying "Sir" to the coaches and principal.

Somehow, innately it seemed, they were attuned to the ways of the adult world long before other boys even knew that those ways existed. Today, one would suppose that they might be the "nerds."

They weren't harmless or weak or even afraid, but something distinguished them from the crowd. When the rest of us went to throw snowballs at cars or to a neighborhood party when parents were gone, they went home. Were they born with good sense?

Tonight was another of the nights of many. After more than twenty-five years in the classrooms and hallways of the local high school, Everett had become a fixture. He was known as a hometown boy who had made good. His high school friends worked at the IGA, the Ford garage and the bowling alley. Roy was the head of buildings and grounds and Kay the superintendent's secretary for the same hometown school district where Everett taught.

Amongst his peers, he had advanced remarkably, yet his education at the local teachers college took him only five blocks away from his high school and within a mile of the elementary school where he had spent his formative years. It was the natural thing to do. As he walked or rode his bicycle home from school some days, he thought of how lucky he was to be traversing the same streets and sidewalks he did as a youth. Many of the bumps and glides of sidewalks and driveways remained the same today.

Passing the homes of long-lost friends, he could replicate the feelings of warmth in their households, the layout of rooms in the homes and even some of the junior high antics that went on in the whitewashed basements. He could recall as yesterday the walk to school in the frigid morning, the rush for home following a Sunday afternoon movie or the walk from church on Christmas Eve.

Right now, he could take you to the spot where he found the five-dollar bill, or retrace for you the route he took step-by-step to get to the grocery store on a summer evening for a seven-cent bottle of Pepsi-Cola.

Right out of high school, Everett finished his summer-time job driving a large dump truck, enrolled in the local teachers college and proceeded to begin the life of academia that he knew was to be his. The shadows of the big limestone outcroppings of the hills and valleys were just too overwhelming.

They kept him and held him to a life that he knew he was destined for—the life of a senior high school mathematics teacher in his home high school. He could have moved on to the field of engineering in a faraway city or to the cockpit of a jet plane that may have taken him to places across the world, but the hills were compelling. After the special fit of the classroom to his personality and the scents of the hills constantly alluring, there could be no other choice.

He was undistinguished as a student, but it felt right. The ideas of books and the structure and beauty of mathematics kept him focused. He knew where he was going. He was headed toward a life of sharing beauty that he felt toward all things natural.

Teaching seemed to be just the place for him. As chaperone of this evening's after-the-game dance, his place was here and now, in the old gymnasium that contained the memories of thirty years ago.

Everett enjoyed his life at home with his wife his high school sweetheart, Jane, whom he had met at a similar after-game dance over thirty years ago. Together they had settled in a big old house on the edge of the valley just out of town. Everett liked to spend his free time refinishing furniture and continuously improving their 100-year-old home—made from the timbers and planks from nearby forests.

He loved the indoor wood surroundings. He enjoyed finding more wooden treasures at Saturday farm auctions in the hills and valleys of God's peace-filled setting. These ventures out with his pickup truck allowed him to bring even more of the natural into their already beautiful home. His days were ever busy serving the needs of kids and families.

At night, he enjoyed his family, fireplace, and the quiet readings of Thoreau after he had corrected his five sets of homework papers from math students.

Just out the back door of home was a small trout stream that invited early morning fishing—heading upstream toward a hole or two that he knew. With a bubbling creek, glorious morning sunrise, Thermos of coffee, garlic-laced sausage sandwich, and anticipated jumps and colors of waiting fish, he found ease in the land of the twenty-third psalm. Stepping over the stream, he often headed up the hillside to his favorite spot overlooking the valley.

With his own kids, he hiked to the top and across the ridge as he did so many years ago with Davey. He circled the cemetery where Ma and Pa resided, rested in the sunshine on the flat rocks at the top of the bluff and ventured down to the entrance of Devil's Cave.

At a small clearing on the side of the hill, Everett and the kids rested and prepared roasted skin-on hotdogs over a small fire. Schumacher was long gone, but they subsisted for the moment on a can of beans and the wieners that came from a second-generation German butcher—with Schumacher's old recipe. He enjoyed telling the kids stories of snipe hunting, woodland campouts and youthful adventure

"Kilroy was here!" The sound of a post-war Harley motorcycle being driven down the street, a neighbor mother hollering "Bergie Allen" at twilight to reclaim her child, and the too-frequent car-train wrecks that occurred in his neighborhood were but some of the sights and sounds that resided in his kaleidoscope of youthful memories. There was no particular order to the set of memories. They were just there.

They were a part of his being. Like thoughts of Woody, they were the "stuff" of life that made it all worthwhile. He only hoped that he would be given the chance to share these and other special memories and senses with his own children and grandchildren—but certainly not the train accidents!

As he approached fifty years of age, he wasn't too certain about the future and his role in it. Classmates had lost more than limbs in their service in Vietnam. Big, tough fellows who lived on the farms and some of those with whom he had played baseball were gone. Hunting accidents, heart attacks, service in Vietnam or any number of calamities or maladies had claimed eight of his friends at last count.

This past summer, he had taken a trip to Alaska to see Davey, his childhood friend of the hills and neighborhood. They hadn't been together in more than twenty-five years. There was, however, an ease about them that transcended the years and the miles between them. They relived old adventures and shared new ones. A day of halibut fishing showed their inherent abilities to work the nets together. A peaceful walk to a mountain trout stream produced great fishing and warm moments in the woods.

On the last day of Everett's visit, Davey and his family had a special dinner of crab and moose steak to celebrate life's goodness. As the evening came to a close, Davey presented him with a bone carving that Davey had commissioned by a native Aleut artisan on the island. Two young boys held a skull between them. With fingers intertwined, they held their uplifted treasure.

As Everett rested in his chair after the dance, his eyes were once again drawn to the mantelpiece. Viewing the beautiful centerpiece carving resting next to a tattered copy of the book *Willie and Joe*, he reflected on true friendship that had been his.